Reconsidering Psychology

Reconsidering Psychology

Perspectives FROM Continental Philosophy

Edited by
James E. Faulconer and
Richard N. Williams

© 1990 Dequesne Univ. Press

Duquesne University Press
Pittsburgh, Pennsylvania

Published by:

Duquesne University Press
600 Forbes Avenue
Pittsburgh, PA 15282–0101

Library of Congress Cataloging-in-Publication Data

Reconsidering psychology : perspectives from continental philosophy /
    edited by James E. Faulconer and Richard N. Williams.
        p.   cm.
    Includes bibliographical references.
    ISBN 0–8207–0223–4
    1. Psychology and philosophy.   2. Psychology—Philosophy.
I. Faulconer, James E., 1947– .   II. Williams, Richard N., 1950–
BF41.R43   1990
150.19′8—dc20   89–78009
                                                            CIP

Printed in the United States of America

To Janice and Camille

Contents

Acknowledgments

Many offered valuable assistance in preparing this volume. To all of them, we offer our thanks. Specifically, we are grateful to Calvin Schrag and Joseph J. Kockelmans for their initial encouragement to put these essays together; to the College of Humanities and the College of Family, Home, and Social Sciences at Brigham Young University for their financial support; and to Susan Wadsworth, editor at Duquesne University Press, for her diligence in seeing this project through to completion. We offer special thanks to Linda Hunter Adams, Director of the College of Humanities Publication Center at Brigham Young University, and to her staff (Rebecca Bennion, Dana Heinzelman, Jonathan Langford, Henry Miles, Tryn Paxton, Camille Oliver, and Jill Terry) for their tireless and patient editorial work with us.

Introduction

This volume intends to make a case—a case against the Western philosophical tradition and thus against contemporary mainstream psychology. It does not claim that this case is the most important case to be made, nor that it is *the* (final and ultimate) case that continental philosophy makes. The philosophical commitment of continental thought precludes that possibility. Instead the essays present *a* case against the tradition, a case arrived at by various continental readings of the tradition. Each essay adds to the case, extends the case, and may even refute parts of it. But at the same time, all participate in this case because they call us to reconsider psychology, and each call has a distinctly continental timbre.

The essays focus on problems facing the field of psychology, problems to which the continental tradition might contribute a useful, alternative perspective. Intended as they are as a serious contribution to the practice and understanding of psychology in the United States, the essays are aimed at those who practice, teach, and study psychology more than they are at philosophers. They offer the intelligent, serious psychologist various preliminary views of the differences continental philosophy can make to psychology. The more optimistic purpose of this book is to present psychologists with a view of some of the central problems of psychology, a perspective that will show the way around many of the most vexing theoretical problems in the discipline, problems that can be avoided when they are cast in the light offered by the continental tradition.

These essays show something of the diversity of the continental movement. Though more contributors take a perspective derived at least in part from the work of the twentieth-century German philosopher Martin Heidegger, the essays represent many points of view, from Edmund Husserl to Jean-Paul Sartre, and from Jacques Derrida to Jürgen Habermas, Hans-Georg Gadamer, and

1

Jacques Lacan. Discussed are several understandings of self-consciousness that take their standpoint in the work of G.W.F. Hegel, also of enormous influence in contemporary continental philosophy. Some essays deal with more strictly philosophical issues, some with methods and methodology, and some with more specifically psychological problems. But whatever particular philosophers or issues they concern themselves with, all the essays share the attempt to understand what makes specifically human behavior, and therefore psychology, possible from within a perspective skeptical of traditional metaphysics and, therefore, skeptical of most of psychology as practiced in the United States today.

We hope the reader will be able to appreciate this diversity and at the same time understand the coherent themes and commitments that run through all the selections. On the basis of this appreciation and coherence, an important and portentous dialogue can be initiated within the discipline of psychology. The essays by Calvin O. Schrag, Joseph J. Kockelmans, James E. Faulconer, and Richard N. Williams grew out of a symposium presented at the American Psychological Association meetings in Washington, D.C., in 1986. That symposium provided the impetus for this volume. All the essays are previously unpublished, either written especially for this volume or adapted for this volume from papers delivered at other conclaves. This work is evidence of the vibrant, growing reconsideration of psychology already underway.

In the title essay, James E. Faulconer and Richard N. Williams take up the question of how individuals relate to the larger group or culture in which they find themselves. Rather than providing an immediate answer to this question, however, Faulconer and Williams review the history of the notion of the self, suggesting that the conundra of psychology are endemic to the way Western culture has conceived the self, and therefore the way psychology has conceived itself. They begin with Plato and Aristotle to compare and contrast the ancient discussion of the self with the modern, showing the difficulties of each, and they end with Heidegger. They argue that the metaphysical anchor of both ancient and modern philosophy is the Greek conception of the *theos*, the transcendent and static divine, and they argue that this anchor has been the source of the difficulties of philosophy and, therefore, of psychology. Heidegger's work shows the possibility of "reconciling" the two views of self (ancient and modern), a reconciliation made possible by rethinking the nature and role of metaphysics, by giving up the traditional anchor. That reformulation makes it possible to rethink the questions of psychology as well as what would count as answers to psychological questions. Therefore the reformulation also makes it possible to see one way in which continental philosophy can make a contribution to contemporary psychology.

In the next essay, "Explanation and Understanding in the Science of Human Behavior," Calvin O. Schrag discusses three issues: (1) the nature of talk about human behavior and the domain of data for a science of human behavior, (2) the relation of theory to practice and concepts to facts, and (3) how one might integrate explanation and understanding. Relying on the work of Thomas Kuhn, Schrag responds to the first question by reminding us that "the constitution of a disciplinary matrix is a conjugated effort proceeding from a *scientific community*, which stands in a certain tradition and conducts its practices either through a normalization of this tradition or through a shift to a revolutionary posture in which the scientific paradigms of the tradition are deconstructed, enabling the emergence of a new paradigm." To the question of theory and practice, Schrag responds: "Praxis has its own insight. It does not need to wait upon the services of an etherialized *theoria* to swoop down from on high to provide the determinations of sense and reference." To answer the third question, "How can one integrate explanation and understanding?," Schrag uses the phenomenon of fear as an illustration and argues that though the metaphysical distinction between explanation and understanding is mistaken because it supposes cleavages in various orders of reality, there is a point to the resulting distinction between the human and the physical sciences. The objects of the latter move but do not act. The objects of the former always act: "The discourse and action of human behavior is always expressive, meaning-laden, infused with intentionality, an event of self-understanding." Such an account of explanation and understanding, Schrag argues, allows for their integration.

In "Some Reflections on Empirical Psychology: Toward an Interpretive Psychology," Joseph J. Kockelmans takes up the question of whether psychology is one of the natural sciences or one of the human sciences in a different way. Beginning with the now commonplace observation that the psychologist's work is interpretive, Kockelmans offers a subtle argument that the division between the natural and the human sciences is an unsatisfactory one because the elements of the disjunction are not mutually exclusive. As an introduction, Kockelmans clarifies what it means for a science to be empirical and in what way it can be said that psychology is empirical. A science is empirical if it can be abstract, formal, and idealized, and, Kockelmans argues, psychology can be empirical, though only within relatively narrow limits. In addition, however, psychology as an essentially interpretive science would use Husserl's phenomenological analysis, reinterpreted in light of Maurice Merleau-Ponty's existential analyses, as well as the methods of hermeneutical phenomenology.

In spite of other differences—such as what to make of the division between natural science and human science—continental philosophers such as Heidegger, Adorno, Gadamer, Foucault, Derrida, and Lyotard share the criticism that Enlightenment discourse, and therefore science based on Enlightenment discourse, has ungrounded assumptions for its fundamental principles. In "Psychology after Philosophy," Donald Polkinghorne discusses the contemporary critique of the Enlightenment presumption that it had discovered a method for uncovering the laws of nature— namely, the method of experimental science—and that experimental science would ultimately give us the solution to all problems. In explaining the critique of the Enlightenment, Polkinghorne focuses on three flawed assumptions: (1) language is an unproblematic and transparent medium for communicating ideas, (2) relations among entities are determinate and describable as absolute laws, and (3) perception opens access to a certain ground against which all knowledge claims can be evaluated.

In spite of the logical inconsistencies of Enlightenment science, psychology has been slow to give up its commitment to Enlightenment principles. Thus, Polkinghorne's critique of the assumptions of Enlightenment science also explains the contemporary criticism of psychology. Polkinghorne discusses two strategies for dealing with the failure of Enlightenment science to provide a basis for psychological science:

> The first strategy is to respond skeptically by locating the error of the Enlightenment in its very attempt to build a system of truth [e.g., the work of Jacques Derrida]. . . . A second strategy is to respond with new efforts to understand the natural and human realms, but with different approaches and with alternate notions of rationality.

Polkinghorne sees one alternative to the traditional notion of rationality in the work of philosophers such as Habermas and Apel, and another in the work of Heidegger and Gadamer. Polkinghorne gives an overview of each of these approaches (the skeptical response, as well as the two reinterpretations of rationality), ending with a brief discussion of the renewal offered by a Heideggerian rethinking of psychology.

Polkinghorne divides the alternative strategies for dealing with Enlightenment discourse between the skeptical (e.g., Derrida) and those that rethink rationality, and for a renewal of psychology he favors the latter, as seen in the work of Heidegger. In his essay, "Heidegger and Psychological Explanation: Taking Account of Derrida," James E. Faulconer takes up the disagreement between these two by taking up Derrida's criticism of Heidegger's work. He argues that either Derrida offers a fruitful rereading of Heidegger's work rather than a criticism or his criticism fails. Faulconer sketches such a fruitful rereading of Heidegger's work, trying to show that rereading Heidegger through Derrida opens Gadamer's hermeneutical work up to a new understanding, an understanding that puts Gadamer's work beyond the usual criticism that his hermeneutics necessarily endorses the status quo. In conclusion, Faulconer offers three observations for psychology about the meaning of the Derridean rereading of Heidegger:

> (1) Psychological explanation must treat both human knowledge and human beings themselves as . . . always already ontologically founded in an understanding of being and already engaged concernfully in the world before any reflection or analysis.
> (2) Existing psychological theories and methods will have to be rethought deconstructively rather than simply destroyed. . . . A deconstructive rethinking involves looking for the seams and cracks in a theory or method to see what it suppressed. [The result would be] a careful and continual rethinking of . . . theories, methods, and practices, . . . a kind of radical skepticism that demands not the dissolution of all claims to explanation, but a constant redoing of them.
> (3) [Such an approach understands] psychological explanation as a richly creative, fictive act rather than as reportage. [Psychological explanation becomes] a kind of storytelling, the best explanations functioning very much like good dramatic and poetic works.

In the sixth essay, "The Metaphysic of Things and Discourse about Them," Richard N. Williams takes up the contemporary critique of metaphysics to show how the problem of metaphysics manifests itself in a more strictly psychological problem—namely, psychologism. Williams understands psychologism to have two manifestations: (1) the reification of mental or psychological states, which become the conditions, antecedents, and explanations for human action; and (2) the adoption of the models and methods of the natural sciences as appropriate for psychology. Psychologism is a problem for psychology because it must always invoke what it should be explaining. According to Williams, the language of psychology carries with it a particular ontological claim about that to which it refers, and the evaluation of such claims should be the task of psychology. But it cannot accomplish its task within a metaphysical language, where the nature of the phenomena goes unchallenged. Distinguishing between metaphysical and practical discourse, Williams argues that the solution of the metaphysical problem lies in the realization that psychology exists as practical discourse rather than as a subspecies of metaphysical inquiry. Only within this practical discourse is an understanding of humanity possible.

Renewed interest in action, consciousness, and ecology has brought as well a renewal of interest in the work of Mark James Baldwin, George Herbert Mead, and Lev Semenovich Vygotsky. Though these three are not usually considered Hegelians, Ivana Markova argues that they base their studies of mind on Hegelian epistemology and that all three think about issues of mind dialectically. Markova's "The Development of Self-Consciousness: Baldwin, Mead, and Vygotsky" gives an overview of the work of each, particularly their understanding of self-consciousness, discussing briefly their relation to William James. Then she shows that each of the three conceives of self-consciousness in a Hegelian manner— namely, as the result of the mutual interaction of self and other— the outcome of the mutual interaction between organism and its environment—and that their methods have a basis in Hegel's dialectical "logic." To make the comparison of Mead, Baldwin, and Vygotsky to Hegel possible, she describes both Hegel's understanding of self-consciousness and his dialectical logic.

The central implication of Markova's paper is also central to the continental perspective: human being is essentially social being. If human being is social being, then interpretation is the only available mode of understanding and language is the only medium. We have no claim to knowledge on either an objective or a private, subjective basis. Markova's essay is interesting also because of the bridge it builds between the work of contemporary "social constructionists" (such as Harré, Gergen, and others) who take their lead from Mead and Vygotsky, and the work of many in the continental tradition.

Given that human being is essentially social and that objectivity fails, the human sciences are confronted with arbitrating between competing claims and perspectives on the world. Simon Glynn's paper, "The Dynamics of Alternative Realities," gives a Sartrean analysis of the possibility of alternative realities: Is there a *real* world that validates some understandings of reality and invalidates others? How, for example, is it possible to judge between those with an accurate or at least acceptable understanding of the world (the sane) and those with an unacceptable and inaccurate reality (the insane)? Drawing on the work of Husserl as well as the Gestalt psychologists, Glynn analyzes what it means for there to be alternative realities—what it means for people's realities to conflict—and argues that there is no transcendent ground for arbitrating between conflicting realities. Therefore, "in all societies, those who are in authority, who have power, control the social construction of reality, and concomitantly of sanity and insanity." With Francis Bacon, Glynn argues that truth and utility turn out to be the same.

An early pioneer in bringing Heidegger's work to the attention of philosophers in the United States, William J. Richardson in "Heidegger and the Problem of World" explains the concept of *world* found in Heidegger's *Being and Time*, using the death of Marilyn Monroe as a focal point for discussing that concept. Richardson shows the relevance of Heidegger's thought to questions of individual perceptions of world by showing the ways in which the word *world* can be understood, especially the distinction between an individual's world and the world as such. In turn, this distinction allows him to discuss the relation between the two such that it is meaningful for a person to say that his or her world has collapsed. Richardson uses this relation to show the way in which the opportunity for authentic existence and the possibility that one's world will collapse have the same origin—namely, the experience of no-thing, that is, anxiety—and he shows that this origin is a temporal origin, an origin oriented toward the future. Perhaps most significantly, like Williams, Richardson goes beyond discussing these issues in theoretical terms, showing how they apply to an understanding of more particular psychological phenomena, in this case that of Marilyn Monroe.

Debra B. Bergoffen continues the continental treatment of psychopathology by turning attention to the psychoanalytic tradition and Jacques Lacan's rereading of Sigmund Freud in "On Becoming a Subject: Lacan's Rereading of Freud." In the United States the usual understanding of Freud is a literalist, metaphysical one—Lacan's interpretation is not widely known outside the psychoanalytic tradition itself. This essay introduces Lacan and, thus, the continental, linguistic reading of Freud.

Bergoffen begins by pointing out the ways in which Freud and Lacan agree: that subjectivity is an achievement, and that this achievement is never an accomplished fact but rather a progressive/regressive movement characterized by lurches toward a higher, more complete mode of integration. But these lurches are fraught with breaks, requiring the subject to return to earlier, more secure modes of being. Freud and Lacan agree that the difficulties of this process are reflected in the fragility of the result. Bergoffen then discusses Freud's *The Three Essays on the Theory of Sexuality* and *The Ego and the Id* and uses Lacan's rereading of the themes of these essays to show the way in which the center of attention moves from sexual identity to language as Lacan questions the ego's claim to occupy the place of the subject. Lacan argues against that claim.

In the final essay of the volume, "Life-World as Depth of Soul: Phenomenology and Psychoanalysis," Robert Romanyshyn shows that psychology is not circumscribed within a larger metaphysical, scientific project. Rather, the subject matter of psychology is as broad as the life-world itself, and to be valuable, psychological explanation must have that same breadth. Romanyshyn takes up three themes: (1) "that the *science of psychology* is a historical appearance of human psychological life, of humanity's soul if you will, which appearance is inseparable from a new physics of nature . . . and a new physiology of the body"; (2) "that phenomenology and psychoanalysis are each in their own respective way responses to this historical appearance of human psychological life as the science of psychology"; and (3) "that a convergence of phenomenology and psychoanalysis leads toward a phenomenological depth-psychology that acknowledges" psychology as a style of vision. As Romanyshyn says, "Soul incarnates itself as world." "A psychology is fleshed out in the way in which an age paints its paintings and builds its buildings, creates its laws and practices its sciences, manages its money, and worships the gods." To demonstrate this third point, Romanyshyn offers a phenomenological/existential analysis of the related problems of eros and technology.

1 • Reconsidering Psychology

James E. Faulconer and Richard N. Williams

An important theme can be traced through contemporary mainstream psychology—namely, the reconciliation of the individuality of human being with the larger group or culture, in other words, with the world. An affirmation of individualism lies at the heart of nearly all formal definitions of psychology. Conceived variously as psyche, self, or organism, the individual is the focus and object of study for psychology, as well as the seat and origin of psychological function. This emphasis on explaining at the level of the individual human being sets psychology apart from and settles it comfortably in its place among related social science disciplines such as anthropology or sociology. Whether individuality is attributed to a unique genetic endowment, a cognitive or developmental structure, an idiosyncratic reinforcement history, a socially prescribed role, or an autonomous ego or self, psychological explanation remains unfinished until it reaches the level of individual beings.

In spite of the attempt by psychologists, including social psychologists, to study behavior at the level of individuals, it is obvious that human beings are always encountered in more complex groups and circumstances and that they do not act wholly independently of the world in which they find themselves. In understanding human beings, then, psychology must also understand the world and how it relates to human being. The psychological tradition has borrowed the word *environment* from the natural sciences to signify the totality of influences, entities, or events outside the individual. By design, this term lacks humanity: it represents the substratum of external determinants of human thought and action. By design and by definition, the environment is conceived to be entirely outside the volitional control of human

9

beings. In this conceptual scheme the humanity of humans, if taken seriously, is found "inside," and the inside is conceived to be individual.

Once the domain of psychology is conceptualized as the study of individuals in environments, the stage is set for asking the fundamental question, a question that has been and continues to be *the* central issue toward which explanatory work in the discipline is directed: what is the nature of the relationship between a human being and the nonhuman environment?

All schools of mainstream psychology can be characterized by how they answer this question. Some, such as the behaviorists, emphasize the pervasive and dominant influence of the environment, essentially reducing the human being to the product of environmental contingencies and forces. Others move the "environment" inside, attributing causality to genetic, biochemical factors or to an autonomous psychic entity such as the traditional Freudian id. The opposite move, basically a Kantian one, makes the environment less important than its active conceptualization. This explanatory scheme, characterized by the traditional psychological humanists, gives preeminence to the directing power of an active autonomous human agent. Another recent approach to reconciling the individual and the environment, cognitive psychology, reaches for a middle ground, stressing the "interaction" between the person and the environment, or between the inner and outer worlds, and most social psychology shares this reach for a middle ground. However, regardless of how they answer the question, all traditional and almost all contemporary psychologies assume their central problem to be the relation between the individual human being and the nonhuman environment.

Owing largely to the very way the fundamental question has been formulated, all these answers to the question regarding the interactions of human beings with their world are fraught with conceptual problems. As formulated in psychology, that question contains within it the seeds of its own insolubility, seeds to be found in the soil of the dominant metaphysics from which psychological theorizing arises, the metaphysics of things, a metaphysics that entails a number of problematic assumptions (Faulconer and Williams 1985, 1987). For the most part, these assumptions, the legacy of our psychology and our culture from a long tradition in Western thought, have gone unexamined in psychology as well as in the other social sciences.

Continental philosophy can make a significant contribution to psychology precisely through its careful examination of these assumptions and their implications, for whatever form it takes, continental philosophy explicitly calls into question the metaphysics that is, at root, the problem. We will outline the issues of traditional metaphysics and some of the forms those issues have taken, as well as one form that the critical examination of that metaphysics takes, and we will show the importance of this examination for psychological theory and practice.

Intentionally or not, psychology has framed its most basic question—the relationship of the individual to the environment—in such a way that it assumes a distinction between mind and world based on the model of mind and world first given us by the seventeenth-century philosopher René Descartes. Descartes proposed that mind and world were two distinct "substances," or basic modes of being. Though most psychologists no longer worry about the metaphysical issue of how many substances there are, they do accept the Cartesian dichotomy of mind and world, wherein the inner and the outer worlds are defined as dissociable and independent.

The self-contradictory task of psychology is to map or catalogue the processes by which these two incommensurable worlds are related. Psychological theories are supposed to give a measure to that which cannot be measured, so they are a reaction to this incommensurability, to the impossibility of coherence in a Cartesian system. For example, behaviorists react to the incommensurability of inner and outer by reducing everything to the outer world. Kantians, on the other hand, emphasize the importance of the inner over the outer. Or commonly, some theorists attempt to avoid the contradiction by taking the inner-outer distinction seriously, but conceiving of the outer as the environment and the inner as the subjective. Such a move is not a solution but instead generally takes the form of an appreciation of the complexity and multiple causality of human behavior. We argue that this complexity grows out of presuppositions that make understanding impossible. Whatever way it handles the Cartesian distinction, however, each of these theories does presuppose it, *even when the theory reduces everything to one or the other of the two possible poles.* (After all, it is the postulating of the two poles, the Cartesian dichotomy, that makes a reduction to one or the other possible.)

In each of these reactions to the Cartesian contradictions, both the inner and the outer realms are conceived in terms of variables in lawful and impersonal interaction with one another (Harré 1977 refers to this as a parametric approach). Once this assumption is made, two very important concerns are conflated: questions of the person and the environment and questions of the individual and the community become the same questions, for the community is external—a collection of things outside the individual, things fundamentally like any other things in interaction with one another. Others are merely part of the environment. Lost in such conceptualizations is the concept of the "world" itself, the "space" in which the inner and the outer occur; lost within a view of humans as subjective individuals situated in an objective environment (consisting of everything not private, not human) is the idea that human beings can be understood only from the perspective of a world within which the individual and other persons and things generally are bound meaningfully and inextricably together from the beginning. This means that "inner" and "outer" are constructions made from the material of the already given, meaningful world. The notion of the inextricable relation of the inner and the outer in the world that precedes each category and makes both possible runs counter to the dominant assumptions of contemporary psychology, but it is a fundamental concern of contemporary continental philosophy. To make sense of the claim we have just made and to understand the possibility to which continental philosophy points, we will have to understand the history of the split between the human inner and the environmental outer, and the resulting split between the individual and the community.

Some, perhaps even most of those within psychology, view the history of psychology as progressive because they view the history of Western culture as progressive overall. We mean *progressive* in the sense that psychological knowledge and expertise have been steadily and systematically expanding, building (as any scientific discipline supposedly should) on previous conceptualizations, resolving inconsistencies and anomalies, and refining what has been established as valid. We suspect that there are scarcely any graduate students in the United States who have not at least heard of Thomas Kuhn's attack (1970) on this model of science (an attack that has been extended and corrected in several ways—for example, Feyerabend 1975, and the essays in Lakatos and Musgrave 1970). For reasons different from Kuhn's, we too believe that this view of psychology is inaccurate. Like the other social sciences, psychology has not been progressive in any fundamental way. Rather, the same questions have continued to be asked, and they have been formulated and asked from within the same unsatisfactory perspective, one that can be described loosely as positivistic, empiricistic, and individualistic: in short, from within traditional Cartesian metaphysics. An overview of the history of the concepts that create the Cartesian split between the inner and the outer worlds, and the problems that result from that split, is essential to seeing those problems clearly and to seeing the alternative we think is suggested by continental philosophy.

In the succeeding sections of this essay, we will make the argument that the history of psychology is not progressive and that the problems psychology faces require a radically new view. No mere fix-up or reconciliation will do. In fact, even an overhaul will not work. Having made that argument, we will then offer a sketch of one version of the theoretical alternative.

The history we will offer will trace the emergence of the notion of the psychological individual (the self) in Western thought, including a survey of the problems with which this tradition has endowed psychology. The sketch of the alternative we will offer will deal briefly with these themes and ideas from the standpoint of a continental thinker who stands at the beginning of the twentieth century, Martin Heidegger.[1] Obviously other thinkers have been and continue to be important and influential in modern psychology, but we choose Heidegger as a starting point because, in one way or another, his work is the starting point for many other contemporary thinkers in the field, because his work is of current interest, and because we feel that his contribution has been substantial, though overlooked in the English-speaking world.

HISTORY OF THE CONCEPT OF THE INDIVIDUAL

The modern idea of the individual, the *self* or *subject* in philosophy, is relatively new. The story of the emergence of that notion, however, is not especially new. (For example, Burckhardt 1983 told us about it in the middle of the nineteenth century.) Briefly, we can tell the story by saying that "anciently there is no notion of the self in the modern sense—that is, of an identity which I can define for myself without reference to what surrounds me and the world in which I am set" (Taylor 1975, p. 6). The modern notion of self begins much later, in the fourteenth century, and does not come to full flower in philosophy until the seventeenth century. The discussion of the individual we find prior to that does not fit into the modern conceptual categories. (That fact alone should give us pause as to the supposedly self-evident nature of the modern understanding of the self.) Thus, an understanding of the ancient notion of the individual and its development into the modern notion will lay the groundwork both for understanding the modern notion and its implications and limitations, and for seeing the importance of the alternatives offered by contemporary continental philosophy, alternatives that overcome the difficulties of both the ancient and modern views while retaining their positive features.

As we read Aristotle's work we find little or no discussion of the psychological individual. His psychology is clearly not a psychology in any modern sense of the term. He does, of course, discuss perception and the different ways of categorizing thought in *On the Soul* (1941a), and both of those are part of what we would consider psychological issues, but Aristotle's discussion of what appear to be psychological issues is distinctly nonpsychological. A similar problem occurs when we look at the other major Greek thinker, Plato: in the *Republic* he divides the soul into three parts and discusses the results of that division (1902, 434d–441c), but that division and discussion would not fall into any category that contemporary psychologists would recognize as psychological. When the psychologies of Plato and Aristotle fail, we might go looking for a psychology of some sort in Aristotle's *Nicomachean Ethics* (1934) or *Politics* (1941c), expecting perhaps to find it implicit in his discussion of the individual, if only in the discussion of the relation of the individual to the community. But we find very little we can construe as the modern self in any of these, and the omission cannot be attributed merely to the primitive state of science in the third and fourth centuries B.C., for what is missing is not a psychology (there is a psychology), but a modern psychology. Perhaps it is more accurate to say that what is missing is the very *possibility* of a modern psychology.

In Aristotle and Plato, rather than the modern self we find discussions of the individual (literally *the one*), as in this passage: "For even if the good is the same for the individual and for the city, it is greater and more harmonious to manifest it and grasp it and preserve it for the city" (Aristotle 1934, 1094b). Rather than being psychological, Greek discussions of the individual tend to deal with the relation of the individual to the community rather than with an analysis of the individual. And, unlike that relation in modern times, the Greeks do not see it as a reconciliation of different beings that are probably alienated to begin with. For the Greeks, the individual is not a psychological self. The individual is simply the smallest unit of the community; the community defines the individual more than the individual defines the community, though neither is ontologically distinct (Aristotle 1934, 1097b). In fact, there is a certain sense in which the individual and the community are identical.

For example, before beginning his defense of the claim that justice is better than injustice, Socrates recommends that we move from an examination of individual justice to an examination of justice in the community in the following analogy:

> The search to which we are putting ourselves is not easy, and I see that we need sharp eyesight. So, since we are not clever, I think we should use this kind of method: if those who do not see sharply were asked to read small letters from far off, and someone noticed that the same letters were somewhere else, larger and on a larger surface, they would call it a godsend, I think, to first read these larger letters and then to examine the smaller ones, if they are the same. [Plato 1902, 368c–d][2]

For Plato and Aristotle, there is neither relation nor opposition between the individual and the community but identity—though one, the city, may be easier to examine than the other. Their notions of both individual and community—and therefore their notion of the psychological self too—must be different from the notions we have of those things. As moderns we expect to find some discussion of the self as individual in political works such as these, but there is none; we find a self in the modern sense neither in ancient science, nor in ancient political science, nor in ancient psychology. However, though the psychology of the ancients will give us no discussion of the self, a look at that psychology will help us clarify both why there is no such discussion and what constitutes the ancient and, therefore, the medieval notion of what we call self. That, in turn, will help us understand the origins of the modern notion.

Let us begin with a look at what the individual was for Greek thinkers. In Greek the subject is "that which has been placed before or in front of something" (*hupokeimenon*), a passive construction.[3] Given this definition, the individual (the subject) is one who has been placed before the world, before what is. Whereas for us the world is passive and placed before the subject for his or her examination, for the ancients the subject is placed before the world. The Greek self does not come to know the world by grasping it and placing it into the container of the mind (as has been generally the metaphor since the seventeenth century). Instead, it comes to know in a way somewhat like being awake. Though not in itself a passive notion, the Greek notion is passive when compared to the modern notion.

For Aristotle, consciousness itself (being able to perceive and understand) is like being awake. It is a kind of openness. "Pure" consciousness is a material; it exists in the same way as does any other pure material—namely, it is conceivable only in relation to what transforms it into a finished product. In other words, there is no material, including mind, that does not already have some attributes, but we can nonetheless consider material as such—in this case, consciousness or mind.

Aristotle's use of the word *material* is quite different from ours, for it does not necessarily refer to something physical. Instead, it refers to what something is made of—whatever that thing is, whether physical or not. It refers to that which something is made of *before* we consider what properties it might come to have. From an Aristotelian point of view, substance or material is whatever it is that has the properties we experience, including but not limited to physical properties. This Aristotelian understanding of material is decisive for much of the history of Western thought. For example, the seventeenth and eighteenth-century discussions of substance in thinkers like John Locke, George Berkeley, and David Hume are discussions of Aristotle's material—compare Locke's discussion of substance (1956) and Berkeley's rejection of the concept of substance or material (1874).[4]

Keeping this meaning of *material* in mind and remembering that the material cause is one of Aristotle's four causes of things (material, formal, final, and efficient—1941b, 194b–195a), we can see that according to Aristotle the mind is one of the causes of ideas, but only as their material, not as an efficient cause; ideas are made of mind, not created by it.

Things in the world are what they are because whatever is real about the world (the "divine") makes them that. We know things in the world because the same reality that shapes them shapes our consciousness. As the signet ring molds wax, the real molds the things of the world *and* molds our minds. Thus, we are together with what we understand, but not because we first grasp something "out there" ready to be taken hold of and then pull it into ourselves, nor because we become joined to it in some mysterious way. Rather, we understand because we are molded and "enformed" by reality through our senses and reason. Like any other material, our consciousness cannot exist without having some form or other, and for Aristotle the form our consciousness takes—our understanding of the world—is a form stamped into it by reality. (See 1941a, particularly 429a.)

This "stamping" of consciousness can obviously but mistakenly be seen as an intellectual precursor to behaviorist conditioning. But such an easy analogue is too facile and, therefore, misleading. For to say that reality stamps consciousness is to make an ontological point, a point about the nature of reality: the stamping or molding is carried out on a metaphysical level in a way that involves all of Aristotle's four causes. But saying that mind is a product of conditioning makes an epistemological point at an entirely physical level involving the single, simple (and transmuted) efficient cause. The similarities of Aristotle's theory of perception and behaviorist models of perception are much more apparent than real.

Given Aristotle's notion of perception and understanding, it is no wonder that most modern and contemporary problems of knowledge (epistemological problems) are not discussed in ancient or medieval literature. With Aristotle's understanding of how we come to know, one need not ask about the correspondence of one's perceptions with the objects in the world; but for the most part, modern understanding insists on that question. With the ancient version of consciousness, understanding is not fundamentally a question of correspondence, but of being enformed, of yielding to what is. Thus, for the ancients there are questions of appearance or illusion on the one hand, and reality on the other, but fundamentally there are no questions of correspondence of subject to object. That is because in ancient thought there are no subjects or objects in the modern sense. Knowledge is a harmony of self (individual) with reality and of thing with reality and, because of that, of self with things.

Thus, for ancient thought, individual and thing are in harmony—the person knows the thing—because they both stand within the whole. They are not directly in harmony with one another, but they are in harmony because they are each what they are in virtue of metaphysical reality. Thus, knowledge is always mediated knowledge, but unlike the case in modern metaphysics, the mediation of knowledge in ancient metaphysics is not one that must overcome a bifurcation of the world into subject and object. Instead, according to the ancient view, the mediation of the world, in its entirety, makes possible what we would call subjects and objects. Because individuals and things are defined in terms of their mutual place within the mediating whole, they are not modern subjects and objects.

We should emphasize that the ancients do not believe we "become one with" the objects we perceive. Instead, to the extent that we perceive something, we become one with whatever reality the things we perceive are one with, with what makes them what they are. We and the things of our perception share a "form." Theaetetus does not, in some magical way, become one with the table in perceiving it, nor does he become one with the Pythagorean theorem in understanding it.

Heidegger explains the view of consciousness we have been discussing:

> Ancient and medieval ontology are not, as the usual ignorance understands them to be, a pure objective ontology with consciousness excluded; rather the peculiarity is precisely that consciousness and the I are taken to be in the same senses as the objective is taken to be. [1975, p. 104]

In other words, ancient ontology does not exclude consciousness, even though it might appear to us to do so. Instead, both consciousness and what we call the objective world are grounded in the same way, in whatever is real, in the truth.

For the Greeks, nature is not the "what is" of the world. It is "that which has been brought forth." Whatever it is that is real (the "divine") has brought forth both the things in the world and our consciousness by enforming the various materials—including consciousness. As a result, any distinction between consciousness and natural things is a distinction of material only, not of being: material is that which can have form, whether physical or not. Consciousness of a chair differs from the chair itself in being made of a different material than the physical chair, much as two chairs might differ in that one is made of wood and the other of plastic. Consciousness of a chair is a particular material—mind—in the form of a chair. The physical chair is a different material—perhaps wood—with the same form. Thus, ancient psychology could not be a science of consciousness itself, for according to Aristotle there could be no science of material itself, only of what gives shape and direction to the material, in other words, form (cf. 1941c, 72a). Ancient psychology is the study of how the material of consciousness is enformed by reality, how consciousness and the real are in harmony. In other words, ancient psychology is clearly a branch of ancient metaphysics.

To understand better this process by which "what is" gives form to consciousness and to see better the connection between ancient psychology and ancient metaphysics, consider Plato's allegory of the cave in the *Republic* (1902). At the end of book 6 Glaucon describes what Socrates is searching for as dialectic knowledge (*dialegesthai episteme*, 511c). Though not etymologically correct, we can learn something about the phrase *dialectical knowledge* by listening to the ideas that might be imputed to the Greek words, by constructing reasonable (though perhaps historically false) etymologies of its parts. Doing this, we can take *episteme* to mean "a place to stand," and in *dialegesthai* we can hear "that which comes via the *logos.*" (*Logos* can mean "language, rule, story, account, explanation," and "ultimate principle," among other things. In this case, the first and the last of these seem most appropriate, *language* and *ultimate principle.*) Putting these together, therefore, we may take the Greek for *dialectical knowledge* to mean something like "a place upon which to stand given through the logos."[5] Socrates agrees that this is, indeed, what he is looking for (1902, 511d), and book 7 is devoted to his discussion of what such a place might be and of how it might be taught to the youth of the community—a discussion that is introduced by the allegory of the cave.

The prisoners in the cave all have the power of speech, the ability to let that which is most fundamental show itself through their speaking. Therefore, they have the ability to name the things that appear before them on the wall (1902, 515b). As we will see, they have confidence in their naming. But though, as the philosopher later discovers, their naming is not altogether wrong, their confidence is misplaced, for the things they name appear and pass away before their eyes. Their naming is only a matter of opinion, not genuine knowledge, even though it takes place through the *logos.* Like the sophists, the prisoners in the cave have an opinion and they are confident of their opinion, and they may even be able to give a reasonable defense of it, one based on the evidence. But because it is grounded in the ephemeral—in the shadows rather than in the light that makes the shadows possible—it is not knowledge. Because it is only the knowledge of appearance, it is only the appearance of knowledge; even though an appearance is an appearance of truth, it is not the truth itself and cannot be the basis for knowledge.

Finally one of the prisoners is dragged out into the light of day. Learning the truth is not something one simply decides to do. It is something one is "compelled" to do. (This is also a theme of Socrates' tale in the *Symposium*, 1980.) This process is not an act of will. Properly speaking, for Plato coming to know the truth is not an act—in the modern sense—even though there are things one must do, even though coming to know is not merely passive. Notice, for example, that in the *Seventh Letter* Plato speaks of this as something that happens to one, but something that requires effort on one's own part:

> It cannot at all be specified [settled] as can other learning, but from continued communion about the subject itself and from living with it, suddenly it is born in the soul, like a light kindled by a leaping spark, and being born, from then on it nourishes itself. [1929, 641d]

This echoes what is said in the *Republic*, that dialectic is the art of turning persons to see what is right rather than the art merely of giving them sight, where *giving them sight* corresponds to teaching in some direct and straightforward manner, and turning persons corresponds to giving them moral character. Though moral character (wisdom) is a result of the practice of dialectic—an activity of both teacher and pupil—Socrates says it is also always partly a result of a divine "gift," something contributed by neither teacher nor pupil (1902, 518c–d).

In the allegory of the cave, the prisoner comes to know the truth through sight. After being dragged out, it takes a while for him to become accustomed to the sun, but once he does he is able to distinguish the objects in this upper world, and finally the sun itself. All the prisoners have had the light in some way. But just as their speech in the cave was only indirectly about real things, the light they have in the cave is only indirect—both in being behind them and in being firelight rather than the light of the sun. The philosopher, however, now knows the light itself. He has seen it directly, though those who remained behind know it only in that it is the unnameable background, the background that *they* cannot name, against which the things they can name appear. He has added knowledge (*episteme*) to speech (*logos*) and now has what Glaucon described, dialectical knowledge (*dialegesthai episteme*): a place in which to stand—from which to speak—that is given through speech by the *logos*. (The word translated "dialectical" [*dialegesthai*] is itself dialectical, for it refers to that which comes to be not only through our speaking—as in Socrates' questioning of others—but also through the *logos*, that which most genuinely is.)

It is tempting to read this allegory with modern eyes, to assume that the prisoners are wrong because there is a lack of correspondence between their names and the things they are naming. However, to fall prey to such a temptation is to misunderstand the point that these prisoners see shadows. It is to overlook the divine element of the story. Shadows are a function of the relation of light—a key metaphor in the allegory, for the sun is the divine good—and the original object. The light is that by which all things are revealed, the whole within which the objects contemplated by the philosopher exist—"[the sun] being in charge of all things in the visible region and, in some way, being the cause of all these things they had seen" (1902, 517b–c). To see only the shadow is not to see that whole; it is to be out of harmony with the whole. The prisoners cannot turn around; they can see only what appears before them. In such a situation, where the darkness of shadows is taken as the reality, the light itself will not be seen. The reason they are wrong is not merely that what they say fails to correspond with the reality outside the cave, but that what they say does not reflect the totality of what is seen, even by them unknowingly— namely, the light and its bringing into being of the things. They are wrong because what they say is not in harmony with the reality within which they already exist, not because it does not correspond to something "over there" and apart from them. They are wrong because *they* are wrong, because they *are* wrong: they are not what they need to be to know the truth. Dialectic is not an art of putting one into correspondence with things. Instead, as was said above, it is the art of learning to look.

For Plato, as for Aristotle, coming to know is a matter of openness. But for us Plato's analogy to sight is more instructive than the analogy to being awake. Sight is not an activity; to open one's eyes at all is to see. However, there is an activity involved in seeing the truth, the activity of looking, of directing one's eyes toward the truth. We can look toward it or away from it. Having looked at the sun, the philosopher has a place in which to stand in his analysis of things. He has the ground that makes the understanding of all things possible, just as the sun makes the sight of all things possible. Since his naming and discussing will now be based on the real source of all that the others see (the light), because he has been through the process necessary to becoming able to see the truth (namely, looking), he will now be able to talk about things with genuine confidence (though, perhaps, not about things ephemeral), because now his talk originates from the light, the *logos*. His explanations do not correspond to the objects about which he speaks nor even to the *logos* itself. Rather, they well up from that ground, they are produced by his place within it.

For us, to understand a thing is to grasp it, to seize it, to take hold of it, to have dominion over it. Many of the metaphors we use to talk about understanding reflect this—for example, "I get it." But for Plato and Aristotle, coming to know is a process in which whatever truly is begets and generates wisdom in us. It is a process in which, by being open to that which we are placed before, we too are given form by that which enforms those things. (As we pointed out earlier and as is important to remember, this openness, though passive from our perspective, is not merely passive; for it includes the careful use of observation and reason.) We become harmonious with the reality of the world; we become one with it. Though it appears so to contemporary ears, Plato's claim that virtue (excellence) is knowledge is not particularly strange; it is no radical departure from the ancient understanding of the world and our life in it. It is a restatement of the ancient epistemology, a restatement that is crucial: the men chained in the cave are not what they need to be; they are said to be thoughtless, lacking sound-mindedness (1902, 515c5). For the ancients, morality (in a broad sense) and understanding are inseparable.

Thinking of understanding as harmony also explains the curious apparent passivity of the philosophic life Aristotle describes at the end of *The Nicomachean Ethics*. The chapters preceding his discussion of the philosophic life make it clear that there are many things the ethical person—ultimately, the philosopher—must do, but as the final chapters make clear, even that doing is a kind of openness. Understanding is responsiveness to the activity (*energeia*, being-at-work) of reality in the things of the world (including ourselves), and both an allowing it to be active and an encouraging it to be active (at-work) in us (see 1934, book 8).

The moral character of thought about the individual and the connection of morality and knowledge mark a major difference between ancient and medieval philosophy on the one hand, and modern philosophy on the other. For the early modern philosophers in the late sixteenth and early seventeenth centuries, moral philosophy takes a back seat to natural philosophy. It is hard to miss the note of displeasure in Francis Bacon's voice when he writes, "When Socrates had drawn down philosophy from heaven to earth, moral philosophy became more fashionable than ever, and diverted the minds of men from the philosophy of nature" (1908, I.79). And Descartes refuses to take up moral philosophy because writings on it "praise the virtues most highly and show them to be more worthy of being prized than anything else in the world, but they do not sufficiently teach us to become acquainted with them" (1972a, part 1). This separation of knowledge and morality is a far cry from what we find in the ancients, for whom to be human at all, to have any understanding of the world, is to be enformed by the "divine." Therefore, for the ancients any degree of excellence—but especially moral excellence—is inseparable from knowledge. For knowing is a way of being, and those who live less excellently live more illusory lives, lives not fully enformed by that which is real, by the truth—regardless of what kinds of propositions they might be able to recite about the objects around them. For the ancients and medievals, the truth is the ultimate order of the world, and rationality is being-in-accordance-with that order. Thus, for the Greeks and medievals, persons are more fully themselves as they come to reflect the cosmic order, and they come to reflect it more as they come to touch with it in the way most suited to it as order—namely, through reason, or—since we often think of "reason" in overly narrow ways—perhaps "thoughtfulness" would be better. The Delphic injunction "Know thyself" is not a call to introspection, as Plato's descriptions of Socrates so vividly demonstrate. It is a call to being full of thought about what is real; to know one's place in the world. For to know oneself and to know the world and to know the divine are one project.

Obviously, we do not understand consciousness in this way today. We may be able to come to understand this view (though not without some struggle), and we may be able to explain it (though not easily). But for us, coming to know is not like that; we do not live this version of consciousness, because it was replaced at the end of the medieval period because of a change in metaphysics. With a significant shift in metaphysics at about the time of the Renaissance came a shift in the understanding of the individual and of individual consciousness. Though the modern understanding of the individual and the individual's consciousness is at the heart of contemporary psychological theory, there is an ancient and intellectually respectable alternative to it. This historical alternative stands as a challenge to any theory basing itself on that contemporary understanding. To have unquestioned confidence in the superiority of the new theory over the old, we would have to show that the new theory is superior to the ancient, incorporating the ancients' insights and making advances on them. To decide whether modern theories of consciousness achieve such advances, we must look at the transition to the modern understanding of consciousness, and to understand that we must at least look briefly at the change in the metaphysics.

THE EMERGENCE OF THE MODERN SELF

Clearly, the change from ancient and medieval to modern philosophy and, therefore, the change in our understanding of consciousness and the individual did not occur overnight (it took about three hundred years); nor did modern philosophy begin with no antecedents in medieval or ancient thought. Neither is it possible to pick out one point from which the change extended, like ripples from a stone dropped in water. The shift is too broad for such an analysis. The shift can be seen in terms of a variety of concepts and problems, all of which intertwine with one another.[6] But for our purposes, it is helpful to look first at the Renaissance discussion of "human dignity." Then we can see how that devolves into the modern equation of knowledge and power, making individual consciousness into the active self of modern thinking rather than the passive "material" of ancient philosophy, and making that active self the center of everything and the standard for knowledge. We believe that in seeing this we will also see that the modern view of consciousness and the individual is not superior to the ancient. Seeing that will require the move to a new view, one that incorporates the insights of each but differs from both.

Based on Genesis 1:26—"God created man in his own image"— there had been discussions of human dignity throughout the medieval period. But those discussions had centered on the high place of humans in the order of creation. *Dignitas* referred to moral or social rank, or the moral qualities expected of and associated with that rank. Thus, to speak of human dignity was to speak of humans' place within the order of creation and what was expected of them as a result. Among the Neoplatonists and church fathers, to speak of human dignity had been, at most, to speak of the human potential to go beyond the limits of being merely in the likeness of God and to become godly by becoming perfectly enformed by God.[7] Fairly clearly, this is a version of ancient psychology applied to the Christian soul.

With the Renaissance, however, and the rise of interest in the individual, the notion of human dignity began to center on the self-worth of the individual human and on the individual's ability to create. Now human dignity came to mean that, like God, humans have control over the world of things, that humans are like God in being creators and in having power, rather than in *being* like God, in becoming godly by being in perfect harmony with God and God's world. Rather than the imitation of God being thought of in moral terms, with the Renaissance it came to be thought of in terms of creation and power.

The change from medieval to modern science illustrates this difference well. Previously the scientific enterprise had been to understand the harmony of the created world and the place of humans in that harmony (and it was in that understanding that mortals became like God). This explains ancient psychology's analysis of perception as a kind of attunement to things and its epistemology's focus on the harmony of the individual with the "divine." On the other hand, in the modern period, to have scientific knowledge was to have power over the things in the world, to be like the traditional God in being able to exercise power. The difference that comes about in this change explains well the superiority of modern science over ancient science—as well as the vacuousness of that superiority. The objects of the two are simply not the same. Where ancient science primarily sought description and understanding as a means to promote harmony with the world, modern science primarily sought power in order to control the world. Thus, to assert the superiority of modern science over ancient is to do two things. It is, first of all, to value power over understanding and, second, to beg the question of what science is to do.

We can see the shift in the notion of human dignity in the work of Pico della Mirandola. By the fifteenth century he speaks of humans as those who are unlike any other creature because they have no fixed location or aspect, or determined form, or laws that determine their nature (*Oratio de hominis dignitate, Opera*, fol. 314ff.; quoted in Cassirer 1963, pp. 85–86).[8] Instead, he says, humans can choose their location, nature, or form for themselves, and they can give their own laws to themselves. The self-defining individual comes into existence with the interest in the individual creation of art and the new version of science (concomitantly, not as cause and effect). Creation and understanding come to mean control rather than bringing forth something from the ground, from reality. (By the time we get to Bacon, for example, the difference between the ancient and medieval world on the one hand, and the modern one on the other, is obvious. He explicitly correlates knowledge with power instead of virtue—1908, "The Plan of the Work.") But since the ancient notion of the proper relation of human beings to meaningfully ordered reality was one of harmony and human acquiescence to that order by ordering oneself, nothing could more clearly reject that ancient view than seeing reality as an object of human control. In fact, we think seeing the world in terms of control and domination assumes that it is not properly ordered (if ordered at all) and that it must be brought to order by one's acts. It assumes that chaos is fundamental and that human power, by analogy to divine power, is required to overcome chaos. One may see this human power exercised directly, as in the ordering power of the mind (a la Kant), or indirectly, as in the apprehension and thus control over laws and conditions of nature, which, in turn, produce the things of the world. Both of these moves are apparent in contemporary psychological theory, the first as humanism and the second as behaviorism.

The analogy of human power to divine power is decisive for the development of the modern notion of self and, therefore, for the possibility of modern psychology. Previously, it was not the objects of the world with which one had to be in harmony. Instead, one had to be in harmony with what is, with ultimate reality (the Forms, God, or whatever else one took to be the ultimate reality). Wisdom was not a relation (in other words, a correspondence) of consciousness to objects for either the ancients or the medievals. With the beginning of the modern period, however, wisdom became such a relation. Now to be wise was to have one's mental representations correspond to the things of the world, just as God's thought corresponded to the world God created. What followed was an analogy of human consciousness to God: to be fully conscious, to be rational, was to be in control of the things in the world, to bring them into order in some way. Human consciousness began to be modeled on the power and creative abilities of the medieval God.

Thus, for the medievals, human consciousness and individuality was found in a relation to God (or the Forms, etc.), but for moderns consciousness was modeled on the ancient and medieval idea of God: self-defining and, in a very real sense, world-defining; atemporal—to the extent that it used the atemporal principles of reason; immaterial; at least in principle capable of certainty about everything; seeking omnipotence (cf. Descartes 1972b). Thus, in

the overall scheme of things, by making the individual and particularly the individual's consciousness into a model of God, the self
replaced ultimate reality as the standard for truth, as the origin of
order in the cosmos.[9] Implicit in this creation of the self-defining
individual was a rejection of the world as defining order, for the
world had previously included the self or individual. Now, however, the individual, like God, is "outside" the world. Whereas, for
the ancients, the search for wisdom was a search for confidence,
for the moderns it became a search for certainty—omnipotence.

In this movement to the individual and to the modern self, the
concept of wisdom was turned topsy-turvy. Previously, being wise
had meant being what one fully is, being in harmony with the
reality of the world. For the ancients, though the wise person had
certainty in regard to the matters about which one can be certain
(matters like geometry), part of wisdom was an understanding that
there is legitimate but noncertain knowledge (craft and ethical/
political knowledge, for example) (cf. Aristotle 1934, 1094–1095a).
For the moderns, however, wisdom meant freeing ourselves from
the world and our harmony with it and drawing back from the
world into ourselves to concentrate on our thinking and our
observations and how we can make sense of and *dis-cover* the truth
of both our thinking and observation on the one hand, and the
things in the world on the other. Descartes's method of doubt, for
example, was proposed to overcome this problem of projected
meaning and to replace it with certainty (see Descartes 1972a and
b, especially a). The question was no longer how we can be
brought to sensibility through understanding the truth, but how
we can make our understanding certain rather than capricious—
and those were, in the final analysis, the only two categories of
knowledge.

It is true, of course, that after the creation of the self- and
world-defining individual, one could still talk about the order of
the world. That kind of talk occurs frequently in the work of those
such as Galileo, Descartes, Bacon, Harvey, and da Vinci. But they
mean something very different by "order." Order is no longer to
be found in the very way in which things in the world are, nor
(especially) in their place within some ultimate order. In fact, to
speak of a place within the order of things is, for the moderns, only
metaphorical—if it is used at all. Instead, nature is secretive and
requires our decipherment. It is a book to be read, something that
stands apart from one and can be understood only with the proper
training—namely, mathematics. Whereas the previous order had

included the individual and was, therefore, available to every rational person, the modern order (in spite of Descartes's claims—1972b, meditation 1) is alien and secretive. Whereas the previous order had been conceived organically, as a growth or emanation, modern order is the order of mathematics, the order of rational, logical thought: the order of the "divine" mind replicated in the mind of the individual. Not only has the understanding of human consciousness changed, but with it the understanding of reality as a whole (in other words, metaphysics) has changed:

> When man becomes the first and only true subject, this means that man becomes, for every being, that being on which all beings are grounded in both their way of being and their truth. Man becomes the center of relation for beings as such. But that is only possible when the comprehension of beings as a whole changes. [Heidegger 1972d, p. 81]

That change in the comprehension of beings as a whole brings with it a great deal. Now, rather than as coexistent beings within a primal reality, both consciousness and things can be thought of in themselves. With the invention of the self-defining individual, subjectivity, we have also the invention of objectivity. The notion of subjectivity comes about because meaning, purpose, and truth are now the exclusive property of human individuals—selves— and not brought into them from the reality of the world in which those individuals live. In other words, meaning, purpose, and truth are now to be determined apart from human participation in the world, and instead from human reflection on the world. It is now possible to have not just imaginings, but genuine meanings that are merely mine and independent of the world in which I live. In fact, for some thinkers and for sound logical reasons, these meanings are the only ones about which certainty is possible (cf. Hume 1888).

On the other hand, the notion of subjectivity gives immediate rise to the notion of objectivity. For now we can ask ourselves, What is there when we set aside our subjective thoughts, meanings, and purposes? In other words, what is there objectively (cf. Taylor 1975, p. 9)? And having the categories of both subjectivity and objectivity, we can now ask a question that was impossible before: What is the relation between our subjective thoughts, feelings, meanings, and purposes and the objective world?[10] Modern epistemology is born at the same time as modern science (and in a very real sense, perhaps they are the same thing).

By the seventeenth century and the solid beginning of modern science, everyone seems to be aware of the change that is occurring in metaphysics and, therefore, in everything else. Galileo's trouble with the Inquisition is a consequence of this change, and Descartes is carefully cognizant of it in his discussion of why he has adopted the method of doubt, a method that explicitly rejects both tradition and some overarching ultimate as the standard of truth and focuses on the individual's thought, the self, as that standard (1972a).[11] Bacon puts the difference perhaps most clearly when he complains that Aristotle is not a good scientist because, "having first determined the question according to his will, he then resorts to experience, and bending her into conformity with his placets leads her about like a captive in a procession" (1908, I.63). In other words, he says that for Aristotle, to understand experience is to find how it conforms to an ultimate, overarching reality, but for Bacon the real is to be deduced by individuals from their experiences of this world. There is an element in Aristotle's discussion of understanding that is missing in Bacon, an element Bacon, and—following him—most moderns, would take to be passivity: in Aristotle, the ultimate reality is in charge; in Bacon, the individual self is.

"RECONCILING" THE ANCIENT AND THE MODERN VIEWS

Our way of describing the creation of the modern notion of the individual or self may make that creation appear to be only an unfortunate event. It might make us long to return to "the good old days," and the temptation might be to advocate such a return. But that is impossible. In spite of the problems of the modern way of thinking (and we will see more of them later), the introduction of the modern self into the history of Western thought cannot be construed as merely an accident, as something to be negated and done away with. To ignore what has been brought about is to ignore what we, in fact, now are. We cannot simply go back to an ancient and medieval conception of ourselves and our world, because we already have the self-defining self as a reality; we cannot simply forget it.

In fact, one might easily argue that whatever advantages the ancient metaphysics and its understanding of consciousness might have had, the modern understanding could not have come about and taken such a footing in the world if it were merely a mistake or an odd flight of human fancy. In the first place, it involves an understanding of something with which, as Descartes reminds us, we are quite familiar (namely, the self). If that understanding were straightforwardly false, it would seem odd indeed for everyone to believe it so thoroughly as we have come to do, or even for it to have been appealing in the beginning. How would it be possible for an utterly or even generally false view of the self to have gained such currency? Perhaps it could be explained as a universal self-deception, a way of avoiding the truth about ourselves. But even if that were true—and we are not at all unwilling to entertain such a possibility—self-deceptions are not simply falsities. They are a way of playing on the truth, of distorting it to suit one's purposes. Thus, even if we go so far as to grant that the notion of the self-defining individual is a self-deception, we must also admit that there is something to it. The modern notion of self at least says something about reality, so we must take account of it if we are to account for the world.

In the second place, to put it crudely but accurately, anything that has done as much for us as has the metaphysics that engendered this notion of the self and the resulting science cannot be all bad. It is difficult to imagine that modern sewage systems, immunization programs, and trips to the moon and back—technologies made possible by the metaphysics found in the work of Descartes, Bacon, and others, a metaphysics that has at its fundament the self-defining individual—are founded on a fundamentally incorrect view of the world and our place in it. It is difficult to imagine that the metaphysics that has given us technology is fundamentally mistaken, even if we are skeptical about technology's benefits or worried about the sway it holds today. Bacon seems to be thinking in the same way when he says "works [the inventions of modern science] themselves are of greater value as pledges of truth than as contributing to the comforts of life" (1908, I.194). In other words, the primary importance of science is not that it improves our lives, though it certainly does, but that it gives strong evidence for the metaphysics that makes it possible, a metaphysics centered in the notion of the self-defining individual, the subject as self.

Finally—and philosophically most importantly—the creation of the idea of the self-defining individual is a response to the failure of the medieval world to make intelligible the split between the divine realm and the human, a failure manifest most clearly in nominalism. Though we have not given particular attention to it, at the heart of ancient and medieval thought was a problem, the problem of the gap between this world, the world of change, and the "real" world, the world of the Forms, God, etc. In spite of the organic modeling of the ancient and medieval understanding of the world and individuals in that world, it contained a fissure in its very foundation, which eventually split that foundation: thinkers began to ask how it was possible for something in this changing world to be in harmony with something absolutely unlike the changing world. Ancient and medieval philosophy could not answer such a question.

In the face of that failure, late medieval and early Renaissance thinkers turned to a discussion of the human world and, in essence, "bracketed" the divine, leaving the question of the divine out of their investigations. Because it could not maintain itself, theology moved from being the center of philosophy to being one more of its areas of investigation. The traditional God moved to the edges of philosophy, and the individual moved to the center to take its place. Whatever advantages we might find in the ancient view of things, we must see the development of the notion of the self-defining self as a positive contribution, and whatever alternatives we propose to modernity, they cannot be a mere return to the ancient view.

In spite of its pretensions otherwise, however, modern philosophy was not completely willing to give up the ancient and medieval appeal to divinity. When the self moved into the center of philosophy to replace God, it imitated the medieval conception of God. The self that comes into existence with the modern period is a being whose realities are its representations. Like the medieval God, the self creates the world it knows by representing that world to itself. In the history of philosophy from Descartes through Immanuel Kant, the self is thinking inasmuch as it has representations. Thus, the thinking activity of the self is an imitation of divine power—acquisition and creation—rather than one of openness to and harmony with divinity as it had been for the ancients. The modern metaphysic of self reduplicates the ancient metaphysic of God in new terms but the same structure. It therefore cannot be expected to escape the problems of that metaphysic.

An analogy to grammar helps explain the metaphysics of the modern self, the "subject." In grammar, that which has predicates is the subject. Analogously, the modern philosophical/psychological subject is that which has representations, and these representations are its predicates. They are what it determines, what it predicates. In grammar, the subject is also that which is qualified by the predicates of an assertion. It is the "about which" in an assertion. Similarly, the modern self is that which lies at the base of all representation. It is the about-which of all assertions of knowledge. To say that any particular such-and-such is true is always to say one knows it is true. It is to say something about the person making the statement as much as it is to say something about the such-and-such. For it is to claim them as that person's representations, predicates. They are what that person, as a knowing entity, knows.

Since, as Descartes points out, the self is only a thinking thing, the having of these predicates is a knowing that I have them (cf. 1972b, meditation 2). *Having predicates* defines the thinking thing as thinking thing. His famous sentence, *cogito ergo sum*, does not mean that I am *because* I am thinking. It means that in thinking, I am. Though Descartes points to this reflectively, it is clear that he does not think reflection is necessary. Reflection reveals the connection between my thinking and my being, but reflection is not necessary to the indubitability of my existence; thinking these predicates, I am also thinking my thinking of them. Thus, I know them immediately and in knowing them I know myself as a thinking being. The ego defines itself in its activity as thinking thing.

The subject is distinct from its predicates; it is not its predicates, but its thinking of them. On the other hand, in having them and in being distinct from them, the subject has its representations, its predicates, as objects—mental objects that supposedly correspond to external objects. The relation of these objects of thought to the objects in the world becomes a major question for modern philosophy. Having set the self off from the world, how can one determine whether one's representations, the things one predicates of the world, correspond to that world? Where can one find the unity which makes it possible to bring together the self that is alienated from its world and that world?

Descartes postulates the self-defining self as thinking thing and resolves the problem of the relation of its representations to the world of objects by reference to God, whom he says can be proven to exist to the satisfaction of the subject. This move is one that has its origins in medieval and ancient philosophy (for the medieval God is the creator, and Descartes's two substances, mind and matter, are God's creations). But Descartes's move is radically different from medieval philosophy in spite of its dependence on that philosophy. Whereas in medieval philosophy God had been the standard by which all else, including the self, came to be and, therefore, could be judged, in the modern period the self is the standard by which even the existence of God must be judged: I am certain of the self; all else requires proof. Moderns put themselves into a position where they can assume the possibility of correspondence between certain of their representations and reality, if they can prove God's existence.

Locke and Berkeley disagree about the status of the objects, but they too postulate the subject as thinking thing and are worried about the relation of its representations to the objects represented. They accept without discussion Descartes's mediation of the subject and object by God. Hume (1980), however, argues that God's existence cannot be proven to the satisfaction of the purely rational subject, which Descartes (1888) has set up as the standard for explanation, and Hume sees that the result is skepticism about any predicates as representations of some external world. In modern metaphysics there is no way to get outside our thinking to check to see whether it represents objects properly—or even to see if there are any objects out there to be represented—and we cannot use God as a guarantor of such correspondence or of the existence of those objects. Thus for Hume, the self knows that it is predicating, and it knows those things of its own invention (like mathematics), but it can know nothing else. Founded in a search for certainty, modern metaphysics ends up in skepticism.

To recapitulate: modern philosophy reduplicates the fatal division of ancient and medieval philosophy. The ancients and medievals divided the divine from the world, centering reality in the divine, and ended up skeptical of the ability to speak meaningfully about the divine. Modern philosophy imitates that division, dividing the individual (interior) from the world (exterior), centering meaning in the individual and ending up skeptical about speaking meaningfully about the world. Descartes's solution to the division is to invoke God, but that solution is the very one that failed the medievals. Hume's criticism of Descartes points to a double failure: not only can we not have access to any divine realm outside this world, as the nominalists came to see, but we cannot even have access to the world. Radical skepticism seems the only answer. Like ancient and medieval metaphysics, modern metaphysics was fissured, and the fissure gradually widened and threatened to split metaphysics wide open.

Immanuel Kant's work is a response to this threat. Whatever the difficulties of healing the split between interior and exterior by reference to the divine, Descartes and Hume had both agreed that the subject is the standard of truth. In fact, it would not be too much to say that the subject is the subject of all modern philosophy from Descartes through Hegel. Kant's genius comes in thinking more seriously about the notion of the subject than had his predecessors; though he does not resort to a proof of God's existence to solve the problem of the fissured metaphysics, he agrees with them in taking up the subject—the individual, the self—as the center of his metaphysics.

Kant (1956) argues that Hume has conflated the knowledge of phenomena (in other words, experience) with knowledge of what is beyond experience, the external world. For Kant, the phenomenal world is properly an object of investigation since the objects of experience are to be found in that world, but the external world (what he calls the *noumenal* world) is not, since it is beyond experience. His resolution of the problem, foreshadowed in Leibniz's monadology, is a brilliant return to the Cartesian subject as thinking thing, showing that we did not need to use God as the guarantor of the accuracy of our representations. Kant takes the notion of the self-defining individual most seriously and, in examining it, finds the possibility for knowledge within the subject itself.

Kant says the question of correspondence has been misunderstood. One need not worry about the relation of one's representations to objects "out there." For knowledge is not knowledge of the "out there," but of the subject, of the conditions for the possibility of the appearance of an object. Since the individual is self-defining, knowledge is correspondence with that self-definition, not with some other object. One has knowledge of experience, of phenomena, when one's knowledge is certain, which certainty one can have without needing to refer to a world beyond any possible experience. One can have knowledge if there is something that guarantees the consistency of one's experience—if there is some transcendental ground to experience—and that ground need not be found in a transcendent external world or in some other thing, like God, which is transcendent of possible human experience. Kant argues that this transcendental ground is found in the categories that make experience possible, those categories (like space, time, and quantity) without which a person could not have any experience whatsoever. This ground, Kant says, is transcendental in that it goes beyond any particular experience. But it is not transcendent; it does not go beyond experience in general.

The secret to Kant's rethinking of the Cartesian position is in remembering that Descartes's *cogito* is not only a thinking of its predicates, but also a knowing that it is thinking them. The characteristic of the subject that makes it possible for Descartes to say *cogito ergo sum* is self-consciousness: in thinking, I am; I know I am thinking my thoughts as I do so. In fact, that is the only characteristic of the subject. Since it is more than its predicates but cannot be thinking apart from predicating, the subject is the self-knowing of predication; it has predicates by knowing that it has them. Thus, given the individual as self-defining, knowledge is to be found in self-knowledge; objective knowledge is to be found in the knowledge of thought objects, in the way in which the self knows its predications.

For Kant, the self, not the external world, is the ground for all representation, so knowledge must be knowledge of the self rather than of the world. With Kant, objectivity, rather than the external world, is a function of the subject. For Kant too, the individual, the self, the subject remains the standard for truth. By taking the idea of the self-defining subject even more seriously than did his predecessors, Kant appears to have solved the problem of the transcendent from within the framework of modern philosophy, replacing the transcendent entity with transcendence. Thus, in reality Kant does not reject the skepticism of Hume. Instead he amends it with a skepticism in which subjective knowledge—Cartesian subjective certainty of the objects of consciousness—is possible. We believe, however, that this emendation did not succeed.

As we have seen, the subjectivization of the world led to the skepticism of Hume, a skepticism that makes human relation impossible. For if one cannot know of one's relation to another, perhaps a spouse—because one can only know his idea of her, not his spouse herself—then he can be related only to his idea of her. Perhaps from some noumenal point of view (which is already a contradiction in terms) it might be said that he is related to her rather than merely to his idea of her, but that relation is for another and not for him. Kant, the most radical of those who make an analysis of subjectivity and the person who shows us its logical culmination, makes it possible for us to have knowledge, knowledge that goes beyond the knowledge of tautological truth still possible for Hume. But Kant does not save us from the alienation inherent in the subject-object approach. Human relation to the objective world may be possible, since that world is a function of the human self. Human relation to others is still impossible. Kant allows one to have certainty about objects in the world of experience and, therefore, he makes science possible, but he does not allow any possibility for relation to other persons as persons rather than as mere objects, since—as he points out in the *Foundations of the Metaphysics of Morals* (1965, pp. 50–52)—persons are not objects, and his metaphysics and epistemology are a metaphysics and epistemology of objects only.

But even at the level of objects, Kant has a problem. The subject-object problem has been overcome, but it has been replaced by a more profound variation of the same problem, the phenomenal-noumenal problem. For Kant, both the world and the self are split, the former into the world of experience and the unexperienced world behind it, and the latter into the self of experience and the transcendent and inaccessible self behind it. Kant has not been able to overcome the alienation implicit in the subjective assumption. In fact, he has redoubled it, even though he has been able to give that subject some confidence in its judgments about the objective world by making that world the world of the subject's experience rather than the world "out there."

Throughout Kant assumes the "out there" as the basis of the phenomenal. Though we can never experience the noumenal world and so can have no knowledge of it, reason demands that we assume it, he says. But he has shown us only that the noumenal world is a necessary condition *if* knowledge as Cartesian certainty is to be possible—in other words, if we adopt a Cartesian metaphysics. Whether knowledge as certainty is possible— whether we ought to adopt a Cartesian metaphysics—is the very question he set out to answer. Thus, reason demands the existence of the noumenal world only if we accept the modern quest for certainty as legitimate. But if we do not accept that quest, a quest resulting from the modeling of the self on the medieval God—and, from an ancient point of view, a question that narrows the notion of knowledge far too much by reducing it to mathematical certainty— Kant's critical philosophy with its distinction of the phenomenal and the noumenal is unnecessary. On the other hand, without some transcendent ground, there is little difference between Kant and Hume—except that Kant has shown us just how complex the alienated inner world that comes from seeking certainty and supposing individuality can be. Kant's attempt to patch the fissure in the cracked foundation of modern metaphysics fails.

The history of German philosophy after Kant and through Johann Fichte and Friedrich Schelling to Hegel is the history of the attempt to patch this fissure, the attempt to give an unalienated account of the possibility of subjective certainty. It is the attempt to give a metaphysics that makes subjective certainty possible without assuming, in one way or another, the existence of an unknown and unknowable realm. And many of our contemporary psychological as well as philosophical and political dilemmas can be seen as responses to the fact that no resolution is offered.

Consider, for example, the problem of freedom. A new notion of freedom comes about in the modern grounding of the truth, of what can be known, in the subject. In fact, previously there had been little discussion of human freedom. Of course there had been some idea of what we might call freedom—we were free to be out of harmony with God or the Forms or whatever; we were free to look in such a way that we did not see the truth; it was possible to live in illusion and remain there—but most discussion of freedom referred merely to freedom from enslavement, liberty. With modern thought, however, we have the innate freedom of the self. In it, like the medieval God, humans found and confirm themselves as the authoritative measure for all truth (echoing Pico's description of them two hundred years earlier). However, built into this new notion of freedom is the problem of free will and determinism, for this freedom is either the arbitrary choice of a self-defining being, or it is conditioned on certainty or confidence in our knowledge of the external world.

In the modern philosophy of the self, the meaning of being is no longer found in the world or in God, but in the individual; and as a consequence, he "need no longer define his perfection or vice, his equilibrium or disharmony, in relation to an external world" (Taylor 1975, p. 9). He is now free from the authority of the church and can legislate for himself. In fact, he *must* legislate for himself. Where previously what was obligatory had been prescribed for him and he was free to act only with those obligations or against them, with the advent of modern metaphysics he is the one who posits what is obligatory. Of course, that positing need not be capricious or merely individual, but even the Kantian ethic of duty is founded on the subjectness of the subject, on shared but individual rationality. At best, what is right is right because it is rational, and the standard for rationality is the subject. The center for virtue is now human being rather than the divine, which seems only fitting considering that human being has taken the position in the metaphysical system that was previously occupied by God.

However, at the same time that we discovered freedom of the self—with the invention/discovery of the self—we also discovered determinism. For there are two things moving through the history of modern thought, both results of the notion of the self-defining individual, and neither entirely compatible with the other. First there is the notion of the self-defining subject and its accompanying freedom, a freedom that comes from the fact that, in a very real sense, the self-defining subject is also world-defining. In other words, the self-defining self has a freedom taken over from the idea of the omnipotence of the medieval God. But second, with the notion of the self-defining subject (subjectivity), we have also the creation of objects in the world to be grasped, manipulated, and understood, objects which exist independently from us and in an ontologically different manner, a manner corresponding to the creations of the medieval God. These objects are not like us because they are not selves like us, so they are not free like us. They constitute the determined, objective world.

Thus, in addition to the metaphysics of the individual—a metaphysics based on the assumption of the self-defining individual—the modern movement has given us the science of objects. But that science has an ironic result: as part of it, in a natural move from the consideration of what we can know about objects unlike ourselves, we begin to ask questions about humans as objects in the world. Humans become part of the world of objects and, therefore, determined. As a result, given the notion of the self-defining individual and the definition of knowledge as certainty, freedom of choice (of the subjective self) is sensible and nonarbitrary only if it is based on sure and certain knowledge of alternatives, alternatives that must actually be there and be dictated by some mechanism—in other words determined, made certain—in order for there to be choices. The question of freedom or determinism is, therefore, an outgrowth of the postulation of the self-defining individual, and our inability to choose between them is a consequence of the fact that the postulation generates them both. (Thus, the Kantian antinomy of freedom and determinism is not a product of reason itself, as he supposes, but of the assumption made by moderns that the individual is self-defining—cf. Kant 1956, B448–449.)

We should notice, in passing, that this understanding of the origin of the dilemma of freedom and determinism shows an asymmetry between the two: determinism is the thinking-out of objectivity, of what it means to speak of the objects that are not like the free subjects we are. That objectivity then gets turned on the subject, asking whether we can take it as an object as well. Here is the asymmetry: objectivity has its origin in the logical reciprocity of subject and object (or there is no sense in talking about the object as opposed to the subject). The self- and world-defining subject, however, is ontologically fundamental to the object. Thus, the subject-object relation, from which objectivity and therefore determinism springs, is itself founded in subjective freedom. Determinism is a child of the modern notion of freedom.

There are other ironies as well. Founded in a claim that the dignity of humans is to be found in their knowledge and power, much of modern philosophy and, therefore, contemporary psychology is a search to overcome the alienation of the individual from the world and the self-alienation that follows from world alienation. Self-defining individuals have lost confidence in their ability to define themselves and can rarely find it in terms they can use. As the center of definition, of meaning, when they turn their activity upon themselves, they are at a loss, for there seems to be no ground from which to give definition to themselves. By definition, they are contentless.

Those who look for self-definition in terms of materialism, scientism, political-isms, or some other objective or semiobjective phenomenon are necessarily dissatisfied, because, without their knowing it, the objects they use to define themselves are already defined by their subjectivity. Because even the scientific search for empirical bases and explanations of social and psychological phenomena is given within this modern subject-object framework, that search is necessarily unsatisfactory. On the other hand, those who look for self-definition in terms that do not involve objects of one sort or another are lost. For only the nothingness of content-lessness seems available to them, and they are, above all, looking for content. That is what self-definition consists of in modernism.

The division of the world into modern subjects and objects presents us with a dilemma: there are two ways to overcome alienation, first through the definition of the self and world given by objects of various sorts that transcend self and world, including scientific laws; or second, through the definition given merely by the subject. The first of these finds self-definition to be illusory self-deception; the second finds it to be nihilism. Having presupposed the self-defining individual—the subject, the Cartesian ego—no other alternatives seem possible for moderns.

At the everyday level, the first of these two alternatives—self-definition in terms of reifications or physical materials of some kind—is most common. In this alternative, either the possibility of the world and the self is given in transcendent objects, like "laws," or that possibility is found in the objects of the world themselves, where they are given transcendent status as objective empirical data rather than particular events.[12] The dangers of this first alternative are most commonly recognized. There are numerous writers who tell us of the terrible alienation brought by scientism, the rise of technology, and various other objective phenomena, like public institutions and social organizations. (They range from the mindless but popular, like Schumacher 1975, to the thoughtful but nearly impenetrable, like Heidegger 1954a.) By splitting the subject from the object, by seeing our relation to objects in the world in terms of their differences from us and in terms of our power over them, we have been transformed into their subjects, those to whom we are in thrall. Those who take on the task of overcoming this alienation using a self-definition that focuses on the objective world (a self-definition that is a function of the modern framework) come to a variety of conclusions, but in each the subjugation we have described is unavoidable.

Also at the everyday level, the second kind of self-definition, definition not in terms of transcendent objects, but of mere self (definition that we have already argued amounts essentially to nihilism) can be found in such places as much modern art and literature, the relatively recent craze for supposedly oriental religions, and 99 percent of pop psychologies. Few who take this second approach to self-definition think it through to its conclusion in nihilism, but when they do, nihilism seems the only alternative to subjugation. This second kind of self-definition, however, does not see that its inability to either find or create meaning is not so much a necessary fact as it is a result of its assumptions about the self. Not surprisingly, in trying to define itself only in terms of itself, the self can find no definition. (After all, no meaningful predication can be self-referential.) Thus, both attempts at self-definition—that in terms of transcendent laws and that in terms of the "objective world"—require something transcendent of self and world as the basis for self- and world-definition, but neither can find such a thing, because both have excluded it in principle: the first by reference to a realm absolutely transcendent of experience; the second by reference to the empty self.

In psychology these two ways are evident in the two primary directions taken by psychological theory, empiricism on the one hand, and various sorts of humanism or subjectivism on the other. Psychological theories that seek to discuss human beings in terms of only the "external world" succumb to the problems of the first way of approaching the self. Humanist, subjectivist theories succumb to the second. Though they appear to be mutually exclusive alternatives, each of these fails because it is based on the mistaken modern metaphysics and its notion of the self, and the resulting mistaken notion of the world. Psychological theory finds itself reliving the failures of modern philosophy. Alternatives to this dilemma will be found only by going between its horns, by finding a way of thinking about the individual and the world that does not presume the modern notion of the self-defining self. (Ironically, by presuming modern metaphysics, social psychology also makes this assumption, *even when it also argues that the self is socially constructed*.)

RECONSIDERING THE PROBLEM OF SELF AND WORLD

In summary of the history of the development of the psychological self, consider the parallel difference between English and Latin terms (and notice the contrast of both with the Greek term *hupokeimenon*). *Subiectum* means "that which lies before or adjacent to," so it names well the Cartesian self: that being closest to us. *Subject*, however, is a latinized English word—originally, it seems, *sugette* —meaning "to be under the dominion of." Thus, in a striking parallel between etymology and the history of ideas, the Latin *subiectum* (corresponding to the Cartesian self) became the English *subject* (the modern alienated and subjugated self). In the search for certainty, a search with the self as its ground, we have come to doubt the possibility of self-certainty and have turned certainty over to the objects and our dealings with them. We have, thus, become alienated from both the objects and ourselves—alienated from objects because the subject-object model of human consciousness begins with the objects already in question, and alienated from self because we can find nothing with which to define the self-defining individual when we make it an object of our search.

As we have already pointed out, we cannot merely return to

some premodern notion of things to solve the problem. To ignore what has been brought about in what we have seen is to ignore the truth. Though the modern view was a response to the failed (because fissured) metaphysics of the ancients and medievals—a metaphysics that divided the world into the two incommensurable parts, God and world—the moderns continued to divide the world into incommensurable pieces, mind and world. Modern philosophy reincorporates the fissure into itself. Thus, modernism also fails, as will any psychology based on that metaphysics. The alternative to the modern understanding of the individual will not be found in the failed understanding of the ancients. We must find some alternative. We must think through both possibilities—the ancient and the modern—and see if there is not some third possibility that can bring about the truth of both these previously seemingly irreconcilable positions. To use Hegel's phrase, we must look for some possibility for understanding the self into which we can be *aufgehoben*—"put up" in the sense of changing in order to preserve. We as authors think continental philosophy provides a basis from which to begin such a work.

MARTIN HEIDEGGER

The most obvious person to whom we can turn in looking for some path "beyond" traditional philosophy is Martin Heidegger. Heidegger was one of the first influential continental thinkers of this century, one who set much of the tone and direction for those who have followed, whether or not they were in any strict sense his disciples. Heidegger's philosophical work has loomed over continental philosophy. Though not often mentioned in Anglo-American literature until recently, Heidegger's influence on continental philosophy has certainly been greater than Jean-Paul Sartre's and perhaps greater even than Karl Marx's in some ways. Heidegger has made a radical critique of traditional metaphysics and, in a not unproblematic sense, he has discussed an alternative to that metaphysics.[13] Since explanation presumes an ontology in presuming what it means to be a thing, as well as what counts as grounds for something else (in other words, an explanation), and since noncontinental methods of explanation to this point are founded in the traditional metaphysics, Heidegger's work provides a radically different starting point for thinking about psychological explanation by providing for the possibility of genuine transcendence.

Heidegger provides for genuine transcendence, but he does not do so by an appeal to a transcendent. (Notice that *transcendence* refers to an activity, a process, etc., while *the transcendent* refers to an entity of some sort, an otherworldly entity. This difference is key to understanding what Heidegger does.) The move to transcendence without an appeal to the transcendent makes psychological explanation possible and provides the groundwork for a fruitful approach to explanation that promises to be radically different from that taken traditionally.[14]

In a lecture course in 1928, Heidegger took up the issue of the metaphor that informs explanation in contemporary psychology, based as it is on modern metaphysics. As we have seen, modern metaphysics, exemplified in Cartesian thought, is a metaphysics in which the subject is known to itself immediately and the world is known only indirectly, known by a mediation of some sort if it is known at all. Describing the situation that results from this metaphysics, Heidegger says:

> Here the subject is thought of as a sort of box with an interior, with the walls of a box, and with an exterior. Of course the crude view is not put forth that consciousness is in fact a box, but what is essential to the analogy and what belongs to the very conception of the transcendent is that a barrier between inner and outer must be crossed. This means that the inner is, first of all, really restricted by the barrier and must first break through it, must first *remove the restrictions.*
>
> [On the view we are criticizing,] transcendence, then, is taken to be the relationship that somehow or other maintains a passageway between the interior and exterior of the box by leaping over or pressing through the wall of the box. So the problem arises of how to explain the possibility of such a passage. [1984, pp. 160–61]

The development of the modern concept of self and this resulting problem of the transcendent turns much of modern philosophy to an analysis of consciousness or to studies based on an analysis of consciousness. (The emphasis of modern philosophy on epistemology is an example of this turn.) But, as we have seen, that analysis fails. The rise of scientific psychology can be seen as a response to philosophy's drive to the analysis of consciousness and its subsequent failure. But psychology, though born in the face of philosophy's failure, dooms itself from the very beginning by assuming the same metaphysics as that which produced the problems faced by philosophy, the metaphysics of the self-defining self. Thus, every attempt at psychological explanation faces the same problems as did modern philosophy. The possibility of scientific psychology will be found only in an alternative to traditional, fissured metaphysics, for that fissure is at the heart of the modern conception of the self and the failure of both the ancient and medieval views.

Psychological explanation occurs within the context of modern (post-Cartesian) philosophy, where the central problem is the problem of the barrier, the inside and the outside separated by the walls of the box.[15] Psychologists offer a variety of answers to the problem of the barrier. Empirical psychologies, for example, seek to explain by moving everything in the interior of the box to the exterior. Cognitive psychologies seek to preserve at least some of the interior. Other psychologies deal with the problem in other ways. But in each case, the explanations given center on the problem of the barrier between inside and outside.

Because the problem is a problem of the barrier, a problem of fissure, psychological theorists—like philosophers—have looked for something that would give unity to the absolute division of the inside from the outside, something that would give a coherent account of both the inside and the outside (the individual and the world), and psychological explanations have relied on the various results of such searches. Because of the way the problem is conceived—because of the metaphor used in thinking about the problem—in most cases this search has been for something that is neither inside nor outside, something that transcends the inside and the outside of the box. But what results in such a notion of the transcendent is not a rethinking or denial of the metaphor, but an addition of another level to it. That which stands, as it were, above the box, holding the inside and the outside—in their division—in a unity is added to the original metaphor. This addition is analogous to the mind of the person viewing the box with its inside, outside, and wall, an analogue with obvious antecedents in traditional theology.

For the medievals, the entity that transcended and explained everything else was God, outside time and space, and the ground of all existence. The modern period abandoned God as the transcendent explanation, but retained the substance of that idea in postulating the inside and the outside, and something that holds together that inside and outside. In God's place modern thinkers put reason, law, etc. Just as was the God that reason and law replaced, these were conceived of as immutable and eternal—unchangeable and atemporal. Though the necessity that explanation be grounded on atemporal and necessary principles does not seem to have been questioned and, therefore, was not defended, underlying the assumption seems to be Aristotle's argument: what needs explanation is change. Change cannot explain itself, so the ground of explanation must be unchanging. Since the ground of explanation must be static, it must also be necessary, for explanations based ultimately on only possibility would not be based on something static (for a static set of possibilities is not genuinely a set of possibilities) (cf. Aristotle 1934, book 6, and Marx 1971, pp. 43–71).

Paradoxically, reducing intelligibility to atemporality and necessity results in the unintelligibility of the world. For that which would make the world intelligible—a grasp of atemporal and necessary principles—lies forever out of reach precisely because those principles, being atemporal and necessary, are themselves not intelligible in a human world that is temporal and possible. Based on the metaphor of consciousness as a box, modern metaphysics has available only three sources of explanation, three places in which one can find the analogue to the medieval God: atemporal and transcendent principles (something beyond both the box and its outside that makes explanation possible), empiricism (something outside the box), and subjectivity (something inside the box).[16] None of these, however, provides a satisfactory explanation, since phenomena, as phenomena, are essentially temporal.

As traditionally conceived, transcendent principles give a common ground for all knowledge. But that ground is inaccessible and, therefore, unknowable, making knowledge impossible. Empiricism, by referring to laws and regularities that are themselves not a part of the sensible world ("behind" or "beyond" it in some sense), turns out to be merely a subspecies of the appeal to the transcendent (cf. Faulconer and Williams 1985, 1987). Thus, though there seem to be three directions to which traditional metaphysics can turn for the possibility of explanation, there turn out to be only two, the transcendent and the subjective. We have seen the case against the transcendent: the transcendent medieval God and the modern transcendent, law, both turn out to be inaccessible and inexplicable, located forever out of human reach.[17] An equally good case can be made against the remaining alternative, subjectivity, for it gives nothing common upon which to ground knowledge. Subjective explanation makes a kind of knowledge possible, but only for the individual and only of the individual (which makes calling it knowledge odd, at least). As a result, in modern metaphysics there is no accounting for knowledge—ironic considering the whole purpose of that metaphysics was to give a ground to knowledge, to make it possible. It follows that in modern metaphysics and its children (like psychology), explanation (the giving of grounds whether psychological or otherwise) is itself without ground.

This failure reveals that the fissure in the foundation of traditional metaphysics, whether ancient and medieval or modern, was irreparable. Founding itself on reason as the atemporal ground and requiring that everything have a ground, reason comes into crisis in the metaphysical tradition, for it has no reasons, no grounds. The medieval God failed as a ground for explanation because it was incomprehensible, ungrounded. Taking its place as ground, the modern self failed for the same reason. As Heidegger says, for the metaphysical tradition *"explanation is the expository interpretation of the incomprehensible"* (1985, p. 217). It is, therefore, doomed to failure.

The ontological analytic begun in *Being and Time* (1976) and continued in Heidegger's later work points the direction for a genuine path of thought about these matters, a path of thought that ought to make explanation in general possible. Psychological explanation would then have a starting point. Without trying to justify them fully, we will sketch some of Heidegger's conclusions.[18]

Heidegger's analytic explicates what is always already disclosed in human being. He argues that when we make that explication, we find the being of consciousness is not found in reflection (as assumed by the metaphysical tradition), but in practical, everyday life. Much of his analysis, therefore, is an analysis of the possibility of everydayness. Rather than accepting the metaphor of the box, with the human subject walled off from the nonhuman, objective world, Heidegger's analysis leads to the conclusion that human being is already being-in-the-world. There is no inside walled off from the outside. A human is not a subject that needs somehow to escape from its subjective immanence into the objective world by a mediation of some sort. Rather, human being (which Heidegger calls *Dasein*[19]) is being-in-the-world (as opposed to "being-in-the-box" and standing over against what is outside it), and being-in-the-world is seen in concern and interest—ultimately in what he calls, semimetaphorically, care.[20] Transcendence is found in human existence, not behind it or outside it.

Because Dasein is characterized by being-in-the-world, it stands out in that world. To be in the world is to have "location," and to have location is to be distinguished from other beings. It is to stand out. (That is why Heidegger speaks of Dasein as *ecstatic*, relying on that word's root meaning—namely, "to stand out.") Because Dasein stands out among other beings and because it is in standing out that it has being, Dasein's being (its activity) is always at issue for itself. In other words, all of Dasein's concernful dealings with the world, even (and perhaps especially) its everyday concerns, are at bottom concerns with its own being. This does not mean that Dasein reflects on itself as a separate entity in those concerns. Rather, since Dasein's dealings in its concerns are inescapably expressions as well as the establishment of its "location" (of its *da*), Dasein's concernful dealings are inescapably and prereflectively concerns with itself (as located and locating rather than as metaphysical entity).

It must be emphasized, however, that since Dasein's being is not a subjective being, this concern with its own being is not a subjectivism. Because it is characterized by being-in-the-world, Dasein is also characterized by being-with. Since to have location is necessarily to have location in a field, as being-in-the-world Dasein is located in the field of the world, and the world always already includes other entities (otherwise it would not be a field). It is primordially both with entities in the world ("being-alongside") and with others like itself ("being-with"). The world—its contents as well as those who share that world—is not something to which the individual comes via reflection. It is given already in what it means to be Dasein. In having location and relation, Dasein already understands the world and it does so as being-alongside and being-with. Being-alongside is seen most obviously in activities like working with tools. Being-with is seen most obviously in activities like speaking: speaking to another, speaking about others and things. To speak about and interpret is a distinctive way for Dasein to be itself. Interpretation is the expressing of the understanding of Dasein made manifest in its being-alongside-and-with. Therefore, interpretation is a taking up of the issue of Dasein's being.

Because it is care, Dasein is ontologically oriented to time. Dasein has this orientation because to have care for activity—to have projects—is necessarily an orientation explicitly toward the future and implicitly (and equiprimordially) toward the past, the "having been" (1976, p. 385). But the time to which Dasein is oriented is not clock time, the eternal succession of a series of "now-points." Instead, it is that which makes clock time possible, the stretching out of Dasein between birth and death, the connectedness of existence (1976, p. 374–75). As Heidegger says in discussing the difference between the ordinary conception of time and primordial time:

> It is exactly when Dasein is immersed in everyday, concernful "living along" [*Dahinleben*] that it does not understand itself as running along in a continuously enduring sequence of pure "nows." The time which Dasein allows itself has what might be called gaps in it because of this covering up [of everyday life and the everyday experience of time]. Often we do not bring a "day" together again if we come back to the time we "used." But this failure of the time which has gaps in it, a failure to come together, is no dismemberment, rather it is a mode of that temporality which has already been disclosed and stretched out ecstatically. [1976, pp. 409–10]

We can only speak of "gaps" in our experience of time, gaps that do not throw our existence into amnesia-induced anxiety, because the time in which these gaps occur is itself based on a more fundamental temporality, a temporality in which there are no gaps. And that temporality cannot be reduced to clock time since it is its origin; it is the connectedness of human existence.

The temporal orientation of Dasein is not just one of the facts about Dasein, not even one of the facts about every particular Dasein. The language of the metaphysical tradition carries so much baggage with it as to present a danger to its users, the danger of unknowingly importing the failures of that tradition, but using that language anyway, we could say that orientation toward time is part of the *essence* of Dasein. Though the details of the argument cannot be replicated here, the investigation of this temporal orientation leads to a conclusion that, rather than being in time, Dasein (standing out with and among others and things) is itself the possibility of time (1985, p. 197).[21]

The resulting ontology (by no means systematic) is one in which temporality rather than atemporality is central.[22] It is important to recognize, however, that by *temporality* Heidegger does not mean any ordinary notion of time. He means, instead, something like *the possibility of time/space*. In doing this ontological work, Heidegger's project was to think through ontological questions—not in order to find some final, metaphysical answer to them (in other words, not in order to build a system), but in order to think through the confusions of that metaphysics, and in order to see what the genuine "ground" of the metaphysics is. For though Heidegger thinks that the metaphysical tradition is mistaken, it is not the kind of mistake where one somehow sees something black and thinks it white. Rather, it is more like seeing something in an odd light as pink though it is ordinarily white. The problem of the object's color will not be resolved merely by looking even more closely at the object. Instead, one must examine the light in which it appears—and part of the understanding of that light is an understanding that this object appears pink in it.

Heidegger's thinking through the problems of metaphysics is similar. He described his method as having three moments—reduction, construction, and deconstruction (1975, pp. 26–32).[23] These terms do not name separate activities, but moments of one activity. Our investigation cannot begin from the ground up. (At best, we could only pretend it does so.) When we discuss the problems of metaphysics, we must use traditional concepts. It is impossible to discuss those problems and at the same time to avoid the traditional constructions of those problems and the baggage that goes with the traditional concepts. Therefore, we "reductively construct" the concepts available (thereby deconstructing them), looking for the difficulties and contradictions in them that will make it possible to come to a new understanding (cf. Heidegger 1985, pp. 135–42, esp. 138). We deconstruct them. Heidegger describes his method in what he says of his analysis of logic:

> We shall try to loosen up the traditional logic in such a way that central problems in it become clear, and from the content of these very problems we shall allow ourselves to be led back into the presuppositions of this logic. [1984, p. 6]

Thus, the deconstruction of metaphysics is not to result in the total dissolution of metaphysics, but in its loosening up. It is to provide what Heidegger calls a clearing in which metaphysics can appear (cf. 1972a, pp. 64–66, for a discussion of the notion of the clearing), a place in which we can see what metaphysics is in order to "use it," to live with and within it without becoming its thralls.

A deconstructive thinking about our usual analysis of consciousness reveals the mistake of thinking of consciousness as a box. Heidegger sees this as a mistake to be expected and only a mistake from the point of view of a more fundamental analysis than is usually given. The mistake is the result of the ordinary everyday experience of things as tools, the most common way of dealing with things. Immersed in such an attitude toward the world, we assume that every being has the same kind of being that tools have (what Heidegger calls *Vorhandensein*, handiness), and there seem to be two categories of such toollike things, the subjective and the objective, the inside of the box and the outside. Though Heidegger's position is that we cannot reduce the being of the world to the status of handiness or tools, there are tools, and virtually anything can be used as a tool. Thus, concepts of subjectivity and objectivity are not simply to be dismissed, for they have their origin in an "accurate" understanding of the world, although in themselves they do not constitute this accurate understanding. Like the other concepts of the metaphysical tradition, subjectivity and objectivity are to be deconstructed.

Because truth is fundamental to traditional metaphysics and also to the problem of explanations, anyone looking for the possibility of psychological explanation must deconstruct the notion of truth. When we examine this notion, we see the general problem of metaphysics repeated, the reduction of grounds to the transcendent and, therefore, incomprehensible. As we saw, in modern metaphysics, truth is a function of the correspondence ordered and made possible by some atemporal and necessary principles: an ordinary statement about the world is true if it (originating inside the box) corresponds to things in the world (found outside the box) via some immutable principle (the transcendent); an explanation is true if it corresponds to the overarching principles that hold the inside and the outside and the flux of the outside together in a unity. The question of truth, therefore, comes to a head in the discussion of representation or correspondence (cf. Heidegger 1967b; 1972d; and 1976, pp. 212–30): Do we explain and understand something by reference to another thing? Is truth to be found in correspondence? If so, where does such a chain of correspondence stop, and how do we understand whatever is at the end of the chain? If not, how do we understand?

In spite of the obvious way in which this describes modern metaphysics, we can see the beginnings of this problem in the philosophy of the pre-Socratic philosopher Parmenides. For him, truth was to be found in an unchanging Entity to which, presumably, all true statements finally refer.[24] For the correspondence theory of truth, the chain of understanding ends with reference to something atemporal, something beyond human experience. As we saw in the discussion of the metaphor of the box of conscious-ness, this is the theme lying at the bottom of metaphysics: to the extent that statements are true and meaningful, it is not enough for them to correspond to things on the outside of the box. Ultimately they must represent (re-present) a transcendent something that makes the correspondence possible. In the tradition, only state-ments are true, and they are true only if they bring the outside into the inside by means of something transcendent, if they carry the outside across the barrier. True statements make something present that is otherwise inaccessible, something immutable.

But we have already seen the failure of this immutable in the failure of traditional metaphysics. The fissure of the metaphysical foundation extends into the question of truth, cracking it beyond repair: How is the immutable, that grounds truth, known? Clearly not by representation, for it stands behind all representation in order to make representation possible. Perhaps by immediate intuition? Then why is representation necessary, and if it is not, how do we explain intuition and what do we do when someone else does not share ours? Or can we explain the immutable by reference to abstraction? Hardly. Abstractions are created, made by finite human minds in a process of moving away from what is represented by the abstraction. They seem, therefore, uniquely precarious as the ground for truth and knowledge.

Metaphysics has consistently pointed to something constant and absolute, something beyond the world, in order to account for the world. As we saw, until the modern period that something was often God. But we also saw that even when God is not postulated as the metaphysical origin of all truth, such a metaphysical origin is postulated (as in, for example, some element from the subject-object dichotomy, usually the self), and this origin occupies the same ontological position as did God. In being beyond the world, however, this transcendent something—whether God, laws of nature, or human nature—remains eternally absent. In being be-yond the world of human experience, the transcendent as the ground of truth is inaccessible and, therefore, incomprehensible. Heidegger's response to this incomprehensibility is to reject the atemporal as the ground of truth and, thus, correspondence as truth's explanation.

As a result, there is in Heidegger's thought no "thing itself," no atemporal, necessary essence to appeal to as a standard of truth. Or more accurately, Heidegger, unlike Kant, makes no such noumenal/phenomenal distinction. Heidegger's thought contains no idea of the "thing itself," atemporal, necessary, and independent of consciousness, but there are "things themselves" as phenomena. This does not mean that the world does not really exist. As Heidegger says, "The world is 'there' before all belief" (1985, p. 217; cf. pp. 214–23). It simply means that there is no metaphysically transcendent world of things in themselves. The things of a transcendent world are unsatisfactory explanations for the things in this world. In fact, they are unintelligible.

Instead of requiring a metaphysically transcendent world to explain its existence, what exists exists as we do, already in the world. Further, it is clear that whatever exists in the world exists with us and "in dialogue" with us. As Heidegger says, knowing makes sense only on the basis of already-being-involved-in (1985, pp. 157–64), and using the term broadly, language is the location of our already-being-involved-in. That which is, including us, exists in and through language. Heidegger quotes from the poetry of Stefan Georg, "*Kein Ding sei wo das Wort Gebricht* [where the word breaks off, no thing can be]" (1959a and b).

This does not mean simply that language (reduced to the mind) creates things in the world ex nihilo, for the converse of this statement is also true, that where there can be something, the word does not break off. Instead, the quotation from Georg suggests that all that is must exist in language (though not because of language); the world is textual. As a consequence, it is possible to speak of atemporal, necessary essences, but to do so is precisely to do that, to speak of them, to bring them into being, and the postulation of extralinguistic, transcendent absolutes is already based on a prior textual understanding of things. Thus if we are to have truth, we must locate it and our knowledge of it in the textual; knowledge and truth, if they are to be genuine, must remain rooted in our textual, preontological understanding. In an analogy to biblical interpretation, Heidegger says this way of proceeding is hermeneutic because it deals with the world as textual (1976, pp. 37f.; 1985, pp. 260–72).

Though there is no objective truth to appeal to, Heidegger's view does not relegate truth to the realm of human subjectivity. That the notion of Dasein cannot be reduced to subjectivity is the first evidence that the notion of truth also cannot be so reduced. The truth is, fundamentally, not a statement; rather, it is the way of being-in-the-world that makes true statements possible, a way of being that permeates all other ways so that there can be no absolutely false way. Truth per se is the way of "being-un-covering" (1976, p. 220). Thus, statements are true to the degree that they have their origin in the way-of-being that is true (a way that reveals and conceals at the same time, since there is no last or final word about the world). Truth is ontologically prior to the thematizing of truth in statements about the world.[25] Thus the necessary tentativeness of all true statements. In our revealing and concealing of the world—its truth—we bring that truth into being. When we thematize that revealing and concealing, we bring propositional truth into being. We might, therefore, say that propositional truth is a "second order" truth.

To say, however, that truth is a feature of our living in the world, that it is something we create, is not to say that it is merely subjective. We do not create truth merely by a subjective act, an act of individual or group mind or will. Objectivity and subjectivity, buzz words of discussions of truth, are both part of the metaphysical framework at issue. They correspond, respectively, to the outside of the box or the viewer of the box of consciousness (depending on whether one is an empiricist or not) and the inside of the box. Only within that metaphor, the very metaphor that has been deconstructed, does the rejection of objective truth require the assertion of subjective truth (or, what is the same, no truth at all).

From a hermeneutical understanding, truth is how things are, but not in an inaccessible or abstract realm of atemporality, and not in mere subjectivity. Things are temporal and textual, not static and otherwordly. If our search for truth is to be located in the place where truth is to be found, it must be a search of and within the temporal. Our search for truth is immersed in a temporal investigation of the textual. Whereas, for the tradition, scientific investigation was supposed to result in statements that mirror the objective world, this temporal investigation of the textual is a creative act, the creation of statements that have their origin in Dasein's being-in-the-world and that, at the same time, go toward making up that world.

CONCLUSION

We are now in a position to reconsider modern psychology and its questions from the perspective offered by contemporary continental philosophy. While the goal of making individual human lives understandable is a reasonable one, we can see that the attempt to explain human action at either the level of the individual or subindividual, or at the level of some superindividual process, is misguided. Both of these are products of the failed metaphysics, misguided because we do not encounter the world in the terms given by metaphysics, and misguided because there is no reason to assume that there is a world that can be accounted for in those terms. As a result, there is no compelling or even sensible reason for believing that any of these grounds (the individual, the environmental, human nature, "law") is the fundamental grounds upon which to build psychological explanation.

If there is to be a human science, it must be able to ask questions that do not make false and misleading assumptions about what it means to be human. Therefore, it must ground itself in the world of temporality (in other words, in truth properly reconceived) rather than in a false metaphysics that leads us to think of human being in terms of categories, dimensions, and definitions that create insoluble problems. For human beings live in meaningful social worlds, and things exist in environments that do not exclude human beings. Human beings have relations with each other and with things within a meaning-full world. Individuality arises from and has meaning only within our temporal situatedness, from our "worldly" existence, not from our private possession of variable qualities or capacities. Failing to be clear about this is to miss what human being-in-the-world means. When this is not made clear, human science, seeking understanding of the human world, will be frustrated, for it will seek its understanding using ideas and tools that not only do not apply, but also distort unnecessarily.

After as well as following Heidegger, continental philosophy has taken for its task the understanding and explanation of that which makes possible all explanation as well as all the false categories and distinctions of modern psychology. In other words, it has set for itself the task of explaining not only how and what we should explain, but how the mistaken alternatives have come about: it has set about to explain the temporal world, the world of concernful dealings. Before the psychological and social scientific disciplines can answer the questions they have posed, they must return to and deal with the more fundamental question of the nature of the world and our being in it; they must return to the understanding of that which makes their questions possible.

We conclude by pointing up the optimistic and egalitarian nature of this project of understanding. Human science must be grounded in the world, and the world is a world of practical and concernful dealings, a world with which all human beings already have intercourse. Though there is a legitimate place for human science in explicating what everyone in some sense already knows, human scientists are not engaged in an activity radically different from that in which every human is always engaged. Honestly understanding our humanity is not the exclusive province of trained experts and practitioners, but of any who are honestly in-the-world.

Notes

1. For obvious heuristic reasons, neither of these sketches (of history, and of Heidegger's work) can be any more than sketches. Though we think them accurate, important distinctions must be flattened out.

2. Translations from the Greek, as well as subsequent translations from the German, are by James E. Faulconer.

3. It can also be translated "that which stands below something else," the origin of the latinate translation: *sub-stance*. Though a common translation, we think it misleading.

4. We can probably locate the equation of physical material with the traditional philosophical notion of substance or material in the work and influence of Locke.

5. It is important to remember that this is not an etymology. It is a reference to what might come to mind for one hearing the words, just as one hearing the English word *sacrifice* might hear its connection to *sacrify* and, thereby, come to understand sacrifice as making something holy. Though, strictly speaking, etymology does not justify such a connection, the connection is very real and can be quite helpful, especially since it is something we see Socrates himself doing in Plato's dialogues.

6. For example, one excellent, if sometimes exaggerated, discussion of this change can be found in Cassirer 1963. There the discussion centers on the problem of knowledge rather than, as does our discussion, on the notion of human dignity.

7. See, for example, the writings of Dionysius the Areopagite (fifth century, A.D.—1970).

8. Note that this claim that humans have no specific location is, implicitly, a denial of the Aristotelian worldview and, therefore, a precursor of Copernican astronomy.

9. Louis Dupré (1984) suggests that this occurred as a consequence of the nominalist doubts about human ability to comprehend God.

10. We see here the basic and more general form of the fundamental question for modern psychology, which we articulated earlier: What is the nature of the relationship between a human being and the nonhuman environment?

11. This is, we think, especially obvious in the beginning of meditation 1 of the *Meditations* (1972b), where Descartes discusses the universality of reason.

12. Though a common approach, the reduction of self-definition to empirical data contains a contradiction analogous to that found in the dilemma of freedom and determinism: within modern metaphysics, the existence of empirical data presupposes the self that is supposedly being defined by the data.

13. There is controversy over the point, but we believe that in the end Heidegger does not think of his alternative as one that sees the problems of the tradition and replaces them with a new metaphysics. (However, Taminiaux 1986 argues that Heidegger did originally see his project in this way.) If we read his early work in light of what comes later, instead of a replacement of metaphysics, Heidegger's work is a rethinking of what metaphysics is. Though he speaks of "overcoming" metaphysics and of its "end," these are not to be taken in the sense of a finished project beyond which we can move to something else (cf. 1972a, p. 24). Thus, the problematic sense of Heidegger's offer of an "alternative" to traditional metaphysics. (Scott 1988 not only discusses the way in which Heidegger's work offers an alternative, he also shows us a way of thinking given within this alternative.)

14. Two points should be made here. First, Heidegger's alternative is radical not only in being quite different from and incompatible with the tradition, but also in going back to the root of the tradition in order to rethink that root. Second, in a certain sense Heidegger's influence in psychology is a relatively longstanding one, for existential psychiatry has, for the most part, been indirectly but profoundly influenced by his work. But it is precisely in that they are existentialists that the problem lies. For existentialism, though influenced by Heidegger, turns out to be a kind of subjectivism, and Heidegger's work is not a subjectivism. For more on the issue of Heidegger's difference with existentialism, see Heidegger 1967a. Heidegger's discussion of being-in-the-world and being-with others (e.g., 1976, pp. 53–125, and 1985, pp. 185–214 and 236–43) should make it clear that Heidegger's work is not a subjectivism, but see also Heidegger 1975, pp. 249–50 and 311–16.

15. But, though psychology's problem is its adoption of the modern turn to the subject and its consciousness, it is important to remember that the problem is not merely a problem of modern philosophy. Its roots lie also in medieval and Greek philosophy. (In addition to the discussion above, see Heidegger 1975, pp. 108–71.)

16. This may seem to ignore a fourth alternative, the Kantian answer, but in the broad sense in which *subjective* is used here, it does not, since, as we have seen, the Kantian structures are subjective in that they are "inside the box," even if they are not individually subjective. Heidegger discusses Kant in some detail in *Kant and the Problem of Metaphysics* (1962) and in chapter 1 of *The Basic Problems of Phenomenology* (1975, pp. 35–107).

17. It does not follow that there can be no God or religion; though commonly assumed, it is not obvious that religion requires the metaphysically transcendent.

18. Heidegger works out the conclusions we will sketch in several

places. Though the later work (e.g., 1972a, b, and c; 1969; and 1954c) is very important, it cannot be understood without a firm base in the early work. Of these, *Being and Time* (1976), published by Heidegger in 1927, is most important. Recently, however, other works have become available and have been translated into English, editions of his lecture notes for the period, such as *History of the Concept of Time: Prolegomena* (1985), *Basic Problems of Phenomenology* (1975), and *The Metaphysical Foundations of Logic* (1984). In these works many of the conclusions we describe are explicated even more fully than in *Being and Time*. Those interested in secondary sources as an introduction to Heidegger's work should look at Steiner (1978) and Biemel (1976). Steiner's book discusses central themes of Heidegger's work; Biemel's discusses the development of Heidegger's thought. Both are excellent, though the latter is more difficult because it is more technical. For more detailed secondary studies, see Kockelmans (1984) or Richardson (1963).

19. The word *Dasein*, though an ordinary word in German, meaning "existence," is used as a technical term by Heidegger. Its roots are in the two terms *da*—there—and *Sein*—being—taking the resulting word quite literally: *there-being*, or "ek-static" being. For Heidegger, human being is characterized by its situatedness (temporal, spatial, emotional, etc.). In philosophic discourse it has passed into English as a technical term not requiring translation.

20. Though one cannot simply take Heidegger's terms—*concern, solicitude, care, death, guilt*—in a straightforward way, his use of these terms as technical terms is closely related to their ordinary and religious usages. Thus, with Heidegger's emphasis on care, it is no coincidence that American pragmatism, in the person of Richard Rorty (1979), has taken up a version of his work.

21. The analogy of Heidegger's concept of time to Augustine's is clear, though the two are not the same (cf. Augustine 1960, book 11). The temptation is to read Heidegger's location of time in Dasein as a claim that time is subjective, but that would be to forget Heidegger's discussion of being-in-the-world and being-with. To say the same thing differently, the temptation to think of this notion of time as subjective occurs only if one accepts the metaphor of the box of consciousness, a metaphor Heidegger explicitly rejects. For an excellent discussion of time and its relation to Dasein (including an explanation of why time is not subjective), see Heidegger 1975, pp. 322–452.

22. In his later work Heidegger ceases to use the term *temporality*, using *Ereignis* instead, and he takes up issues of temporality from within the discussion of *Ereignis/Enteignis* ("appropriation/disappropriation"). (*Ereignis* is translated "appropriating event," but it is important to remember as well its ordinary meaning, "the coming to pass.") This shift in terminology may be partly because of the easy confusion of the terms *temporality* and *time*. It is certainly the result of a change in Heidegger's thinking about the philosophic issues with which he was concerned, a change about which there is a good deal of discussion in Heidegger literature but which need not concern us directly here, except to say that Heidegger was concerned that his early work was still too wedded to the subjective metaphysics of modernism. (The essay "Time and Being" and

the subsequent seminar on that essay are probably the best discussion of *Ereignis* and related ideas—Heidegger 1972b and 1972c. Scott 1987 gives an excellent discussion of the philosophical issues involved in the changes that show themselves in Heidegger's work, pointing out that they can already be seen in *Being and Time*.)

23. We have avoided the usual English translation of *Abbau* as *destruction*, feeling that *deconstruction* is more accurate, though it has the problem of perhaps misleading those already familiar with the French philosopher Jacques Derrida's different use of the same term. Gadamer (1986) has suggested that *uncovering sedimentation* might be a more appropriate translation. Though descriptively accurate, we do not use that translation because it is somewhat unwieldy and because we think the parallel with Derrida's different use of the same term an instructive one—in spite of its possibility of misleading.

24. Though, for heuristic reasons, we use the standard interpretation of Parmenides as a starting point, Heidegger argues that this movement to transcendence begins fully in Plato's interpretation of Parmenides (cf. 1954b and c).

25. Thus, the connection between Gadamer's hermeneutics, discussed in *Truth and Method* (1972), and his claim that truth is that which creates methods and not the reverse.

References

Aristotle (1934). *Nicomachean ethics* (H. Rackham, trans.). Cambridge, Mass.: Harvard University.

——— (1941a). *On the soul*, The basic works of Aristotle (R. Mckeon, ed.). New York: Random House, 535–603.

——— (1941b). *Politics*, The basic works of Aristotle (R. Mckeon, ed.). New York: Random House, 1127–1316.

Augustine (1960). *The confessions of St. Augustine* (J. K. Ryan, trans.). Garden City, N. Y.: Image.

Bacon, F. (1908). *Novum organum*, The advancement of learning and novum organum. New York: Colonial.

Berkeley, G. (1874). *A treatise concerning the principles of human knowledge* (C. P. Krauth, ed.). Philadelphia: Lippincott.

Biemel, W. (1976). *Martin Heidegger: An illustrated study* (J. L. Mehta, trans.). New York: Harcourt, Brace, Jovanovich.

Burckhardt, J. (1983). *The civilization of the renaissance in Italy*. Salem, N. H.: Salem House.

Cassirer, E. (1963). *The individual and the cosmos in renaissance philosophy*. Philadelphia: University of Pennsylvania.

Descartes, R. (1972a). *Discourse on method*, The philosophical works of Descartes I (E. S. Haldane and G. T. Ross, trans.). Cambridge: Cambridge University, 88–130.

——— (1972b). *Meditations on first philosophy*, The philosophical works of Descartes I (E. S. Haldane and G. T. Ross, trans.). Cambridge: Cambridge University, 133–99.

Dionysius Areopagita (1970). *Opera*. Frankfurt: Minerva.

Dupré, L. (1984). "The shape of modernity." Unpublished lectures delivered at Brigham Young University.

Faulconer, J., and Williams, R. (1985). "Temporality in human action: An alternative to positivism and historicism," *American psychologist*, 40.11 (November), 1179–88.

—— (1987). "More on temporality in human action," *American psychologist*, 42.2 (February), 197–99.

Feyerabend, P. (1975). *Against method*. London: Verso.

Gadamer, H.-G. (1972). *Wahrheit und Methode*. Tübingen: Mohr (Paul Siebeck).

—— (1986). Personal interview. Perugia, Italy, July 16.

Harré, R. (1977). "The ethnogenic approach: Theory and practice," *Advances in experimental social psychology*, vol. 10 (L. Berkowitz, ed.). New York: Academic, 283–314.

Heidegger, M. (1954a). "Die Frage nach der Technik," *Vorträge und Aufsätze*. Pfüllingen: Neske, 9–40.

—— (1954b). "Moira" (Parmenides, fragment 8, 34–41), *Vorträge und Aufsätze*. Pfüllingen: Neske, 223–48.

—— (1954c). "Platons Lehre von der Wahrheit," *Wegmarken*. Frankfurt: Klostermann, 201–36.

—— (1959a). "Das Wesen der Sprache," *Unterwegs zur Sprache*. Pfüllingen: Neske, 157–216.

—— (1959b). "Das Wort," *Unterwegs zur Sprache*. Pfüllingen: Neske, 217–38.

—— (1962). *Kant and the problem of metaphysics* (J. Churchill, trans.). Bloomington: Indiana University.

—— (1967a). "Brief über den Humanismus," *Wegmarken*. Frankfurt: Klostermann, 311–60.

—— (1967b). "Vom Wesen der Wahrheit," *Wegmarken*. Frankfurt: Klostermann, 175–99.

—— (1969). *Identity and difference* (J. Stambaugh, trans.). New York: Harper & Row.

—— (1972a). "The end of philosophy and the task of thinking," *On time and being* (J. Stambaugh, trans.). New York: Harper & Row, 55–73.

—— (1972b). "Summary of a seminar on the lecture 'Time and being,'" *On time and being* (J. Stambaugh, trans.). New York: Harper & Row, 25–54.

—— (1972c). "Time and being," *On time and being* (J. Stambaugh, trans.). New York: Harper & Row, 1–24.

—— (1972d). "Die Zeit des Weltbildes," *Holzwege*. Frankfurt: Klostermann, 69–104.

—— (1975). *Die Grundprobleme der Phänomenologie*, Martin Heidegger Gesamtausgabe, Bd. 24 (F.-W. von Herrmann, ed.). Frankfurt: Klostermann.

—— (1976). *Sein und Zeit*, 4th ed. Tübingen: Neomarius.

—— (1984). *The metaphysical foundations of logic* (M. Heim, trans.). Bloomington: Indiana University.

—— (1985). *History of the concept of time: Prolegomena* (T. Kisiel, trans.). Bloomington: Indiana University.

Hume, D. (1888). *A treatise of human nature* (L. A. Selby-Bigge, ed.). Oxford: Clarendon; repr. 1968.

———— (1980). "Dialogues concerning natural religion," *Dialogues concerning natural religion and the posthumous essays* (R. Popkin, ed.). Indianapolis: Hackett.

Kant, I. (1956). *Kritik der reinen Vernunft*. Hamburg: Meiner.

———— (1965). *Grundlegung zur Metaphysik der Sitten* (K. Vorländer, ed.). Hamburg: Meiner.

Kockelmans, J. (1984). *On the truth of being: Reflections on Heidegger's later philosophy*. Bloomington: Indiana University.

Kuhn, T. (1970). *The structure of scientific revolutions*. Chicago: University of Chicago.

Lakatos, I., and Musgrave, A. (1970). *Criticism and the growth of knowledge*. Cambridge: Cambridge University.

Locke, J. (1956). *An essay concerning human understanding*. Chicago: Regnery.

Marx, W. (1971). *Heidegger and the tradition* (T. Kisiel and M. Greene, trans.). Evanston: Northwestern University.

Plato (1902). *Politeias*, Platonis opera I (J. Burnet, ed.). Oxford: Oxford University.

———— (1929). *Epistles 7*, Plato in 12 volumes, vol. 9. Cambridge, Mass.: Harvard University.

———— (1980). *Symposium* (K. Dover, ed.). Cambridge: Cambridge University.

Richardson, W. (1963). *From phenomenology to thought*. The Hague: Nijhoff.

Rorty, R. (1979). *Philosophy and the mirror of nature*. Princeton: Princeton University.

Schumacher, E. F. (1975). *Small is beautiful*. New York: Harper & Row.

Scott, C. (1987). *The language of difference*. Atlantic Highlands, N. J.: Humanities Press.

Steiner, G. (1978). *Heidegger*. New York: Viking.

Taminiaux, J. (1986). Public lectures. *Collegium phaenomenologicum*. Perugia, Italy, July 28–31.

Taylor, C. (1975). *Hegel*. Cambridge: Cambridge University.

2 • Explanation and Understanding in the Science of Human Behavior

Calvin O. Schrag

Philosophy and psychology have gone their separate ways for some time now. Each has developed its own grammar and its own vocabulary. Efforts toward translation have been made now and then, and there have been intermittent recognitions that somewhere down the line there are common concerns and interests, of both a theoretical and practical sort. This is certainly the case in the recent developments of cognitive science, and it surely was the case in the heyday of classical behaviorism when behaviorists in psychology and positivists in philosophy approached a common perspective on things. Also, in the days of introspective psychology, philosophical presuppositions, drawn principally from the garden varieties of philosophical idealism, significantly informed the theory construction of the psychological discipline.

Yet, the alliances between psychology and philosophy have not been all that durable. They have been more like marriages of convenience in which the bond was provided by the most recent philosophical or psychological theory in the neighborhood. But when the theory construction underwent a paradigm shift in one or the other discipline, the fragility of the conjugal bond of convenience became readily apparent. Somewhere at the center of things in this seesaw of alliances is the wider issue of the proper placement of both psychology and philosophy against the backdrop of the history of the special sciences as they marked out for themselves spaces of inquiry distinct from those of the humanistic disciplines. This created tensions not only between the disciplines of philosophy and psychology but within each of them as well. To observe the tensions one has but to become a member of a core curriculum committee at any of our institutions of higher learning in which the central task is that of integrating the required courses for a general education in the arts and the sciences. There appears to be little consensus on the part of psychologists regarding the proper placement of their discipline on the continuum (if we indeed speak of such) of the humanities/special sciences spectrum. Philosophers, too, are divided on the issue. Logicians, for the most part, are more comfortable with bridges to departments of mathematics than with conversations with more traditionally oriented humanists.

My goal in the current exercise is to mark out three interrelated issues (questions, if you will) that might function as pivots in a conversation among the practitioners in the two disciplines. The first concerns matters pertaining to the constitution of the domain of discourse and the region of data for a science of human behavior; the second has to do with the theory/practice and concept/fact problematic—an issue that would appear to be germane to all knowledge endeavors; and the third involves a suggestion for integrating explanation and understanding within a wider space of interpretation.

THE CONSTITUTION OF THE DISCIPLINE

In formulating the general topic we land on "Explanation and Understanding in the Science of Human Behavior." A host of questions circle around this formulation, pertaining to the grammars of "explanation," "understanding," "science," and "human behavior." We are searching for a general topic that has something to do with psychology, looking for some species of entrée to the field, the area, the region, the *topos* of psychology. Using the language of the historian and philosopher of science Thomas Kuhn, we begin inquiring about the "disciplinary matrix" that defines the practice of psychology. The term "psychology" by itself is not of much help. To inform a beginning student that psychology is the "logos" of the "psyche" may get the conversation going—but it does little more than that. A host of questions are elicited in the moment one becomes aware of the evident polysemy of *logos* (word, discourse, reason, structure, study, theory, science—and no doubt more) and the correlated polysemy of *pscyhe* (self, mind, consciousness, experiencing subject, behavior, and so on). We thus immediately gravitate into a quandary of multiple vocabularies that seek to define the subject matter at hand.

It was thought at one time that psychologists studied "human nature," but now we know that only fuzzy-minded philosophers speak this way. And those not yet liberated from gender discrimination continue to talk about the "essence of man." "Self" and "ego" are surely out. Their conceptual lubriciousness has by now become evident to all, philosophers and psychologists alike. "Consciousness" is still suspect in many circles. And "human experience" is so encompassing and noodlelike that it can be claimed by every investigator on any given topic. Admittedly, "mind" is getting some renewed approval nowadays. This is particularly the case in the proliferation of the literature on cognitive science, but it is not all that clear that "mind" carries cognate significations across the board.

We thus begin with a problem in the effort to identify the province of our discourse on matters psychological. The referents of our scientific talk take on features of inscrutability and indeterminacy. Signifiers appear to display an ineluctable waywardness, and vocabularies seem to succumb to an elasticity that appears to have no determinable boundaries. Yet if we are to talk about explanation and understanding within a certain region of inquiry, we should have some sense of what this explanation and understanding is *about*. Presuppositions with respect to the disciplinary matrix at issue need to be clarified, and certainly some of these presuppositions have to do with the referents of our discourse, modes of inquiry, conceptual models, and procedures and strategies of experimentation. Some consensus on the "aboutness" of a particular science needs to be achieved before the results can congeal into a body of knowledge. Might it be the case that the quandary of reference that we have articulated is to a great degree the result of a substance-oriented prejudice of thought, which would have us look for a monolithic subject matter somewhere in the neighborhood, a unified entity of some sort, a definable object that answers to a specific nominal determination? This is a prejudice deeply ingrained in our tradition, going back to René Descartes—and possibly even further.

The task is not to detail the history of this tradition of substance-attribute and subject-predicate oriented reflection, or to recount its deconstruction by such notables as Wittgenstein,

Heidegger, Derrida, and others. Rather, it is to suggest that the constitution of the disciplinary matrix at issue might proceed differently, taking note of references to the plurality and multiplicity of phenomena that make up "human behavior." This plurality and mutiplicity includes human capacities, skills, habits, attitudes, desires, volitions, beliefs, and social and institutional practices. Could we agree that this is what our discourse on human behavior is about? Might it be that our referent is not a singular, insular entitative subject, monadic self, or encapsulated ego? Nor would it be an invariant essence or nature of such an entity, but rather a panoply of human capacities and practices. Although we have landed on "human behavior" as a kind of general designator, we need to recognize that this is a bloodless abstraction that at best points us to the concrete performances of discursive and nondiscursive activities that define the region where the action truly i's.

Already at this stage an observation of some consequence needs to be made. In the constitution of the disciplinary matrix, which involves at once a selection of vocabulary and a demarcation of regions of subject matter, interpretation is at work. The inquirer, always along with other inquirers, constitutes the region of inquiry and the data within this region by taking something *as* something—that is, taking events and occurrences as dispositions, attitudes, desires, skills, etc. This is what Heidegger has called the "as-structure" of interpretation (1962, pp. 188–95), which is at least on one level as much at work in the physical as in the social sciences. Even physicists constitute their disciplinary matrix and select their data by taking events and happenings in the physical world as signifying such and such, and by making methodological decisions for including x and excluding y. In all this, interpretation is already operative. Interpretation rides the crest of all disciplinary constitution, selection and determination of data, methodological decisions, and entertainment of hypotheses. On this level there is no interesting distinction between the physical and the psychological sciences. Both are, if you will, contextualized within a history of interpretive practices (Kuhn 1979, pp. 267–300). In this respect both sciences are hermeneutical.

The preceding remark about constitution as the workings of an inquirer "always along with other inquirers" is a point that needs to receive some emphasis. The constitution of a disciplinary matrix, whether in the physical or the social sciences, is a corporate result of the performances of a community of investigators/ interpreters. No investigator/interpreter is an island unto himself or herself, but is rather part of the mainland of investigators and interpreters working out of a tradition and from a ground of sedimented theories and practices. The constitution of a disciplinary matrix is a conjugated effort proceeding from a scientific *community*, which stands in a certain tradition and conducts its practices either through a normalization of this tradition or through a shift to a revolutionary posture in which the scientific paradigms of the tradition are deconstructed, enabling the emergence of a new paradigm (Kuhn 1962).

THEORY VERSUS PRACTICE AND CONCEPT VERSUS FACT

We have already alluded to the second issue/question in the preceding discussion. This will be named the theory/practice problematic. It is a "problematic" precisely because the issue of the nature of theory and its relation to practice is one that continues to occasion puzzlement in the various disciplines of human knowledge. Since the time of the Greeks there have been recurring tendencies to draw the distinction between theory and practice rather sharply. According to Aristotle, *theoria* provides us with knowledge that carries the weight of universality and necessity. *Theoria* is about the universal rather than the particular, and about the necessary rather than the probable. The foundations for such knowledge, Aristotle argued, are to be supplied by a formal logic and a doctrine of categories.

Modern theory construction, unlike that of the ancients, is not as closely wed to the requirements of universality, necessity, apodicticity, incontrovertibility, and claims for a discovery of what is really there. Theories are articulated in the grammar of a calculus of probability, principles of uncertainty, degrees of predictability, provisional rules, and the like. Nonetheless the question of the relation of theory to practice, and the adjunct question of the relation of concepts to facts, still await an unambiguous answer. The story of the various efforts to define these relationships is uncommonly complex, involving longstanding disputes between rationalists and empiricists, idealists and materialists, essentialists and existentialists, cognitivists and behaviorists, and I suspect a host of others. This is not the time and place to rehearse the story. What we wish to suggest is that our vocabularies about theory and practice, concepts and facts, may require some retrenchment. We need to reexamine the recurring intolerable oppositions between the theoretical and the practical, the conceptual and the empirical, and particularly with respect to the role that these oppositions play in the sciences of human behavior.

It is a rather common view of our empirical age that the genuine bugbear in scientific enterprises, to say nothing of philosophical speculation, is grand theorizing, unifying conceptual schemes, abstract ideas, and (God forbid) value judgments. We have been informed by our empiricist friends that these are the slippery slopes down which the scientist and philosopher alike are wont to slide if the proper vigilance is not exercised. But apparently there need be no worries about the nature and use of facts. Facts are simply there for everyone to see. They are the brute givens in our world of experience and obtrude upon our consciousness like specks in our field of vision. A fact is simply a fact, somehow fully transparent to the attentive mind, indubitably given. A moment of reflection will bear out that this common and taken-for-granted view of fact is already rather heavily laden with interpretation and with theory. Indeed what we have before us is the "bare bones" theory of fact.

Let us suppose that facts are not somehow given willy-nilly, stumbled upon like pebbles on the seashore, but that they *become* facts only through a process of selection, classification, description, and thus interpretation. The vocabulary of fact takes on meaning only against the backdrop of methodological decisions involving the identifying and sorting out of what is taken as given within a particular field of inquiry. What is sorted out is then grouped into "physical facts," "psychic facts," "social facts," and "cultural facts." There may also be "aesthetic facts," "political facts," "economic facts," and "religious facts"—and I suspect some others as well. It would seem that in the house of facts there are many mansions, and until such time as a fact enters one of these mansions it is difficult to grant an intelligibility to any fact. A fact becomes a fact when it is *taken as something*. This is the interpretive moment in the apprehension of facts. There are no facts without interpretation. Facts are selected by the practitioner of an art or a science as holding a certain significance within a constituted disciplinary matrix.

The point at issue could be put another way. Facts are intelligible as facts only against a background of scientific practices, skills, and habits of thought that have become normalized and are taken for granted by a community of investigators. Facts emerge only within a context of interpretive practices, guided by a discernment that determines the proper fit of the selected facts to these practices.

This is a different story about facts than that told in the narratives of empiricism from Hume to logical positivism. What makes the story different is that the account of facts is contextualized within the interpretive practices of the community of investigators. An interesting consequence of this different story of facts is that it occasions a different story about theory. As much as fact, theory is a fallout of the communicative praxis that situates our variegated projects of knowledge about ourselves and our world. Both theories and facts take their rise from the dynamics and the history of interpretation. There are no facts without interpretation, and there are no theories without interpretation. Interpretation goes all the way down.

In this way the ideals of pure objectivity, unimpeachable epistemic foundations, and context-free categories and rules are decisively placed into question. The designs of "grand theory" are indeed undermined, and undermined in the same moment, as it were, that are the designs of an abstract empiricism. This leads to a reformulation of the issue of the relation of theory and fact. Theories are no longer viewed as immaculate conceptual schemes and untrammeled paradigms that can be called upon from time to time to order the facts. They are no longer seen as conclaves of invariant rules that can be applied to our discursive and institutional practices. They are themselves emergents from the history of these practices. The construal of theory as a *mathesis* of rules that are "applied" in our messing around with facts entails at once a misconstrual of the texture of *applicatio* as Hans-Georg Gadamer has perceptively shown (1975, pp. 274–78). It also entails an occlusion of the background features that inform the construction of theory and the constitution of facts. The vagaries of grand theory travel with an abstract empiricism.

The move beyond the unacceptable dichotomy between grand theory and abstracted empiricist facts opens up a new space. We name this new space the *hermeneutical space of communicative praxis*. In this space, theory and fact alike are seen as inscriptions left by the workings of interpretive practices that are geared to an understanding of ourselves and our world. It is important to recognize that this understanding, manifest in these interpretive practices, does not come about through a reception of brute, isolated, atomistic, nonintentional facts (the fallacy of fact in empiricism) and the taking up of a predelineated, innate, a priori, or infrastructural

conceptual scheme that alone is able to confer upon them a significance (the fallacy of theory in rationalism). Interestingly enough,
these two fallacies are two sides of the same coin. The rationalism
of grand theory simply buys into the empiricistic notion of fact.
Communicative practices, involving both our discourse and action,
through which we make our way about in the world, already
display an understanding of self and world. Praxis has its own
insight. It does not need to wait upon the services of an etherialized *theoria* to swoop down from on high to provide the determinations of sense and reference.

THE BINDING TOPOS OF INTERPRETATION

Thus far we have been discussing issues that relate to all the
sciences—physical, life, psychological, social, historical—indeed to
any discipline that purports to provide a body of knowledge.
Questions having to do with the constitution of the region of
inquiry or disciplinary matrix and with the relation of theory and
fact cut orthogonally across the humanistic and scientific disciplines. The third and final issue to be raised deals more specifically
with the peculiarities of a science of human behavior as distinct
from the spate of subdisciplines commonly grouped under the
rubric "the sciences of nature." Although the requirement for
interpretation in defining a disciplinary matrix is common to both
the human sciences and the natural sciences, the constituted
subject matter would appear to be different in the two cases—at
least so it is claimed by some.

Rather early in the history of the human sciences this alleged
difference of subject matter was cited as the critical distinction
between the social and the natural sciences. The German philosopher Wilhelm Dilthey, who played a consequential role in the
debates on this issue, attempted to sort out the domains of the
Geisteswissenschaften and the *Naturwissenschaften* with the help of
the distinction between understanding (*Verstehen*) and explanation
(*Erklárung*). "Nature we explain; man we understand" is his oft-
quoted one-liner. For Dilthey and others in this tradition, this
distinction between explanation and understanding arose from a
more basic metaphysical distinction between the order of nature
and the order of mind. "Nature" and "Spirit" were the shorthand
designators used in the service of this metaphysical distinction.
And as the proverbial "every schoolboy" knows, this distinction

reaches far back into the tradition. It received an accentuated articulation in the Cartesian dualism of the *res cogitans* versus the *res extensa*, and it was given various expressions in the history of modern idealism from Kant to Hegel and onward. The specific fallout of all this for the developing structure of academe was the polarization of disciplines along a spectrum of those that were modeled after the study of matter and those modeled after the study of mind.

What we wish to propose is a detour around the metaphysical separation of the two domains as traditionally formulated and a strategy for refiguring the understanding/explanation distinction. In the discussion of the constitution of the disciplinary matrix of a science of human behavior, we already concluded that the proper referent of the discipline cannot be defined by chasing down substances, entities, and essences. The likes of these appear to be perpetually deferred as objects of reference. I suggested that the vocabulary of human capacities, skills, performances, and practices might be more suitable for the task at hand. What is at issue in a human science, in a study of *humanitas*, is a field of activity in which the performances of speech acts, gestures, bodily comportments, dialogical transactions, and institutional practices interplay and inscribe various patterns of communicative behavior. The speakers, hearers, and actors who make up this panoply of practices already understand themselves in their discourse and action as they encounter the discourse and action of other speakers and actors. This understanding may be implicit and inchoate, precognitive and affective, incomplete and at times fractured—but it is a self-understanding and self-interpretation nonetheless.

Although we should reject the metaphysical distinction between the two domains as formulated by traditional metaphysicians, we should agree with their intent, if you will. A distinction between the human and the natural sciences needs to be maintained, but it is not located by discovering cleavages in the various orders of reality. A science of human behavior explores the terrain of discursive and nondiscursive practices in which the behavior at issue is that of self-interpreting speakers and actors who already understand themselves in their speech and action. Physics also deals with "behavior," but in the case of physics what is at issue is the behavior of subatomic particles and bodies, whose movements can be described, measured, and predicted with a certain degree of accuracy. Only by committing a rather grievous category mistake can we transfer the sense of behavior from the domain of human action to the behavior of entities in motion. Subatomic particles do not interpret and understand their behavior as they undergo it. They do not confer significance upon the motion that they exhibit. They are mute and devoid of speech. They move, but they do not act. The distinctive feature of human behavior is that in speaking and acting humans endow their activities and performances with meaning. They understand themselves in and through their activities, skills, and social practices. The discourse and action of human behavior is always expressive, meaning-laden, infused with intentionality, an event of self-understanding.

This all mandates a distinction between the physical and the human sciences, and confers upon the latter a special demand or requirement—namely, to provide an account of that which is itself an event of interpretive understanding. Although both the physical and the human sciences are interpretive in the constitution of their regions of inquiry, the human sciences are interpretive in a double sense. They provide interpretations of that which is itself an event of interpreting.

The problem now (and it is a problem of some magnitude) becomes that of determining in what sense the patterns of human discourse and action as ongoing processes of interpretation can become the proper subject matter of a "science." If talk of a science of human behavior is to be justified, it will need to be in terms of a sense of science different from that of physics and chemistry. But there is no a priori reason why there cannot be a polysemy of *science* as there is a polysemy of everything else. One needs to recognize the play of a plurality of grammars, a multiplicity of language games, and a heterogeneity of methodological decisions in the doing of science. Not all sciences are cut from the same cloth.

A science of human behavior would need to locate itself somewhere in the interstices of explanation and understanding. Explanation is not to be jettisoned in the project of a human science; rather the task is that of seeing its intercalation with understanding. Dilthey simply overstated the case when he summarized matters: "Nature we explain; man we understand." We have already seen how interpretive understanding is at work in the physical scientists' constitution of their disciplinary matrix. Now we need to recognize how explanation is at work in a science of human behavior. Surely explanations of various sorts are offered by the human sciences. A political scientist is able to devise explanations of voting behavior patterns in the different segments of society. A sociologist can provide explanations of differences of family structure in a comparative analysis of the industrialized West and the Third World. A psychologist of religion can devise measurements of religious attitudes. In the practices of these several human sciences, various aspects of human behavior are selected for controlled observations, measurement, and prediction. This comprises the explanatory function of the human sciences.

The conditions for such explanation are provided by the possibility of objectification through analysis. A slice of human behavior is objectified through an analysis of its constitutive parts. We shall call this the *elementalist* matrix of explanation. Explanation requires a matrix of elemental units that can be broken down for analysis to discern if the matrix might yield recurring patterns. The distinctive feature of the human sciences, however, is that the configurations of the discursive and nondiscursive practices under investigation are understood by the subjects of these practices against the background of contextual wholes. The political act of voting, a father-son relationship in a particular society, and a religious ritual have sense or meaning only as the subjects stand within a context of wider institutionalized political, social, and religious practices, in which they already understand themselves by virtue of their participation in the activities. We shall call this the *holist* matrix of understanding.

The peculiar task of a science of human behavior involves the requirements of both explanation and understanding. Explanation, moving out from an elementalist matrix, proceeds via reductive analysis of the constitutive units under investigation. Understanding proceeds via a recognition of the genealogy of meaning that unfolds against the background of configurative and contextual wholes. It is thus that the particular "theory," "science," or *"logos"* that informs such a discipline is one that binds the moments of explanation and understanding. Such a science of human behavior forges an analysis of elemental units while it recognizes the display of meaning-formation on the part of the participatory subjects as they are situated within the holistic background of their beliefs and practices. Insofar as both explanation and understanding arise from interpretive projects (although in different ways), one can properly speak of explanation and understanding as correlative moments of interpretive comprehension.[1] A science of human behavior thus falls out as an *interpretive* science, bonded by the moments of explanation and understanding.

The study of the human emotions provides an illuminating example of the uses of explanation and understanding by the community of investigators in the human sciences. The range of human emotions—anger, fear, shame, love, hate, pity, sympathy, melancholy, grief, suffering, anxiety, despair—details virtually inexhaustible phenomena for scientific and philosophic investigation.[2] An interpretive comprehension of these phenomena requires that they be both explained and understood. The dynamics of this comprehension knits together the moments of explanation and understanding as it moves to and fro between elemental units and contextual wholes.

The phenomenon of fear affords a peculiarly appropriate example. Fear announces its presence in the arena of the human emotions as a globally contextualized experience. This experience is informed by a background of associated events, practices, and dispositions that mark out an inner and an outer horizon—in which the phenomenon comes to be, intensifies, subsides, and passes away. The inner horizon is the space of the multiple profiles of the feared object and of the variable dispositions that are solicited by the object-as-feared. The sleazy figure emerging from the alley occasions the experience of fear in a variety of possible profiles of presentment—fear of an alienating stare, verbal abuse, being shoved, robbed, raped, beaten, or annihilated. These profiles of presentment are accompanied by variations in the affective dispositions of the fearing subject, whereby fear at one juncture aligns itself with anger, at another juncture with hate, at still another juncture with disgust, and so on. This all comprises the contextual background of the inner horizon in the undergoing of the fearful experience. But there is a wider, outer horizon that envelopes the phenomenon of fear. This includes the spate of societal expectancies, sedimented folkways, cultural myths, and historical memories, all of which in various ways condition and channel the expression of fear. The point at issue here is that the background features of both the inner and the outer horizon are constitutive of fear as a global phenomenon. The expressive meaning of fear resides as much in these background features as in the psychic episodes of the fearful subject.

Admittedly, this abbreviated description of the background conditions, the inner and outer horizon, of the emotion of fear needs to be fleshed out through careful, detailed, and painstaking elaboration. The hope, however, is that it provides sufficient clues for marking out the comprehension of the contextual and holistic configuration of the phenomenon. Understanding is geared to an apprehension of the phenomenon of fear in its holistic presentment. The dynamic of this holistic presentment unfolds as a self-understanding of the subjects in their situations of being afraid and a disclosure of the world as threatening. In the grammar of phenomenology this is referred to as the *intentional structure* of fear. Fear exhibits an intentionality, a making-manifest, a disclosure of the fearful subject and the threatening situation. On this level of experience fear is not yet determined as an objectified mental or affective state. It is, as Heidegger would say, *a mode of being-in-the-world*, which unfolds as a simultaneous disclosure of self and world (1962, pp. 179–82). This mode of being is at once a project of understanding.

The comprehension of the phenomenon of fear within the disciplinary matrix of a science of human behavior, however, also needs to make room for the strategy of explanation. Although this strategy always proceeds in concert with the project of understanding, it does comprise a distinct, although not separable, moment. The moment of explanation marks out a shift of attention from fear as a globally contextualized phenomenon to fear as an isolable and objectifiable psychic state or condition. As a result of this shift, fear is rendered as a *datum*, a datable occurrence within a bracketed time-space frame of reference, subject to analysis and to tests of reliability, repeatability, and public validation. Here attention focuses on the elemental components of the phenomenon—intensities of affective response, correlates with neurological processes, solicited verbal reports, and observed bits of segmented nonverbal behavior. This provides the space and the determinants of explanation. Explanation proceeds via an objectification, identification, analysis, and formalization of the constitutive elements that make up the phenomenon at issue. Such a strategy of explanation, which proceeds according to the rules of method adopted by the community of investigators in a special scientific field, is not to be denigrated, disparaged, or despised. Explanation as an analytic and methodic strategy of investigation retains its propriety and legitimacy. Things go awry only when one succumbs to the postanalytic fallacy and severs the objectified analytical contents from the inner and outer horizon of the phenomenon, from the holistic background of social practices in which the elemental components always remain embedded.

It is thus that the dual requirement for explanation and understanding needs to be acknowledged, and each needs to be given its proper due in a science of human behavior. The task, however, is not simply to juxtapose them, place them side by side, but rather to integrate them as mutually corrective and jointly reinforcing moments within a unifying comprehension.

Notes

1. Ricoeur has grasped this point with penetrating clarity in his observation that explanation and understanding are "two different stages of a unique hermeneutical arc" (Ricoeur 1976, p. 87). Elsewhere he speaks of explanation as the analytical moment of interpretation as correlated with the envelopment of understanding. "Understanding precedes, accompanies, closes, and thus *envelops* explanation. In return, explanation *develops* understanding analytically" (Reagan and Stewart 1978, p. 165).

2. Scheler's classic study, *The Nature of Sympathy* (1954), offers a detailed and penetrating investigation of some salient features of the affective life of humankind. Properly characterized as a phenomenology of the human emotions, Scheler's extensive study gives particular attention to the affective phenomena of sympathy, empathy, love, hate, and resentment. This is a study that still awaits the recognition from contemporary psychology and philosophy that it so richly deserves.

References

Heidegger, M. (1962). *Being and time* (J. Macquarrie and E. Robinson, trans.). New York: Harper and Row.

Gadamer, H.-G. (1975). *Truth and method.* New York: Seabury.

Kuhn, T. (1962). *The structure of scientific revolutions.* Chicago: University of Chicago.

—— (1979). "The relations between history and history of science," *Interpretive social science: A reader* (P. Rabinow and W. Sullivan, eds.). Berkeley: University of California, 267–300.

Reagan, C. E., and Stewart, D. (eds.) (1978). *The philosophy of Paul Ricoeur.* Boston: Beacon.

Ricoeur, P. (1976). *Interpretation theory: Discourse and the surplus of meaning.* Fort Worth: Texas Christian University.

Scheler, M. (1954). *The nature of sympathy* (P. Heath, trans.). London: Routledge and Kegan Paul.

3 • Some Reflections on Empirical Psychology: Toward an Interpretive Psychology

Joseph J. Kockelmans

The work every psychologist actually engages in as a psychologist is a form of interpretation. For psychologists try to give a scientific account of human behavior and to make a practical use of this knowledge in their dealings with human beings. The account psychologists give of human behavior is one that flows from the conceptual framework that has been formulated carefully in the theoretical part of the discipline. It has taken almost one hundred years to bring this underlying conceptual framework to its current form. If one grants that giving an account of human behavior on the basis of a carefully formulated conceptual framework is the work of finite understanding, and also grants that all understanding, to the degree that it is finite, is interpretation, then it is obvious that the psychologist's work is the work of interpretation.

Yet it is not this issue that I would like to raise in these brief reflections; rather I would like to focus on a second thesis: that in contemporary psychology there is a definite need for a special interpretive component (von Uslar 1970, pp. 337–52). Before turning to the main issue, however, I would like to offer some introductory observations.

In treatises on philosophy of science, one very often finds a distinction mentioned between the natural and the social sciences. This distinction runs parallel to Wilhelm Dilthey's distinction between *Naturwissenschaften* and *Geisteswissenschaften*. Phenomenologists and existentialists, on the other hand, prefer to make a distinction between the "sciences of nature" and the "sciences of man," or between the "natural sciences" and the "human sciences." Those who defend the first distinction quite often argue that the natural and the social sciences rest on the same logical, methodological, and epistemological principles, and that the distinction mentioned is merely connected with the subject matters studied in the various sciences. Those who defend the second distinction are obviously aware of the fact that to a certain degree human beings are part of nature and thus can be studied in the natural sciences; this is the case mainly in biochemistry, biology, physiology, and psychophysics. On the other hand, they argue, what is characteristic for humans as human lies beyond the realm of nature and that is why a scientific study of human behavior must be listed among the human sciences. It is also frequently argued in the second approach that the natural and the human sciences rest on different sets of logical, methodological, and epistemological principles, and that for this reason we must distinguish between two different types of objectivity. Those who adopt the first point of view often argue that psychology (with the exception of social psychology) is to be listed among the natural sciences, whereas phenomenologists and existentialists place psychology among the human sciences (Strasser 1963).

Both of these distinctions are unsatisfactory. Evidence for this is found in the fact that among those who defend the first distinction there is an ever-growing number of philosophers and psychologists who argue either that psychology is not a natural science, or that one must distinguish between a natural psychology and a *verstehende* psychology. On the other hand, the leading phenomenologists are quite suspicious of the thesis that one should distinguish two types of objectivity. In the pages that follow I would like to suggest that one can come to a more satisfactory distinction by using labels that refer to the *methods* to be used rather than labels taken from the subject matters of the various sciences.

Since the end of the nineteenth century, three quite different approaches to human behavior have been suggested; they are generally labeled with the expressions experimental psychology, introspective psychology, and *verstehende* psychology. Each of these approaches may be found today (albeit in a substantially modified form) in what is generally called *empirical psychology, phenomenological psychology*, and *hermeneutic psychology*. In this essay I wish to defend the thesis that these approaches, provided they be properly understood and provided their limitations be carefully stipulated, are *not* mutually exclusive, but should be related to one another positively, if psychology is to fulfill its meaning and function in our society.

In formulating this thesis more carefully and also in my attempt to justify it, I am writing from a *philosophical* point of view. The philosophical position underlying this approach may perhaps be indicated with the help of the label *hermeneutic phenomenology*. For my purposes, it is of the greatest importance to state explicitly that the disciplines I wish to consider here are, taken in themselves, *not philosophical* disciplines. Furthermore, the view I wish to develop in their regard does not depend exclusively on the philosophical position that happens to be my own (the ambiguity suggested by the labels *phenomenological psychology* and *hermeneutic psychology* notwithstanding). What I am trying to say can be said from any other philosophical point of view, provided that view does not a priori exclude any appeal to immediate experience (to be taken here in the Hegelian sense) and provided one admits that phenomena inherently historical cannot be understood except by interpretation. For the meaning and function of a science are not to be determined in regard to the "intentional noeses" of the philosopher who examines this science, but in regard to the "intentional noeses" of those who are actually involved in the scientific pursuit—that is, the scientists and the clinicians. Also, the thesis I wish to defend can easily be stated in a language in which there are no expressions used that are interpretable only from within the thesis. I merely wish to state that psychology has the possibility of solving its relevant problems if and only if one is willing to admit descriptive and interpretive methods in addition to empirical methods.

EMPIRICAL PSYCHOLOGY

In characterizing the most important views proposed in regard to the possibility of a strictly empirical psychology over the past forty years,[1] it is important to make a clear distinction between the views suggested by phenomenologists and those proposed outside the realm of phenomenology. It seems that in the nonphenomenological literature basically three views have been defended.

The first view states that the methods of the natural and the human sciences are fundamentally similar and, thus, that a science of humans based on the model of the natural sciences is possible. It is further stated that the questions of whether an empirical psychology is possible and of whether the scientific method can deal with *all* aspects of human behavior must be evaluated pragmatically in terms of its actual achievements, rather than on any a priori contention or by philosophical speculation on the meaning and presuppositions of concepts used to identify human actions. Finally, according to this view, contemporary empirical psychology has accumulated sufficient empirical evidence to demonstrate the feasibility of a strictly empirical study of human behavior. In other words, an empirical study of human behavior is a well-established discipline. This view has been and still is defended by the majority of American psychologists actually involved in psychological research, as well as by a great number of Anglo-American philosophers.

However, the psychologists and philosophers constituting this large group of authors by no means form a harmonious unity. For among the psychologists defending this view we still find those who defend a rather radical form of behaviorism, whereas most contemporary psychologists are more oriented toward neobehaviorism. Neobehaviorism distinguishes itself from classical behaviorism mainly in the three following characteristics: (1) elimination of metaphysical overtones as found in classical behaviorism; (2) operationism as introduced by Percy Bridgman; (3) a strong affiliation with neopositivism, particularly insofar as epistemological, logical, and methodological issues are concerned. Finally, we find today a group of liberal neobehaviorists who have completely abandoned the thesis that stimuli can be uniformly reduced to a physical description, and responses to mere movements in space. In their view it is impossible to avoid describing stimuli in perceptual terms and to conceive of them as something that has meaning for the responding organism. Equally, responses cannot be reduced to mere component movements in space. The neobehaviorist view has been defended by Hull, Tolman, Guthrie, Skinner, Spence, Miller, Brunswik, Estes, Meehl and others; whereas the more liberal form of neobehaviorism has been defended by Guthrie and Miller (in their latest publications), as well as by Gibson, Hebb, Koch, and others.

Furthermore for the philosophers in the group there has been the famous dispute as to whether or not Carl Hempel's covering-law position in regard to scientific explanation should be accepted as a further specification of this view. Whereas this conception has been defended by Popper, Hempel, and Oppenheim on the one hand, and Skinner, Brunswik, Spence, Newell, and others on the other hand, a great number of people feel that this view describes scientific explanation inaccurately either for both the natural and human sciences (Nagel, Hanson, Rescher, Helmer) or at least for the human sciences (Scriven, Chisholm, Brodbeck, Heidelberger, and others).

This was one of the reasons a number of psychologists and philosophers were led to a second view, which states that a science such as that defended by the first view may indeed be desirable, but that it is only partially realized in the various sciences. Psychology in particular is an "inexact" science, somehow comparable to meteorology. This view, first defended by John Stuart Mill, is, in addition to those just mentioned, found among a great number of psychologists actively involved in psychological research into complex human phenomena.

The third view states that a strictly empirical psychology, if it is to account for the most distinctive features of human behavior, is simply impossible. The reason for this is that (1) such a science cannot account for the *meaning* of human action, although perhaps it can deal with the physiological aspects; (2) human behavior is not governed by uniformities and laws, because it is *essentially* intentional, purposive, free, temporal, historical, and reflexive. This "separatist" view is defended, for example, by Hodges, Peters, Tajfel, Winch, Gewirth, Turner, Malcolm, and others. Some of these authors have suggested that a further development of Dilthey's *geisteswissenschaftliche* or *verstehende* psychology could ultimately lead to a nonempirical but strictly scientific study of human behavior.

If we turn now to the phenomenological literature, we find first the view that *every* empirical approach to human reality is doomed to failure and that the only legitimate approach to human beings is to be found in the phenomenological, this latter term to be interpreted either in the sense given to it by Husserl in his *Phänomenologische Psychologie* (1962), or in the sense given to it by Heidegger in *Being and Time* (1962). Although these phenomenologists point to a solution other than that suggested by the protagonists of the third view—that is, that there is no empirical psychology—those defending this fourth view nonetheless use mainly the same arguments to substantiate their view as the arguments suggested by the members of the third group.

Other phenomenologists have argued that an empirical approach to human behavior is indeed possible within certain limits, but that the genuinely human meaning of the results of this type of investigation is to be clarified by a *philosophical* study of human-kind, which at the same time must give the ultimate foundation to empirical research and its results. It is assumed here that this "phenomenological anthropology" is to be developed within the confines of phenomenological or, even better, existential philosophy. It seems to me that this fifth view is quite frequently found among American psychologists influenced by phenomenology and existential philosophy.

Finally, many phenomenologists defend the view that empirical research in the realm of human phenomena is possible and neces-sary, but that such an approach is to be complemented by descrip-tive as well as hermeneutic approaches that as such *are not yet* philosophical in nature. This sixth view has been further inter-preted in two ways: (1) according to a first group of phenomenolo-gists, which includes Husserl and some of his followers, empirical psychology is not the study of human behavior, but of psychic life or of consciousness; (2) the protagonists of the other group (in-cluding Sartre, Buytendijk, Linschoten, and others), on the other hand, conceive of empirical psychology as the study of human behavior.

Comparing these different views, we find in the phenomeno-logical as well as in the nonphenomenological literature a number of scholars defending the possibility of a strictly empirical psychol-ogy, and others who categorically exclude this possibility, at least as long as the term *empirical* is used in a sense similar to that found in the natural sciences, and physics in particular. One might be inclined to conclude from this that we may reduce these six alternatives to only four, the last two being subspecies of the fourth—that is, the phenomenological. In the following pages I hope to show that and why this is not so, but before doing so I wish to make a few general remarks that will help later in clarifying my position more precisely.

First of all, it is important to note that those who defend the first view (natural science) often do not exclude, and in some instances even explicitly refer to, the possibility of developing and applying to the realm of psychology certain methods in addition to empirical methods, but to the best of my knowledge they have never devel-oped these ideas in any detail. Furthermore, most of them describe this possibility exclusively in connection with and as a function of empirical research. In other words, in this view these additional methods are meaningful only insofar as they are presupposed by and have a constructive function within empirical research itself (Carnap 1955).

Secondly, the arguments set forth in the third view (that empirical psychology is impossible) do not always lead to the conclusion that empirical psychology is really impossible, but rather to the view that other methods are to be used in psychology also. It seems that Spence, Chisholm, and Krimerman have realized the possibility of maintaining the third view without having to abandon the first completely.

Thirdly, those defending this third view have never pointed to the possibilities opened up by Husserl's phenomenological psychology. Most persons seem to suggest that a *verstehende* psychology, as suggested by Dilthey, must be conceived of as the genuine forerunner of the psychology one is seeking. It is not impossible that Max Weber's sociological writings have had some influence here.

If we now turn to the basic issues underlying this complex dispute, it seems to me that at least three questions should be asked: (1) Precisely what is the subject matter of psychology? Is it human psychic life or is it human behavior? And if the latter is the case, what does the term *behavior* precisely mean in this context? (2) What is meant by the expression *empirical science* in this connection? (3) Does applying empirical methods to human behavior indeed imply such a form of reduction of the original phenomena that a *genuine* empirical study of human behavior is excluded in principle?

As for the first issue, it seems that contemporary philosophy, analytic as well as "existential," has pointed out sufficiently convincing arguments to show that any form of classical (that is, Cartesian) dualism is unacceptable. From this it follows at once that empirical psychology as a study of human psychic or inner life is to be excluded. It seems to be much more reasonable to conceive of psychology as the empirical science of human behavior.

As for the meaning of the term *behavior* in this context, it seems to be equally clear that the arguments set forth against classic behaviorism are so convincing that we have to rule out any conception of behavior that remains within John Watson's stimulus-response schema. Influenced by ideas developed by Edwin Guthrie and Edward Tolman on the one hand, and Maurice Merleau-Ponty on the other, I am inclined to believe that it is reasonable to say that by the expression *human behavior* we should understand any form of a person's orientation toward the world in which he or she lives. One might argue that I am guided here by a philosophical a priori for which only an existentialist will be sensitive. However, it is my conviction that although this manner of speaking may have its origin in existentialist literature, to conceive of human behavior in terms of its orientation toward the world surrounding humans and to the things and fellow beings they encounter there is by no means tantamount to conceiving of human behavior in a manner that could be understood and justified only from an existentialist point of view.

One might also argue that by conceiving of human behavior in terms of concrete forms of orientation toward the world, one by no means radically transcends classic dualism and that there, too, unavoidably makes a distinction between the "inside" and the "outside," the "mental" and the "visible," the "private" and the "public," the "psychical" and the "physiological." Many things should be said about this issue, but I wish to limit myself to a few remarks only. First of all, in studying human behavior one must realize that in each concrete form of orientation toward the world a person simultaneously constitutes meaning and expresses it in such a way that the constituted and expressed meaning form an indissoluble unity. Thus it is not correct to say that a person's behavior consists in a set of bodily activities that express and communicate a meaning that *as such* is found in his or her *psyche* or "inner life." As Merleau-Ponty correctly observes, when I am faced with an angry gesture, the gesture does not make me think of anger as something to be found somehow *in* the other's inner life and of which I can have knowledge only by recalling the feelings I myself experienced when I used similar gestures; the gesture itself *is* the other person's anger (Merleau-Ponty 1962, p. 184).

It is obviously true that there are a great number of thoughts, intentions, ideas, beliefs, feelings, moods, imaginations, hopes, desires, and the like, which do not manifest themselves *directly* in overt behavior. But I would not hesitate to exclude all this from the subject matter of empirical psychology, except insofar as it manifests itself at least indirectly in a person's overt behavior. The question of how far psychoanalysis is able to deal with these "private" states effectively, as well as the question of how far these states motivate my behavior in a manner sometimes not known to myself nor immediately observable by others, must remain unanswered here. One thing is clear, however; psychoanalysis, insofar as it deals with these "private" states directly, is certainly not an *empirical* science in the sense under consideration here.

We must turn now to the complicated question of what precisely is to be understood by the expression *empirical science* in this connection. Before attempting to specify exactly what is meant by this expression, we should take note of certain distinctions that will help us avoid misunderstanding. First of all, it is obvious that the empirical sciences can be studied from different perspectives: from a historical point of view in the history of science, from a social view in the social sciences, from a logical point of view in the logic of science, and from the philosophical point of view in either epistemology (neo-Kantianism) or fundamental ontology (hermeneutic phenomenology) (see Kockelmans 1969, pp. 77–168).

It is also important to make a distinction between science taken as a process and science taken as a result. When one speaks of the logic of science, one very seldom deals directly with science as a process, but mainly with science taken as a result, and as already expressed in the linguistic statements of a natural or artificial language. Logic is then interested in the logical relationships between the statements in which the results of a science taken as a process are expressed (Rudner 1966, pp. 4–18). This relationship can then, for example, be described in terms of a deductive-nomic scheme as suggested by the covering-law position, which presupposes that there is an essential unity of method between the natural and social sciences. The following theses seem to be essential to Hempel's position (1965, pp. 331ff.):

1) Every science seeks to establish empirical laws that can be used to explain and predict specific events or regularities.
2) Proposed laws must be tested by means of the hypothetico-deductive method—that is, by deriving empirical consequences from the suggested universal hypotheses and comparing these consequences with the results of direct observation.
3) Empirical laws must not be conceived of as analytic statements; they are basically falsifiable descriptions of uniformities.
4) An explanation of a particular event or set of events is scientifically acceptable, if and only if it is able to subsume the event under or deduce it from empirical laws together with statements describing conditions antecedent to the event or set of events. It is to be noted that many empirical

laws have the form of statistical correlations. But regardless of the form of these laws, their primary function in scientific inquiry is to serve as major premises in explanations and predictions.

5) Explanations of past events and predictions of future events have an identical logical form. Thus explanation and prediction are symmetrical.

I have already pointed to the fact that the covering-law position has been ardently debated; it is rejected by some, reformulated by others, or accepted by many as describing just one alternative among others. It seems that many positive arguments can be set forth for Hempel's theory. But it is also undeniable that this view describes an ideal that has not yet materialized in all natural sciences and most certainly not yet in the social sciences. It seems reasonable, with O. Helmer and Nicholas Rescher (1959, pp. 25–52), to distinguish between exact and inexact sciences, and furthermore with respect to the inexact sciences to allow for other alternatives in addition to the covering-law model. Some of these alternatives have been discussed in the literature and a number of them point to valuable perspectives (Hanson 1958; Scriven 1956, pp. 105–30; and others).

For my purpose here it is important to realize that the discussion concerning the covering-law position (one which focuses mainly on the latter's fourth and fifth theses) has not pointed up any arguments against the possibility of a strictly empirical psychology, nor against the thesis that psychology as an empirical science is essentially similar to the natural sciences. I do not deny that in the discussion of the covering-law position in its application to psychology and the social sciences, many persons have raised very serious doubts in regard to such an empirical psychology, but as I understand it, this is not connected with the logical and epistemological status of the empirical sciences as such, but mainly with the "reduction" that all empirical research necessarily implies. For this reason we must turn now to this important issue.

Rudolf Carnap has stated that underlying the empirical enterprise as a whole is the basic assumption that the "principle of reducibility" can and should be accepted universally. This principle states that in all scientific discourse a term x is reducible to the terms y, z, etc., if the term x is such that the conditions for its application can be formulated with the help of the terms y, z, etc.; the statement containing the terms y, z, etc., is called the *reduction statement* for x in terms of y, z, etc. According to Carnap, for the realm of psychology this means that there is a behavioristic method of determination for any term used in psychology; and also, that any term for which there is a behavioristic reduction is itself reducible to the language which we use in speaking about the properties of the observable, natural things surrounding us. Speaking concretely, this means that concepts referring to a person's intentions, beliefs, attitudes, and feelings can and should be translated into terms characteristic of things that are open to immediate observation and measurement (Carnap 1955, pp. 52ff.).

Although many philosophers and scientists have strongly objected to Carnap's interpretation of the meaning of the principle for psychology, I think it is rather obvious that empirical research as such, of necessity, presupposes this principle. A similar remark can be made in regard to operationism, which is merely a further specification of the reductionist principle: although one can justly object strongly to Bridgman's interpretation of it, nonetheless it is clear also that no empirical science can function if operationally defined terms are excluded altogether. Since this essay is not the proper place to treat these important issues in detail, I shall limit myself to two observations that are of the greatest importance for psychology as an empirical science.

First of all, in an attempt to determine the precise meaning of the reductionist principle as well as operationism in psychology, we should carefully avoid any form of dualism. It seems that most persons who have objected to the views suggested by Carnap and Bridgman have encountered this pitfall; they try to argue that the "inside" cannot be reduced to the "outside," the "mental" to the "observable," and the "psychical" to the "physical." As I have pointed out previously, psychology as an empirical science is not interested in the "mental" or the "psychical," but merely in human behavior.

Secondly, the problem connected with the reductionist principle and operationism should be approached from a point of view in which science is taken as a process rather than as result. But this leads us from the logic of science to an ontology of science (Linschoten 1964, pp. 15–64; Heidegger 1962, pp. 401–18). In all their scientific activities, empirical scientists thematize their subject matter in a way that *essentially* involves objectivation. Objectivation, in turn, implies abstraction, formalization, and to a certain degree idealization, in view of the fact that objectivation, as found in empirical science, is oriented toward functionalization.

In other words, the question of whether empirical sciences of persons are possible, and if so, in what sense and under what conditions, is not primarily one of whether the statements that constitute the human sciences can be systematically related to one another in one way or another. Rather, that question is connected with the question of whether human behavior as such allows for a thematization that essentially implies abstraction, formalization, and idealization. It is clear that the question of whether one is to allow for mathematization in this context is a derivative one that perhaps can be answered positively, provided one acknowledges the importance of statistical procedures and conceives of mathematics in a sufficiently broad way.

As far as the first question is concerned, it seems that idealization, abstraction, and formalization, if applied to human phenomena, necessarily imply that certain aspects of the *meaning* of the human phenomena must be left out of consideration in the sense that this part of their meaning as such does not and cannot constitute the immediate subject matter of such a science. This does not entail, however, that consequently an empirical science of persons is impossible, but merely that such a science has meaning within relatively narrow limits and that, therefore, there is a place and need for other approaches to human phenomena that are neither philosophical nor empirical.

Most logicians will argue that description and interpretation, if separated from the empirical approach, can never have an objective meaning in that the principle of verification does not apply in these realms. In my view these authors exclude without sufficient ground a form of *scientific* and intersubjectively verifiable discourse, in which the verification does not presuppose a logical relationship between the statements of the discourse (namely, that between premises and conclusions), but in which the verification consists in the fact that scientists examine the acceptability and adequacy of the statements taken separately on the basis of the actual and humanly possible experiences they themselves have had or could have.

To give an example: in an eidetic description of the *meaning* of human emotions, an author may use a number of sentences to explain that there is an essential difference between "being afraid" and "being in a state of anxiety." In such a description the sentences used do not have the purpose of operationally or otherwise a priori defining what the meaning of fear and anxiety is, nor are the statements related to one another as are the statements found in strictly empirical discourse where explanation, prediction, and verification go hand in hand. Yet the description is intersubjectively verifiable in that those persons reading these statements can test them against their own experiences, actual or possible. It will not do to say that all persons will describe their own emotions in their own, merely subjective, way. For first of all, the *eidetic* description is not oriented toward any one concrete, emotional experience, but toward the essential structure of the emotion in question. Furthermore, it may very well be the case that the analyses given by various psychologists will vary in many instances, in that, indeed, it is very difficult to eliminate *all* subjective prejudices from such a description. But I still believe that, in principle, by means of positive criticism, discussion, and comparison, one can come to an accurate description of the human meaning of an emotion. Finally, neither will it do to object that in various cultures people experience emotions differently. For insofar as there is a core of truth in this remark, this aspect of the problem will be accounted for by a subsequent hermeneutic approach to the issues involved.

DESCRIPTIVE AND HERMENEUTIC PHENOMENOLOGY[2]

In the previous section I tried to explain what I think should be understood by the expression *empirical science* and in what sense this expression can be meaningfully applied to a scientific study of human behavior. I have indicated, also, that many difficulties can be brought forth against such an attempt. But instead of conceiving of these difficulties as making an empirical science of persons impossible, I have taken these difficulties to refer to the necessity of developing other approaches to the human reality in addition to the empirical ones, approaches that, although still scientific and not philosophical, nonetheless cannot be called empirical. We must now turn our attention to these approaches.

I first wish to examine the question of what the expression *descriptive psychology* precisely means in this context. The paradigm of what is called here *descriptive psychology* is what Husserl meant by his phenomenological psychology, which he conceived as the regional ontology of human psychic life. Translating Husserl's view into a slightly different language, we may say that the expression *descriptive psychology* means the regional ontology that tries to bring to light the essential and necessary structures of the various modes of persons' orientation toward the world. As for the methods to be used in this science, Husserl suggests that in each regional ontology the methods of free variation and intentional analysis are of prime importance (see Kockelmans 1967, pp. 138–84). In his view both of these methods belong together in principle and practically always go hand in hand.

It seems that the method of free variation is a very important one for the human sciences. However, we must realize also that its practical applicability within the realm of a descriptive study of human behavior is rather limited and that Husserl's conception of essences should be reinterpreted. Merleau-Ponty rightly remarks that the essences about which Husserl speaks cannot be an end in themselves; they have merely the meaning of a means. What the human sciences try to understand is persons' effective involvement in the world. In the various orientations toward the world we are usually too tightly bound to the world to be able to know ourselves as such at the moment of our actual involvement. That is why our own *ek-sistence* requires insight into the field of ideality in order to understand and to prevail over our facticity (Merleau-Ponty 1945, pp. ix–x).

We must realize further, as Husserl explicitly does, that the various modes of our orientation toward the world do not just "bear" or "contain" meaning, but they precisely bring meaning about and constitute it. That is why these forms of orientation toward the world cannot be adequately described solely by employing the method of free variation. This method must go hand in hand with intentional and constitutive analyses—that is, analyses that try to show how each form of orientation toward the world in its own way brings meaning to light by constituting that meaning on the basis of the given situation. However, here too a reinterpretation of Husserl's original conception seems mandatory. It seems Heidegger has correctly argued that the originally given phenomena that constitute the immediate subject matter of the analysis are not so much to be analyzed and described but to be interpreted according to the laws and rules of hermeneutic phenomenology (Heidegger 1962, pp. 61–62, 197–203, 486–87).

Although I am convinced that the last remark is important, as I hope to show shortly, I nevertheless believe also that most later phenomenologists have underestimated the practical value of Husserl's conceptions for a descriptive human science. It seems that relatively little is gained in many instances by immediately proceeding to the Sartrean "ek-sistential project," which indeed constitutes the root of all authentically human conduct. For as Ricoeur correctly observes, in so doing one takes the risk of missing the specificity of the problem at hand, and of pushing the contours of the different modes of orientation toward the world in a kind of indistinct existentialist monism that repeatedly tells the same story when speaking about perception, emotion, sexuality, speech, imagination, and so on (1952, pp. 115–23).

However, to say that Husserl's intentional analysis, reinterpreted in the sense of Merleau-Ponty's existential analyses (1945, pp. 160, 377), is and remains a method of inestimable value for a descriptive study of persons is not tantamount to denying the necessity of hermeneutic procedures. The reason hermeneutics is indispensable in a descriptive human science lies in the fact that all forms of human conduct are *essentially* temporal and historical, and thus cannot be understood adequately if they are not "understood" within the context of a person's past and the history and tradition of the society to which that person belongs. But to say that a person's conduct cannot be understood adequately except by "understanding" it within the context of the person's past and the tradition in which he or she lives amounts to saying that one adopts a reflexive attitude in regard to the past and that tradition. This in turn means that I "interpret" the person's conduct within that context. Gadamer has rightly pointed out that such an interpretation necessarily implies dialectics—that is, a continuous methodical switch of perspectives (necessary to critically examine the presuppositions that are preunderstood in any interpretation) in order to separate mere prejudices from legitimate assumptions (Gadamer 1975a; 1975b, pp. 153–341).

Yet there is still another important reason why a good psychologist has to turn to interpretive and critical methods. For many important insights made available to us by contemporary psychology can be applied in various ways when the psychologist is concerned with concrete human beings in concrete situations. In this application of psychological insights, the psychologist must take the individual person or group within the world in which they actually live, if he or she is to understand their position, needs, problems, and motives, and be able to help them. It is obvious that because of the essential historicity of persons and their world, this "taking into account" must imply interpretation and critique. This is why hermeneutics, too, opens up a great number of possibilities precisely in the realm of the *practical application* of psychological insights, in addition to the important contributions it can make to the psychologist's *theoretical* concern (von Uslar 1970, p. 349).

Notes

1. Of the vast amount of literature available on the subject, I mention here merely the most important studies referred to in the following: Brodbeck 1962, pp. 231–72; Brunswik 1952; Carnap 1955; Chisholm 1955–1956, pp. 125–48; Hanson 1958; Helmer and Rescher 1959, pp. 25–52; Hempel 1965; Nagel 1961; Popper 1957, 1959; Scriven 1956, pp. 105–30; 1962, pp. 170–230; Winch 1958.

2. I refer to the following as a sample of the most important views: Buytendijk 1959, pp. 78–98; Gurwitsch 1966; Husserl 1954, 1962; Linschoten 1963, pp. 113–22; Merleau-Ponty 1942, 1945; Sartre 1936, 1939; Strasser 1963. For a more complete bibliography, see Kockelmans 1967.

References

Brodbeck, M. (1962). "Explanation, prediction, and 'imperfect' knowledge," *Minnesota studies in the philosophy of science*, vol. 3 (H. Feigl and G. Maxwell, eds.). Minneapolis: University of Minnesota, 231–72.

Brunswik, E. (1952). *The conceptual framework of psychology*. Chicago: University of Chicago.

Buytendijk, F. J. J. (1959). "Die Bedeutung der Phänomenologie Husserls für die Psychologie der Gegenwart," *Husserl et la pensée moderne* (H. L. Van Breda and J. Taminiaux, eds.). The Hague: Nijhoff, 78–98.

Carnap, R. (1955). "Logical foundations of the unity of science," *International encyclopedia of unified science* (O. Neurath, ed.). Chicago: University of Chicago.

Chisholm, R. (1955–1956). "Sentences about believing," *Proceedings of the Aristotelian society*, 56, pp. 125–248.

Gadamer, H.-G. (1975a). *Truth and method*. New York: Seabury.

——— (1975b). "The problem of historical consciousness" (J. L. Close, trans.), *Graduate faculty philosophy journal*, 5.1, pp. 2–52.

Gurwitsch, A. (1966). *Studies in phenomenology and psychology*. Evanston: Northwestern University.

Hanson, N. (1958). *Patterns of discovery*. London: Cambridge University.

Heidegger, M. (1962). *Being and time* (J. Macquarrie and E. Robinson, trans.). New York: Harper and Row.

Helmer, O., and Rescher, N. (1959). "On the epistemology of the inexact sciences," *Management science*, 61, pp. 25–52.

Hempel, C. G. (1965). *Aspects of scientific explanation*. New York: Free Press.

Husserl, E. (1954). *Die Krisis der europäischen Wissenschaften und die transzendentale Phänomenologie*. The Hague: Nijhof.

——— (1962). *Phänomenologische Psychologie*, Husserliana, vol. 9 (W. Biemal, ed.). The Hague: Nijhoff.

Kockelmans, J. (1967). *Edmund Husserl's phenomenological psychology*. Pittsburgh: Duquesne University.

——— (1969). *World in science and philosophy*. Milwaukee: Bruce.

Linschoten, J. (1963). "Fenomenologie en psychologie," *Algemeen Neder-lands tijdschrift voor wijsbegeerte en psychologie*, 55, pp. 113–22.
—— (1964). *Idolen van de psycholoog*. Utrecht: Bijleveld, 15–64.
Merleau-Ponty, M. (1942). *La structure du comportement*. Paris: Presses Universitaires de France.
—— (1945). *Phénoménologie de la perception*. Paris: Gallimard.
—— (1962). *The phenomenology of perception*. New York: Humanities.
Nagel, E. (1961). *The structure of science*. London: Routledge and Kegan Paul.
Popper, K. (1957). *The poverty of historicism*. London: Routledge and Kegan Paul.
—— (1959). *The logic of scientific discovery*. New York: Basic Books.
Ricoeur, P. (1952). "Méthodes et tâches d'une phénoménologie de la volunté," *Problèmes actuels de la phénoménologie* (H. L. Van Breda, ed.). Paris: de Brouwer, 115–23.
Rudner, R. (1966). *Philosophy of social science*. Englewood Cliffs, N. J.: Prentice-Hall.
Sartre, J.-P. (1936). *L'imagination*. Paris: Alcan.
—— (1939). *Esquisse d'une théorie des émotions*. Paris: Hermann.
Scriven, M. (1956). "A study of radical behaviorism," *Minnesota studies in philosophy of science*, vol. 1 (H. Feigl and M. Scriven, eds.). Minneapolis: University of Minnesota, 105–30.
—— (1962). "Explanations, predictions, and laws," *Minnesota studies in the philosophy of science*, vol. 3 (H. Feigl and G. Maxwell, eds.). Minneapolis: University of Minnesota, 170–230.
Strasser, S. (1963). *Phenomenology and the human sciences*. Pittsburgh: Duquesne University.
von Uslar, Detlev (1970). "Das Problem der Deutung in der Psychologie," *Hermeneutik und Dialektik*, (R. Bubner, K. Cramer, and R. Wiehl, eds.). Tübingen: Mohr, vol. 2, pp. 337–52.
Winch, P. (1958). *The idea of a social science*. New York: Humanities.

4 • Psychology after Philosophy

Donald Polkinghorne

Contemporary European philosophers describe their work as taking place at the beginning of a new, postmodern era that marks the end of philosophy—that is, the Western attempt to ground knowledge on a sure foundation. The epistemological search for certainty of the previous era has been referred to by a variety of terms—*philosophy, modernism, metaphysics,* and *Enlightenment discourse.* The new purpose of those who previously would have been called philosophers is "to bring about the end of philosophy," "to overcome the tradition," or "to silence modernism" (see Baynes, Bohman, and McCarthy 1987). At the core of modernism or Enlightenment discourse was the belief that a method for uncovering the laws of nature had been discovered, and that the use of this method would eventually accumulate enough knowledge to build "the heavenly kingdom on earth." The method was the one advocated by Francis Bacon—experimental science—and through it the idols of belief that shielded ordinary understanding could be penetrated and certain knowledge produced. The present discipline of psychology grew up as a participant in the modern commitment to experimental principles. Now that the principles of its parent discourse are being called into question by continental philosophers, the present practices of the human sciences in general, and psychology in particular, are also in question.

The modernist idea was that formal reasoning applied to sense data provided a foundation for certain knowledge. This notion became an unquestioned supposition of its discourse. Beginning with Nietzsche, however, a series of thinkers have challenged these assumptions and have sought to expose their limits and errors. Included among these scholars are Martin Heidegger, Theodor Adorno, Hans-Georg Gadamer, Michel Foucault, Jacques Derrida, and François Lyotard. They have sought to deconstruct the Enlightenment discourse by showing that its foundational principles are merely ungrounded assumptions.

Deconstruction of the Enlightenment tradition is based on the notion that language is opaque. This opaqueness prevents language from being an unobtrusive vehicle for ideas and perceptions. Language contributes its own artifacts to a discussion, and these artifacts are often overlooked by the participants who believe that their talk is a transparent vehicle for carrying their ideas. It becomes difficult to distinguish the part of the conversation that is generated by language itself from the part that is derived from the referents of the language. Because contemporary European philosophers believe that no position can be taken up outside a discourse system, their own critique is contained within the limits of a specific network of meaning. This difficulty is compounded in the attempt to disclose the situated assumptions of the Enlightenment discourse, for it is precisely the Enlightenment's "language game," its conversation, that shapes our contemporary experience. Thus, the deconstructive approach looks for anomalies and contradictions within modern philosophy and tries to uncover its hidden layers in order to reveal the historical and firmly situated nature of what it has taken for granted as ultimate truth.

The deconstruction of the modern or Enlightenment discourse is taking place in two overlapping conversations in philosophy—a more general conversation, whose contemporary representatives are Foucault (1973), Derrida (1974), and Lyotard (1984), and a conversation focused on the philosophy of science. Participants in the first conversation describe the error of seeking a foundation to assure the truth of our epistemological beliefs and call for us to be comfortable living without certainty. The topic of the second conversation is more limited and is focused on the break up of the Enlightenment consensus about science, and the participants in this discussion talk about ways in which a "postempirical" or "postpositivist" science might be practiced. The purpose of this essay is to examine the themes of this second discussion (philosophy of science) by contemporary European philosophers and to relate their conversation to the practice of psychology.

FORMAL SCIENCE AND THE ENLIGHTENMENT DISCOURSE

The deconstructive discussants recognize that the knowledge produced by the epistemological principles of the modern belief system during the three hundred years of its use has brought about a transformation of the human environment. The industrial and informational revolutions—as well as political revolutions— have achieved what is generally acknowledged to be an improvement in the quality of human life. These beliefs have produced significant advances in the control of natural processes. The discussants' doubts are directed at modernism's basic assumption and belief that it is founded on a sure foundation that guarantees that its knowledge statements are accurate and assured descriptions of reality.

The Enlightenment was historically situated after two previous discourses through which the Western tradition had passed—the classical discourse of the Greek period and its replacement, the revelatory discourse of the Middle Ages. The Enlightenment discourse retained elements of both periods. Many of its assumptions were carried over from the revelatory period against which it was in rebellion, and its inspiration was drawn from the classical period, which it rediscovered. The idea of human science and the notion that the human being was an empirical entity that could be studied in the manner of other entities was invented by the Enlightenment discourse (Foucault 1973, p. 344). The idea was formed in the late seventeenth century as part of the Enlightenment vision of making a new and better world, but it was almost two hundred years later before the idea overcame the residuary resistance from the revelatory discourse. Disciplines for the scientific study of human beings were created at that time, and in the century since then the idea has gained such scope and power that it currently holds a central position in our understandings of our selves and our societies.

The Enlightenment discourse contains rules set for the language game of science. The postmodern conversation seeks to change these rules and, in particular, to reform the approach to the study of human beings. At the beginning, the Enlightenment's notions were subordinate to the notions of the dominant Christian revelatory discourse. The Enlightenment notions began to gain strength in Western Europe during the seventeenth century and were enlivened by the breakthroughs in astronomy, especially Galileo's dismissal of teleological explanations for planetary motion. The rediscovery of traces of the classical discourse and the culminating accomplishments of Isaac Newton gave further support to the developing Enlightenment faith. Francis Bacon, René Descartes, and John Locke were the early spokesmen for the movement and provided the warrants for breaking out of the structures of the revelatory or medieval discourse. The central themes of the Enlightenment discourse were preserved from skeptical threats by Immanuel Kant in the late eighteenth century, and the last refinements were proposed at the beginning of this century and developed between the world wars by the Vienna Circle.

Assumptions about the nature of reality were radically challenged by the Enlightenment discourse. The old assumptions held that reality was created as a stage on which human salvation was to be worked out and on which God's purposes and interventions determined the movements of the heavens as well as the events on earth, but the new conversation pictured reality as ultimately something more like a machine that ran according to universal regularities. These regularities functioned as mathematical relations, and because the human mind has the capacity to comprehend mathematics it is competent to understand the basic operations of the universe. Although the precision of the regularities was not apparent to everyday observations, it could be discovered through careful, measured observations and logical calculation using inductive procedures. It was believed that humans, by gaining an understanding of the regularities, would gain the power to predict how reality would respond to their interventions and, thus, could secure control over the natural and human environments. Evidence of early scientific successes using this model led to the notion that humans would progressively accumulate knowledge until ultimately they would have the power to build an earthly kingdom that would be equal to the heavenly kingdom of the revelatory discourse, which had been understood to be possible only through God's grace at the end of time. Antagonism between the formal science of the Enlightenment and the sacred knowledge of revelatory discourse has been present from the start. It is evident in Galileo's conflicts with religious authorities over his defense of the Copernican system, as well as the contemporary campaign to include creationism in high school textbooks.

Eventually, the main force of the revelatory and scholastic tradition collapsed under the weight of the continuous success of formal science in generating new discoveries that resulted in increased human control over natural processes. The modern conversation based on reason was taken up in a popularized form throughout Europe. The ideas and concepts of the discourse were spread by the writings of the French philosophes and the English periodicalists (see Eagleton 1984, pp. 9–27). The ideals and hopes of the age of reason and the Enlightenment became instrumental in the movements for reform of social and political organizations throughout the European world and fostered the American and French revolutions. As Western technological achievements have become adopted by non-Western ' countries, the Enlightenment discourse and its commitment to progress through science has now become the dominant international discourse about knowledge.

The agenda for the Enlightenment discourse called for the accumulation of objective knowledge of the mathematically ordered reality that lies beneath the varied and disordered appearance of the flux of everyday experience. The excitement of the early participants in the discourse came from the notion that human existence is governed by underlying laws that resemble the laws that order the movements of the heavens.[1] It was believed that, just as superstitions about the movements of the stars and the earth had been cleared away, so too would the superstitions and errors that had deformed human institutions and relations be cleared away by formal science. When the natural order underlying human existence became known, new institutions could be built that would conform to this order and would support the natural development of human happiness.

It was believed that when all the laws of nature were finally known, the Enlightenment would culminate with the full happiness of humankind. During the three centuries in which this conversation has been the focal concern of the discourse about knowledge, however, the trend has been in the opposite direction. The enthusiastic commitment to the scientific method as the vehicle for discovering ultimate and eternal truths has been corroded over the years and contemporary European philosophers of science now doubt the possibility of attaining absolute and unchanging truths about reality (cf. Polkinghorne 1983, pp. 94–103).

In spite of challenges from these philosophers of science, belief in the presuppositions of formal science continues to inform mainstream practice in psychological research.[2] The Enlightenment discourse is built on four basic assumptions—that the real is unchanging, that ordinary knowledge is flawed, that objective truth can be known by using specific methods of inquiry, and that humans have access to a foundation on which truth claims can be based. The presumptive character of these themes has been buried below the proclamations of formal science. They have lost their tentativeness and have assumed the status of obvious truths.

DECONSTRUCTION OF THE ENLIGHTENMENT DISCOURSE

The focus of the postmodern conversation is the deconstruction of the Enlightenment's assumptions and its idea that science is grounded on a sure foundation. The talk has uncovered three mistaken assumptions: (1) language is an unproblematic and transparent medium for communicating ideas; (2) relations among entities are determinate and describable as absolute laws; and (3) perception opens access to a certain ground against which all knowledge claims can be evaluated.

Language and Reality

The Enlightenment discourse adopted the commonsense notion that words "stand for" or "refer to" particular objects. However, in addition to individual objects, formal science was interested in naming the categories of which particular entities were manifestations. It was at the level of categories that relations and laws could be understood. Although it was recognized that words existed that referred to categories, the issue was whether these categories actually existed independently of the words that named them. This controversy about language was a carryover from the medieval discussion about the external referents to categorical words. Nominalists held that reality consisted only of particulars, and thus a general term such as *dog* did not represent a universal reality of "doghood" but was only a term (*nomen*, name) that referred to thoughts constructed by the mind. The question raised for formal science by the remnants of this controversy concerned the status of categories and the proposed lawful relations among them. Because the goal of objective knowledge was to develop general statements, the question was asked: What is the status of the reality that these statements refer to? Further: Do the statements refer to actual laws and rules of nature, or are they merely mental constructions that are not descriptive of anything real? Are they only pragmatic tools useful for making predictions?[3] The unfinished debate concerns whether the theories of science—that is, the statements of relation among categories—are descriptions of a real theoretical realm or merely mental models useful for predicting events.

A second development in understanding the nature of language also undercuts the Enlightenment assumption that language is transparent and unproblematic. Ferdinand de Saussure (1966) transformed linguistics from the study of the historical changes through which language developed to a study of the way a single language system distributes meaning. According to Saussure, the relationship between words does not reflect the external relationship among the things the words signify. Words evince only the organization internal to a language system. The particular way in which a language breaks down its ideas is arbitrary. The meaning of an idea in a language is determined by the other ideas in the language rather than by external objects. Various language systems divide the spectrum of conceptual possibilities in different ways, so the categorical expressions of a language are not drawn from nor are they representational of an external, independent, objective realm.

A third theory of the limits to language as the representation of the objective realm has been presented by Ludwig Wittgenstein (1968) in his later writings. He argues that the meanings of words are social constructions and are parts of a language game one has learned to play. The meanings of words are linked to the following of rules that allow members of a community to understand one another. Words are not pictures of the world, and they are not derived from private ideas in the mind. They are created by social practice, and in order to participate in the practice of speaking, one needs to know the rules which the community uses to define its particular words. Thus, there is no neutral language by means of which reality as it is in itself can be described.

The nominalist controversy, Saussure's notion of language systems, and Wittgenstein's language-game theory undercut the Enlightenment assumption that formal science statements are clear representations of the objective realm and are free of subjective elements. There had been a modernist attempt to remove all subjective aspects from scientific language by creating an ideal language in which the ordinary meanings of words were set aside and replaced by meanings that were either true by definition or were limited to empirical referents (see Hempel 1959, pp. 108–29). The move to an ideal language has been particularly influential in the practice of formal science by psychology, especially in its adoption of technical terms with precise operational definitions.[4]

The position inherent in all three of these discussions of language is that in spite of the attempt to create an ideal language for formal science, there remains a gap between the categories of any language and those of objective reality. Moreover, these notions of the limits of language challenge the purity of observation reports, because they imply that the text of experience is a conflation that cannot be disentangled in order to separate out pure perception from language. Consequently, pure perception is not available as a certain referent for the words of an ideal language nor as a foundation on which the knowledge statements of a formal science can be grounded.

Determinate Laws and Probability

There was an expectation in the Enlightenment discourse that the laws that existed among categories could be described in the exact terms required for valid formal logical deductions and mathematical operations. The basic thrust of the formal science position was that there were underlying lawlike principles that governed all activity. The exemplar for these laws was the law of gravity, where a clear and determinate description could be given of the relations that held among categories (a constant force among objects in space and time). But the efforts to discover laws or exact relations have not been uniformly successful, especially in the study of human actions.

Formal science research in psychology has not produced many determinate descriptions of laws or relation among variables. Much of the research has ended with findings in which there are variations in the actions of entities under the same circumstances. The first hope was that the reason absolutely determinate laws were not discovered as guides for all activity was because knowledge was still incomplete. Presumably, when further observations were made and more sophisticated theoretical laws proposed, the apparent variability would give way and the determinate assumption would be saved. However, the later discovery of the apparent random activity of individual subatomic particles raised further doubts about the whole notion of a reality determined by universal principles. In the realm of small particles the determinate model has had to be changed to acknowledge a certain amount of real nonconformity and randomness of activity. The response within formal science to the variant activity that continued to appear, even in research with large objects and human behavior, was to adopt the notion of statistical laws. These laws are statements about the probability of a single instance conforming to a prediction instead of statements about how all instances will respond. (See Hacking 1975 for a historical study of the development of probability theory.) For example, of a hundred instances one could expect that sixty would respond according to the proposed rule, but one would not know in advance which sixty.

A different area of doubt, which also brought about a retreat from exact law statements to probability statements, concerned the limits of inductive logic for the demonstration and verification of knowledge claims. The hope of formal science was that methodologically controlled experiments could be used to demonstrate the truth that some proposed law statements were representations of actual natural laws. But the inductive logic that guided scientific reasoning was insufficient to provide certain verification. Ampliative induction yielded only a probable indication that an inferred generalization was true. No number of successful predictions could prove that a law would continue to hold in all circumstances and for all time. (See Swinburne 1974 for a selection of essays that address the problem of induction.)

This "scandal of inductionism" brought about another retreat from the ideal that formal science could demonstrate certain knowledge about the unchanging reality that determined changing events. The knowledge goals were altered so that science no longer sought to verify or demonstrate absolutely that scientific statements were true. It aimed, instead, to justify belief in a law by showing that it was highly probable. Walter Weimer uses the term *justificationism* to describe the position that a method for ascertaining the certainty of knowledge claims could be developed, and he uses the term *neojustificationism* to designate the new strategy that the best that could be achieved is a high probability of the truth of a statement (1979, pp. 8–19). Neojustificationists moved from the idea that statements could be proved true or false to the idea that the probability of a statement could be confirmed. For neojustificationists, the body of accepted scientific propositions was no longer composed of certain indubitable lawlike propositions; rather, it contained only highly probable propositions. Formal science thus changed its position from the claim that it produced absolutely true knowledge to the claim that it produced knowledge that was probably true. Hans Reichenbach, a leading proponent of formal science, described the abandonment of verification by formal science:

> Thus there are left no propositions at all which can be absolutely verified. The predicate of truth-value of a proposition, therefore, is a mere fictive quality. . . . Actual science instead employs throughout the predicate of weight. . . . We regard a high weight as equivalent

to truth, and a low weight as equivalent to falsehood. . . . The conception of science as a system of true propositions is therefore nothing but a schematization. [1938, p. 188]

This retreat from the early Enlightenment belief in a demonstrably true knowledge of the objective realm did not bring with it an abandonment of the spirit of the belief. Probable truth was understood to be preferable to a return to knowledge by authority or a giving over to complete subjectivity and relativism. Imre Lakatos has described the position: Neojustificationists "thought that even if science does not produce certainty, it produces near-certainty" (1968, p. 322). Despite the philosophical difficulties of providing a warrant for the use of induction to confirm hypotheses, the use of experimentally developed data to provide probabilistic support for hypotheses is the basic format used by contemporary formal science.

Observation as Foundational

By the late 1950s and early sixties, the idea that observations were mirror reflections of external reality was increasingly under attack (see Rorty 1979, pp. 165–212). Observation came to be understood as a constructive effort of the observer. What was experienced as a fact was the result of a theoretical network of meanings and expectations as well as of the stimulation of the sensate system by physical changes in the external or internal environments. The formal science position accepted two kinds of terms—theoretical terms, which were defined negatively as consisting of those self-definitional terms that are not observational, and observational terms, which were words that described direct experiential evidence. Although the meaning of theoretical terms was thoroughly scrutinized, it was thought that the meaning of observational terms was unproblematic because they were simple accounts of direct experience.

Mary Hesse (1980) produced a summary of the arguments developed by philosophers of science that undermined the notion that observational statements were clear, unproblematic reflections of the extralinguistic reality. Because words are learned in empirical situations where the observer is taught to classify certain similarities of individual experiences under single words, information about the dissimilar elements of an experience is lost in all descriptions reporting observations. The particular sectioning of experience into a language of classification is dependent on the theoretical, cultural, and valuing schemes the observer has learned. Any experience can be divided or punctuated in various ways. This idea that there are different ways of dividing up a sequence of events has been developed by Gregory Bateson. Two persons can link the sequence of events into different chains and create different meaning from the same events (see Watzlawick, Beavin, and Jackson 1967, pp. 54–59).

In addition to the problem created by the fact that observational reports are dependent on which of the multiple classificatory schemes is used to describe an experience, contemporary philosophers of science have noted that observations are not independent of the theories they are supposed to test, and thus they cannot be used as the ground on which the truth of a theory can rest. Willard Quine (1953) has reaffirmed Pierre Duhem's notion that facts are theory-dependent. The idea that there are two separate languages, one theoretical and the other observational, and that the observational can serve as a neutral validation of theory, is mistaken. There is one language network in which the meaning of observational words is dependent on theoretical assumptions. If observational descriptions appear not to confirm a theory, the whole network of meaning can accommodate itself to retain the theory. For example, measuring instruments, which are supposed to produce independent observations, are dependent on theoretical assumptions about how the instruments function. (See Polkinghorne 1983 and Suppe 1977 for discussions of the corrosion of the idea of objective and pure observation statements.)

The epistemological principles of formal science have been undercut by the deconstructive philosophers of science. Using the Enlightenment's own conception of rationality and formal logic, the postpositivist philosophers have found formal science to have been built with inconsistent and ungrounded assumptions. Their thrust has been to demonstrate the logical dissonance in the system, but not to propose alternatives. The critique has produced instability at the very borders that were supposed to demarcate the procedures that would guarantee true and objective results from those that could produce only biased and subjective outcomes.

A first reaction in psychology to these critiques was to continue to accept the basic premises of the Enlightenment program regarding the attainment of a better world through science, but with the realization of the limits of formal science to produce an actual picture of reality. The view of science was adjusted to a more pragmatic appreciation, which stated that although science may have philosophical inconsistencies, it has produced formulas that do predict the probable responses of nature. This view has been the general reaction to the critiques of formal science and is the one held by many in the mainstream of psychology. The plan is to continue with the basic thrust of Enlightenment science but to work for better controls and greater purity of method. Thus, in spite of the demonstrated logical inconsistencies in the system of formal science, psychological science has been slow to give up its commitment to the Enlightenment principles. It has taken some hesitant first steps toward expanding its methodology beyond the basic formal science design by accepting quasi-experimental designs and field studies.[5]

PSYCHOLOGY AFTER THE ENLIGHTENMENT

The Skeptical Response

A more radical response to the deconstruction of the modernist or Enlightenment assumptions has been called for by contemporary European philosophers. They hold that the inconsistencies in formal science are a demonstration of the error of the system and that the Enlightenment misrepresented reality when it assumed that it was organized according to the principles of formal logic. Two strategies are possible if one accepts that the Enlightenment system itself was in error. The first strategy is to respond skeptically by locating the error of the Enlightenment in its very attempt to build a system of truth. This strategy sees the Enlightenment as the last Western try to ground knowledge, and views its failure as a demonstration that there can be no system that grounds us in reality. According to this strategy, we need to learn to live in the world without belief that we have access to ultimate truths. A second strategy is to respond with new efforts to understand the natural and human realms, but with different approaches and with alternate notions of rationality.

A representative of the first strategy is Jacques Derrida. He seeks to undo "metaphysics"—that is, any thought system that depends on an indubitable and unassailable foundation, first principle, or ground on which a hierarchy of truths and meanings can be constructed. Derrida reads the works of Enlightenment writers to show how their texts come to embarrass their own system of logic. He does this by focusing on their "symptomatic" points, the aporia or impasses of meaning, where the texts contradict themselves and come unstuck. Derrida believes that there is something in writing itself that finally evades all systems and logics. The categories and the structure of a text cannot restrain its surplus of meaning, which diffuses and spills over. All language displays this surplus of meaning, and writing itself challenges the Enlightenment concept of a fixed structure of meaning.

Derrida also holds that there is nothing outside the text and, therefore, that the reading and interpretation of a text is an endless play that has no connection to an extralinguistic reference. In his *Of Grammatology* (1973), Derrida condemns the Western (Enlightenment) tradition for its commitment to the ultimate possibility of literal truth. Western history has preferred speech to writing, for speech is understood as the locus of presence in which the possibility of intelligibility and contact with truth could occur. His opposition to the "Western tradition" is radical and unyielding. He attacks Edmund Husserl's commitment to a direct intuition of the contents of consciousness as a sure foundation on which the structures of consciousness can be known (Derrida 1973).

The skeptical strategy of Derrida and others does not provide a context in which a new science can be constructed for psychology. Instead, it stresses the limits of any attempt at truth. The second strategy, however, does offer the possibility of a new framework for psychology. This strategy calls for the exploration of alternate logics in the attempt to understand human existence. It allows for the use of communicative and hermeneutic rationality in the investigation of the various orders of human existence. The strategy does not begin with the Enlightenment commitment to formal logic and observation statements as the requirements for knowledge. Instead, it explores human existence with nonformal modes of understanding in the expectation that areas of the human realm can be made comprehensible. Its call for a renewed attempt at understanding does provide the opportunity for a renewal of psychology.

The Reconstructive Response

There are two contemporary nonskeptical responses in continental philosophy to the critiques of the Enlightenment and the loss of belief in its epistemological foundations. The first is exemplified by Jürgen Habermas and Karl-Otto Apel, who retain a commitment to a type of universal reason that can serve as the vehicle for grounding statements. The second is exemplified by Heidegger and Gadamer, who attempt a reexamination of ontology through the recovery of hermeneutic rationality as the principal means by which humans understand reality. Both responses provide support for the reconstruction of psychology as a human-centered science.

One of the assumptions of the Enlightenment discourse was that rationality was limited to the kind of thought that adhered to the principles of formal logic, and that this is the only legitimate way to reach valid conclusions. By setting aside the term *reason* to refer only to the type of thinking process that uses calculative, hierarchical ordering operations, the implication was made that all other approaches are unreasonable or irrational. The reconstructive philosophers argue that it is this limited understanding of reason that has prevented the human sciences from displaying an understanding of human existence. They recognize a broader notion of reason, which includes any knowledge process used by human beings to understand their world and to solve problems. The characteristics of their enlarged notion of reason include coherence and consistency but not necessarily the disengaged perspective of theoretical understanding. Rationality is defined by them as articulations in some media of the sensibleness of activities within a domain (see Taylor 1982, pp. 80–105). A postpositivist psychology would incorporate this expanded notion of rationality.

Communicative Reason

Karl-Otto Apel and Jürgen Habermas hold that knowledge is grounded not in a subjective but rather an intersubjective interaction. Habermas attempts to construct a theory of truth that stands midway between the Enlightenment notions of objectivism and truth as correspondence and the skeptical notions that all statements are conditioned and relative to the language games in which they are spoken. Habermas does this by appealing to the idea of universal pragmatics or the theory of communicative competence (1984, pp. 1–141). Unlike Chomskian linguistic competence, which addresses an individual speaker's ability to form grammatical sentences, communicative competence refers to the general structures that appear in every possible speech situation. A speech situation necessarily involves both the speaker and the listener in certain agreements and assumptions in order for the communication to proceed. Some of these assumptions are that the communication is understandable, that its propositional content is true, that the speaker is sincere, and that the communication given is appropriate in the situation. However, if an assumption is called into question while the communication is taking place, it cannot be reestablished by simply making an appeal to an outside ground —to direct observation, for instance. For such an appeal needs to be brought back to the conversation as the field in which agreement occurs. Agreement is finally reestablished only discursively, through argumentation. At the same time, if the force of the better argument is to hold sway in the conversation, there cannot be obstacles in the way of a free and just exchange of views. In the ideal speech situation, the goal of achieving truth directs the conversation of the community. In this ideal situation, it is the cogency or soundness of argument and warranted assertibility that motivate the members to accept a claim of truth or correctness. Although Habermas admits that the ideal speech situation exists as a potentiality rather than as an actuality, it serves as a point from which to evaluate any particular communal search for truth.

Habermas believes that in such an open and free argument the truth will win out and bring the group to a consensus. It is rationality itself that convinces the members of the rightness of a position, he says. This rationality is not the same as formal logic, however. It includes a logic of the practical as well as a logic of the theoretical. The force of the rationality is not conditioned by the particular language game in which it is used—it has a universal power. For his attempt to renew a notion of nonrelative rationality, Habermas has received extensive criticism from those skeptical of any attempt to ground knowledge or move beyond the limits of the language games (e.g., Lyotard 1984, p. xxv). Although he accepts the notion that all attempts to provide indubitable foundations for philosophical reason have broken down and that grand epistemological systems can no longer be developed, Habermas seeks to vindicate the Enlightenment notion that truth of some sort is possible. The meaning of the *truth* he uses is different, however, from the Enlightenment idea of truth as objective representation of what is. For Habermas, the truth or falsity of a statement is a function of the community's response. The speaker who claims that a statement or action is true must submit it to communal critique where it can be justified or "defended" in order to produce a rational communal consensus as to its truth or correctness. In Habermas's consensual theory of truth, a statement is justified as true when the community is convinced of its truth after hearing and participating in arguments for it and countering arguments against it (McCarthy 1978, pp. 291–310).

Habermas believes that there has been an evolutionary expansion of the rational competence of communities to recognize arguments for truth and of their ability to direct critical judgment against the disorder and disequilibrium that exists within society. He holds that the rationality that operates to move a communication community to agreement on a knowledge statement has a role in the natural and social sciences because it can serve in the process of reconstructing, after the event, the rational content of the field of research or subject matter. A reconstructive science addresses the activities that persons carry out without explicitly being able to give an account of the concepts and schema on which their performances are based. The aim of the rational reconstruction is to render explicit the structure and elements of the practically mastered and implicitly carried out actions (McCarthy 1978, p. 276). For example, people know how to speak and tell stories, but they are not able to give an account of how they accomplish such tasks. A rational reconstruction would aim to uncover the processes by means of which they present their performances.

Habermas's concept of rationality presupposes that open and free communication exists among people so that they can justify to one another what has been said or done. Habermas's idea of open communication involves the presence of conditions that make possible the settling of arguments and the reaching of agreements about the justification of statements. He believes that these conditions transcend particular situations because they are necessary for any open communication to occur. Thus Habermas overcomes relativism and skepticism about the end of philosophy of finding universal givens in the act of communication.

Habermas's notions of consensual truth and rational reconstruction are useful tools for the development of a post-Enlightenment psychology. His concept of an expanded rationality that includes hermeneutical reasoning opens up the idea of the reasonable beyond the limits of formal logic.

Hermeneutic Reason

Martin Heidegger (1962) has proposed that the primary mode in which human beings make sense of their existence is hermeneutic understanding—the application of a nonformal set of reasoning principles. This kind of rationality is also used to understand the meaning of human expressions and performances—for example, making sense of texts, metaphors, and models, and comprehending what a painting means. At times Heidegger accepted that the formal science approach does work in giving technically correct information about how to induce expected reactions in certain aspects of nature, but he was opposed to the extension of these technological insights to statements about the actual organization of reality. He believed that the picture of the human being as an entity made up of component parts organized according to the prescriptions of formal science is mistaken. When this picture is enlarged to describe human experience and action as parts that are formally organized into categories and determined by fixed relations, he believed that it is in error and that it destroys the full potential of human existence. In his later pieces Heidegger points beyond a projected end of philosophy and of modern technological thinking toward a totally new beginning.

Three principles of understanding make up hermeneutic rationality: (1) parts are understood from the perspective on the whole; (2) context sensitivity is crucial to reaching conclusions; and (3) knowledge of meaning is derived from a continual correction and expansion of first heuristic approximations by search and review of the various aspects that compose the object of inquiry (the hermeneutical circle method of inquiry). One can make judgments about whether these principles have been applied correctly. Heidegger understands hermeneutic reasoning to be a type of human rationality that is more rigorous than conceptual rationality (Faulconer and Williams 1985).

Heidegger's work can be divided into two phases, the deconstructive phase and the "recollective" or reconstructive phase.[6] My interest here is with Heidegger's attempts to develop a new discourse that overcomes the limits of the Enlightenment. He sees that the end of philosophy poses a new task of thinking open to the fullness of reality, a fullness that has been progressively concealed by Western metaphysics. The new task of thinking takes the form of listening to and understanding reality. The Enlightenment idea that our ordinary experience is untrustworthy has taught us that the real is removed and hidden from us and can be known only through logical methods that make it appear. For Heidegger, these methods stand in the way of our ordinary awareness of reality's closeness. He proposes that we give up categorical discourse as a form of "objectifying" thought. This mode of thought has been inherent in the Western understanding that knowledge occurs between a worldless subject on one side and a distanced objective realm on the other. The bridge over this distance is crossed by the ideas in the subject's mind. These ideas are supposed to be mirror reflections from physical objects that cross the gap between the world and the mind. Heidegger believes that this description of knowledge creation neglects the point that human beings are already a part of the world they seek to know. The idea that the knower is separate from the known is an artificial construction in which the human capacity to detach oneself imaginatively from the immediate situation is elevated to an ontological reality.

Humans have the capability of imagining themselves removed from the historical moment and the local situation where they are standing at a particular moment. This capability allows them to take a point of view that appears free of egocentricity. The process of creating a point of view outside one's own experience is derived from the ability to create by imagination the self as observer, standing at a distance from and detached from one's own experiential field. From this imagined distant point of view, one can suppress most of the contents of the flow of experience in order to concentrate on a particular part of one's experience, thus making the part appear as a figure and making the rest of experience recede into the background. The original fullness of experience becomes a shadow while the focal object is abstracted into a clarity. "The original phenomena become reduced to more or less ideal entities which are abstract in comparison to the originally given phenomena" (see Kockelmans 1973, p. 254). The full and rich original experience is filtered to bring before the imagined distant point of view only that part of the whole field that is of interest (see Polkinghorne 1983, pp. 283–92). It appears as if knowers are looking at their own experience and that they are outside this experience, free of perspective and of cultural and personal bias. The standpoint that such knowers seek to create is a standpoint that does not interfere with what is experienced. The advantage gained from the disciplined imaginative point of view and the reduction of ordinary experience is that the aspects of experience that are abstracted or pulled out stand out more clearly and can be subjected to close scrutiny.

What the Enlightenment discourse and its classical predecessor did was to emphasize the distanced viewpoint and say that this was the manner in which knowledge and truth were to be derived.

Heidegger's response to the end of philosophy was to start over and revive the "problem of Being" by beginning with the fullness of the original experience before it is partitioned into figure and ground by the imaginatively created distanced viewpoint. His effort was directed at giving a clear and detailed description of experience in its original condition. He concluded from his investigation that the Enlightenment understanding that knowledge results from developing an accurate picture of a foreign substance was in error. He reminded us that the notion of a gap between a point from which to view (the knowing subject) and that which is to be known (the object as experienced) is a creation of our own efforts and is not the actual and original condition. Thus, the problem of how to overcome the split of the subject from the object, which has engaged so much of Western philosophy, is a fabricated pseudoproblem. The Enlightenment assumed that the mentally manufactured distancing of a point of view was the original and given condition, and that the problem of knowledge was the way in which experience could represent a separate objective world. Instead of concerning himself with this manufactured problem, Heidegger proposed that we attend directly to the more primordial condition, which is the fullness of experience prior to the construction of a separate viewing point.

Heidegger believed that when one attends to experience in its original form reality appears as something conjoined with us and not as something separate and distant. It has been understood in Western thought that what is real is material and objectlike—that is, that what is "really real" are physical things that are removed from us and placed "out there." These things are indifferent to us, and reality would continue in its fullness without any human presence. Heidegger's notion of reality is more inclusive. It takes into account the order of meaning as well as the physical order. To clarify his idea, he uses the analogy of reading a poem. When looking at a poem a person has not understood its full reality if all that is recognized is the physical order of paper and bits of black ink. These materials are the conveyors of meaning, and to know what is really there one must attend to the meaning of the poem as well as to the materials that carry its message. Without a reader to attend to and understand the meaning in the poem, the meaning cannot display itself. The analogy breaks down if one thinks of the reader as separate and removed from the message. For Heidegger reality is one. It is not a duality of reader and poem or knower and known. It is as if reality, through the human order of meaning, creates a clearing for itself so that its message can be made meaningful through our understanding. Thus, reality comprises not only its own expressiveness but also its own understanding in the awareness that is human being.

Heidegger proposes that we give up the Enlightenment's visual metaphor with its inferences of a disinterested subject gazing at a distant object. In its place he suggests an aural metaphor in which experience is conceived of as hearing reality. The aural metaphor is not meant, however, to describe a mechanical process in which sound waves strike the ear and stimulate the aural sensory apparatus. It refers to the process of listening to and comprehending a speech—that is, to the process of understanding what someone has to say. The aural metaphor suggests that experience is the presence of reality. It is the equivalent of the statement that when we hear a poem we are in the midst of its meaning. When we engage in listening to a poem and understanding it, we are no longer separate from the poem. We are a part of it in the sense that its meaning is in us.[7]

For Heidegger the kind of process involved in experiencing reality as meaningful is the same kind of process that is entailed in experiencing speech as meaningful. As mentioned before, this kind of knowing is called "hermeneutic" knowing and involves processes of thought in which the whole text is understood by successive heuristic interpretive guesses as to the pattern of meaning connecting the parts of the message. The hermeneutic process advances by moving to and fro between the parts and a continuously more refined interpretive understanding until a point of most likely fit is developed and each part is seen as significant in relation to the assumed whole meaning. For Heidegger, the primary transactions of consciousness—those that take place prior to the operation of detachment and abstraction—are hermeneutic or interpretive in form. The transactions of calculation and figuring are secondary operations and come into play only after the reduction of experience to objective figures.

Heidegger's attempt to develop an alternative discourse about human existence can provide psychology with a model for a new phase of development in which a positive, post-Enlightenment, reformed human science can emerge. This new psychology would include hermeneutic reasoning among the logical forms through which it would approach human experience and action. Using Heidegger's analysis of human existence, it would approach human actions as the expression of hermeneutic understandings that are planned and informed according to configured and linguistic schemes, such as narratives and stories. Such a psychology would produce results more closely aligned with the experience humans have of their own lives. It would develop an inventory of hermeneutic schemes as a system to suggest similarities among episodes and still retain in its descriptions what is distinct and dissimilar in particular situations. Thus, its outcomes would be statements describing the significance of events in relation to their role in larger episodes, and the function of these statements would be to give clarity and depth to the understanding of human existence.

The renewed psychology would operate more like a humanities discipline than like a natural science discipline, and the kind of validity its conclusions would have would be more like the valid interpretations of literary expressions than like the valid conclusions of logical and mathematical deductions. Although it would retain the capacity to use the tools of formal science, these tools would be understood to be aids to description rather than means for prediction and control.

Notes

1. Veyne uses Aristotle's distinction between the "lunary world" and the "sublunary world" in discussing the kind of knowledge appropriate for use in historical writing (1984, pp. 28–29). He holds that in the sublunary world "man is free; chance exists, events have causes whose effect remains doubtful; the future is uncertain; becoming is contigent." He compares these properties to the determinate effect of laws in the lunary world.

2. Howard (1984) surveyed 42 editors of psychology journals, asking them to rate a form of Galassi's eleven components in the training of skilled researchers. The "ability to evaluate research critically" received the highest rating, and eight other items were ranked close together. "Philosophy of science" was ranked tenth, just above "computer skills," and both were considerably below the eighth item. The point of Howard's paper is that the philosophy of science is considered by journal editors and training directors of APA-approved counseling psychology programs to be of little importance in the training of researchers.

3. Two recent efforts to defend both sides of the realism/nominalism (currently called *conventionalism* and *instrumentalism*) controversy have been made by Newton-Smith (1981), defending the realist construal of theories, and van Frassen (1980), defending a pragmatic or instrumental position of theory acceptance.

4. See Kerlinger (1973) for an example of the application of the principles of an ideal language to formal science research in the behavioral sciences. The first part of this leading textbook on research design is entitled "The Language and Approach of Science." Kerlinger (1973, p. 29) writes: "A construct is a concept. It has the added meaning, however, of having been deliberately and consciously invented or adopted for a special scientific purpose."

5. See Gelso (1979, pp. 7–35) for a description of methods used in psychology that do not meet the strict criteria of formal science and its laboratory experiment exemplar. The extension has occurred in the random sampling requirement, where less control over the "all else being equal" principle has been accepted, and in the laboratory-precision-in-observation requirement, where field study and interview data have been allowed.

6. This summary presentation of Heidegger's response to the "end of philosophy" is based on statements made throughout his works. It is highly condensed, and I have tried to convey the thrust of his ideas without using his extensive specialized vocabulary. My statements are not drawn from specific references in Heidegger's texts, but from ideas developed in various of his works. Some interpreters of Heidegger divide his work into "early" and "late" periods. The early period has an existential emphasis and is represented by *Being and Time* (1962), first published in 1927. His late period is distinguished by its concern with poetry and language and is said to begin with his essay "The Origin of the Work of Art" (Heidegger 1971, pp. 17–87), first published in 1935. I have not made this two-period distinction in my discussion, but I use the later works as keys to understanding the existential discussion. Hofstadter has translated and collected seven of the later works under the title *Poetry Language Thought* (Heidegger 1971).

7. See Ihde (1976) for a full discussion of the effect of the visual metaphor on Western philosophy and important suggestions and corrections.

References

Baynes, K., Bohman, J., and McCarthy, T., (eds.) (1987). *After philosophy: End or transformation?* Cambridge, Mass.: MIT.

Cranston, M. (1967). "Bacon, Francis," *The encyclopedia of philosophy* (P. Richards, ed.). New York: Collier Macmillan.

Derrida, J. (1973). *Speech and phenomena: And other essays on Husserl's theory of signs* (D. B. Allison, trans.). Evanston: Northwestern University.

——— (1974). *Of grammatology* (G. Chakravorty, trans.). Baltimore: Johns Hopkins University.

Eagleton, T. (1984). *The function of criticism*. Thetford, England: Thetford.

Faulconer, J. E., and Williams, R. N. (1985). "Temporality in human action: An alternative to positivism and historicism," *American psychologist*, 40 (November), 1179–88.

Foucault, M. (1973). *The order of things: An archaeology of the human sciences.* New York: Random House.

Gelso, C. J. (1979). "Research in counseling: Methodological and professional issues," *Counseling psychologist,* 8, pp. 7–35.

Habermas, J. (1984). *The theory of communicative action,* vol. 1: *Reason and rationalization of society* (T. McCarthy, trans.). Boston: Beacon.

Hacking, I. (1975). *The emergence of probability.* Cambridge: Cambridge University.

Heidegger, M. (1962). *Being and time* (J. Macquarrie and E. Robinson, trans.). New York: Harper and Row.

———— (1971). *Poetry, language, thought* (A. Hofstadter, trans.). New York: Harper and Row.

Hempel, C. G. (1959). "The empiricist criterion of meaning," *Logical positivism* (A. J. Ayer, ed.). New York: Free Press, 108–29.

Hesse, M. (1980). "Theory and observation," *Revolutions and reconstruction in the philosophy of science.* Bloomington: Indiana University, 63–110.

Howard, G. (1984). "The queen is dead! Long live the queen!" Unpublished manuscript.

Ihde, D. (1976). *Listening voice: A phenomenology of sound.* Athens: Ohio University.

Jay, M. (1985). "Habermas and modernism," *Habermas and modernity* (R. J. Berstein, ed.). Cambridge, Mass.: MIT, 125–39.

Kerlinger, F. N. (1973). *Foundations of behavioral research,* 2nd ed. New York: Holt, Rhinehart, Winston.

Kockelmans, J. J. (1973). "Theoretical problems in phenomenological psychology," *Phenomenology and the social sciences,* vol. 1 (M. Natanson, ed.). Evanston: Northwestern University, 225–80.

Lakatos, I. (1968). "Changes in the problem of inductive logic," *The problem of inductive logic* (I. Lakatos, ed.). Amsterdam: North-Holland, 315–417.

Lyotard, Jean-François (1979). *The postmodern condition: A report on knowledge* (G. Bennington and B. Massumi, trans.). Minneapolis: University of Minnesota; repr. 1984.

McCarthy, Thomas (1978). *The critical theory of Jürgen Habermas.* Cambridge, Mass.: MIT.

Newton-Smith, W. H. (1981). *The rationality of science.* Boston: Routledge and Kegan Paul.

Polkinghorne, D. E. (1983a). "The reductions and existence: Bases for epistemology," *Analecta Hesserliana,* vol. 15, *Foundations of morality, human rights, and the human sciences* (Anna-Teresa Tymieniecka and C. O. Schrag, eds.). Dordrecht, Holland: D. Reidel, 283–92.

———— (1983b). *Methodology for the human sciences: Systems of inquiry.* Albany: State University of New York.

Quine, Willard van Orman (1953). "Two dogmas of empiricism," *From a logical point of view.* Cambridge, Mass.: Harvard University.

Reichenbach, Hans (1938). *Experience and prediction.* Chicago: University of Chicago.

Rorty, Richard (1979). *Philosophy and the mirror of nature.* Princeton: Princeton University.

Saussure, Ferdinand de (1907–1911). *Course in general linguistics.* (C. Bally and A. Sechehaye, eds.; W. Baskin, trans.). New York: McGraw-Hill; repr. 1966.
Suppe, Frederick (ed.) (1977). *The structure of scientific theories,* 2nd ed. Urbana: University of Illinois.
Swinburne, Richard (ed.) (1974). *The justification of induction.* Oxford: Oxford University.
Taylor, Charles (1971). "Interpretation and the science of man," *Philosophy and the human sciences.* (Charles Taylor, ed.). Cambridge: Cambridge University.
——— (1982). "Rationality," *Rationality and relativism.* (M. Hollis and S. Lukes, eds.). Cambridge, Mass.: MIT, 80–105.
van Fraasen, Bas C. (1980). *The scientific image* Oxford: Clarendon.
Veyne, Paul. (1984). *Writing history, essay on epistomology.* (Mina-Moore-Rinvoleri, trans.). Middletown, Mass.: Wesleyan University.
Watzlawick, Paul, Helmick Beavin, Janet, and Jackson, Don D. (1967). *Pragmatics of human communication.* New York: Norton.
Weimer, W. B. (1979). *Notes on the methodology of scientific philosophy.* Hillsdale, N. J.: Lawrence Erlbaum.
Winch, Peter (1958). *The idea of a social science and its relation to philosophy.* London: Routledge and Kegan Paul.
Wittgenstein, Ludwig (1968). *Philosophical investigations,* 3rd ed. (G. E. M. Anscombe, trans.). New York: Macmillan.

5 • Heidegger and Psychological Explanation: Taking Account of Derrida

James E. Faulconer

As arguably the most important thinker of twentieth-century continental Europe and one of the two most important thinkers of the century (Ludwig Wittgenstein being the other), Martin Heidegger offered a genuine alternative to the metaphysical tradition of substances in his discussion of the basic question of philosophy, "What does it mean to be something?" In doing this, he laid a foundation for an alternative to traditional approaches in the human sciences such as psychology, history, and literature. Rather than assuming that to be something is to be a substance of some kind (using *substance* as it is traditionally used in philosophy, so that it can refer both to mind and to material entities), in his early work Heidegger argued that what is (being) is that which is revealed in human activity in the world. The result was a quite different view of both what it means to be and what it means to be human. Though his later work took a different turn, it too can be said to focus on the relation of being and human being (Kockelmans 1984, p. 33). This new view of being, including human being, paves the way for an overhaul of psychological theory, for a new understanding of psychological explanation.

Central to the new understanding of human being which follows from Heidegger's ontology is the notion that consciousness cannot be conceived as a box (Heidegger 1984, pp. 160ff.) and that explanations of human phenomena in terms of transcendent, atemporal principles—for example, immutable laws of nature—are in principle undesirable (cf. Faulconer and Williams 1985, 1987).

Once we reject substances as the basis of what is, we no longer have "things in themselves" apart from any possible human interaction and behind all supposedly mere appearances. Rather, the "thing in itself" appears in human life—in speech and activity— and there are no atemporal, static principles that can encapsulate what is essentially temporal and subject to change—namely, what appears in human life. The details of approaches to psychology engendered by Heidegger's view have not yet been fully worked out, though some sketch of them is given in this volume (e.g., Kockelmans, Polkinghorne, and Schrag) as well as in other places. However, these approaches can be summarized briefly.

A Heideggerian psychology rejects the notion of atemporality and, therefore, the notion of laws of behavior, but contrary to what is commonly assumed, such a psychology is not a subjective psychology. For the idea of the subject is based at least on the assumption that substances are the basis for being, if not also on the assumption that the subject is itself one of the substances. Instead, what follows from Heidegger's ontology are human sciences that find their work and meaning in interpretation: hermeneutics. Psychological explanation, therefore, has more in common with literary interpretation than it does with physics, though it is important to reiterate that this does not mean that a hermeneutic psychology rejects the empirical in favor of the subjective. (From a hermeneutic point of view, literary criticism need not be subjective.)

Heidegger's hermeneutic ontology and its implications spawned, directly and indirectly, a variety of further work, much of it clearly relevant to questions of psychology. As examples, consider the work of those obviously hermeneutical, like Hans-Georg Gadamer and Paul Ricoeur; or the work of those identified more with social construction and Marxism, like Jürgen Habermas; or the work of Jacques Derrida, someone known in this country more as a literary figure, but clearly a philosopher in his own right (cf. the essays in Sallis 1987, and the discussion in Caputo 1987, pp. 120–206). In spite of the competing claims of and the disagreements among these philosophers, two things are clear: first, their debt to Heidegger and second, their relevance to rethinking psychological explanation along new lines. Theoretical discussions of psychological explanation that take Heidegger's viewpoint into account tend to take positions outlined by these philosophers and others like them.

To date the major critic of Heidegger's work has been Derrida.

Much heralded and much condemned in the United States, Derrida's work is dense and difficult and, at first glance, it has little to say about psychological explanation. In fact, from a Derridean standpoint, psychological explanation might be a mere will-o'-the-wisp. Derrida's criticism of Heidegger, therefore, forces us to reevaluate Heidegger's work and its relevance to psychology. In this paper, I will examine that criticism, arguing that though it does not work as a criticism, it does provide a lever point for understanding Heidegger. Therefore, it also enables us to understand what psychological theory and psychological explanation would be like from a Heideggerian viewpoint. I will point to Gadamer's work as an example of an approach to understanding that makes psychological explanation possible, an approach based on Heidegger's ontological alternative.

DERRIDA CONTRA HEIDEGGER

Derrida's criticism of Heidegger amounts to the claim that Heidegger has not gone far enough. In rejecting the atemporal transcendent as the basis for explanation, Heidegger has seen the problem of traditional metaphysics—namely, the supposition of a metaphysically exterior origin of truth, a primal ground that accounts for everything else but is not itself accounted for. Heidegger has made a convincing case against the possibility of any such primal ground. But, says Derrida, in its place Heidegger seeks another origin, another ground, for explanation—first in temporality, then in language, then in *Ereignis* (appropriation, a technical term often translated "appropriating event" to keep in mind, as Heidegger intends, the root meaning of "coming to pass").[1] On Derrida's reading, Heidegger has replaced the atemporal transcendent with a temporal transcendent (e.g., language), when temporality and atemporality are not the problem. The problem arises from metaphysical transcendence—in other words, the supposition of a metaphysical origin.

There must be transcendence in some sense. Understanding and experience must go beyond the moment. Without transcendence there would be nothing but the chaotic play of light, sounds, and smells on our senses. In fact, there would not even be that, for the naming of that impossible possibility requires transcendence. It requires something to connect the moments of concrete experience. Heidegger's answer is that transcendence is found in temporality. But Derrida argues that Heidegger's search for a new origin, temporality, to replace the old one, substance, is merely a species of the same movement that manifests itself in the tradition Heidegger is criticizing.

Derrida claims to go further. In a move reminiscent of Heidegger's discussion of metaphysical truth as representation (1972b), Derrida says the metaphysics of things can, more generally, be called the metaphysics of presence (i.e., of re-presenting some metaphysical entity). Heidegger, Derrida says, has not seen this more general formulation, so he has attacked the metaphysics of things without attacking the metaphysics of presence, and he has postulated another metaphysics of presence in the place of the old one. Thus, since Heidegger's work, like traditional metaphysics, is a search for such an origin, it fails to escape the problem of the history of Western thought. It falls within what it attempts to overcome. Though in many ways Heidegger's work is both radical and productive, says Derrida, it contains the same flaw that it finds in the tradition.

On the traditional view, explanations give us understanding of particulars by showing us, by re-presenting, a transcendent entity or collection of entities. Plato, for example, seeks to bring the heavenly forms before our gaze. Medieval theology wants to show us God. Modern science wants to present the immutable laws of nature for our inspection. In each case, Derrida says, the idea is to make what is otherwise unseen present to us in order to account for what is seen. Similarly, Heidegger's search for an origin is a search for something that becomes present in any re-presentation, in any theory. It does not get beyond the appeal to the transcendent even if it temporalizes that transcendent.

Derrida says that in taking up Immanuel Kant and casting everything in terms of temporality, Heidegger still relies on the notion of time as presence, and the notion of presence is the hallmark of metaphysical transcendence, the search for *the* transcendent (Derrida 1982, pp. 46ff.). Thus, though in a certain sense Heidegger makes a giant step forward, according to Derrida, he does not escape the problem he brings so forcefully to our attention. If Derrida is right, Heidegger's alternative to the tradition is not a genuine alternative. If he is right, Heidegger's alternative will not give us a sufficient basis for explanations, psychological or otherwise.

In contrast, Derrida's response to the problem of presence (the problem of the transcendent) is to give up the search for a genuine origin, as contrasted to the supposedly mistaken origins of the tradition. Like Heidegger, Derrida aims to allow appearances—phenomena—to stand on their own, to allow them existence without appeal to something behind them that makes them possible, without recourse to representation, and he thinks he has gone further than Heidegger in doing so.[2]

Derrida describes his work as work on a general theory of systems (1973, p. 132), and Rodolphe Gasché has compared it, by analogy, to Kurt Gödel's work on completeness and incompleteness in arithmetic (1985). Indeed, the term *system* appears over and over again in the interviews in *Positions* (1981b). The point of Derrida's discussion of *différance* (a neologism and one among several names he uses for what he is talking about) is to show the origin of systems in difference (the "space" between the elements or threads of any system) and deferral (the deferral of any "last word," of any metaphysical resolution in the transcendent, of any final re-presentation)—in play, if play is conceived not as arbitrariness, but as give and take.[3]

Classically philosophy has dealt with binary differences—being and nothingness, space and time, plenitude and emptiness, true and false, sameness and otherness, male and female. However, one or another member of these sets of dyads has always held the upper hand, has always been the origin in terms of which the other was discussed: being has been taken to be a more fundamental concept than nothingness, space more than time, plenitude more than emptiness, true more than false, sameness more than otherness, and male more than female. In each case, one of the elements of these pairs has been made fundamental, has been privileged, and the other has been explained in terms of it. In each case, one of these elements is the presence (the transcendent) we make manifest in expression and explanation, and the other element is supposedly made absent.

Such privileging of one element of a pair idealizes closure, bringing explanation (and indeed, all discourse) to a halt if the privileged element succeeds in taking on the ontological status of the medieval God, the unchanging source of all being. Any adequate explanation would re-present the unchanging source fully; it would no longer need to be spoken. Nothing more could be said once the adequate explanation was given; continued explanation would merely mark a previous failure to explain adequately.

Thus, on this traditional, privileging view, the end of thinking and explanation is absolute silence, the silence of a god who needs no longer to speak, for everything has been said. Of course, those who accept the traditional metaphysics will say, "Exactly, the scientific goal is knowing silence rather than ignorant loquaciousness." But my essay presupposes that the Heideggerian deconstruction of traditional metaphysics is a deconstruction that adequately reveals the failures and inadequacies of that metaphysics, the impossibility for speech to bring about final closure.

To those within the metaphysical tradition, loquaciousness—that is, babbling sophistry—might seem the only alternative to the quest for ultimate, metaphysical silence. But from Heideggerian and Derridean viewpoints there is an alternative to the choice between absolute loquaciousness and absolute silence. Faced with the chimera of metaphysics, we need not throw up our hands in despair unless we are despairing for the presence that has turned out to be a chimera. Genuine explanation of human beings is possible. That explanation will give us insight into the matters we take up, but it will not come to an end, unless human being comes to an end. There are genuine and true things to be said about matters, but there is no "last word." Speech continues of necessity rather than because it fails. It is the necessary continuation of speech that interests Derrida, and his criticism of Heidegger amounts to a claim that Heidegger does not adequately account for the necessity of continuation because, like those he criticizes, Heidegger proposes not just transcendence, but the transcendent.

Différance—difference, the space between the pairs of the metaphysical tradition, and deferral, the deferral of the final presencing promised by privileging one element of those pairs—accounts for the necessity of continued speaking. The space between the pairs is the space from which any presence springs, the space from which any privileging of one thing over another is possible. Presence is not a result only of the privileged term itself. It is a result of the play of the elements, a play that makes the elements, as elements of metaphysical pairs, possible. Because the elements of the pairs exist only in play with one another, the privileging of one element always carries with it the denied member of the pair; the denied member insinuates itself in every re-presentation of the privileged member.

The necessity of continuing to speak comes from the system of metaphysical pairs. Explanation is necessarily metaphysical; it necessarily privileges one element of any pair over the other. There can be no explanation if something is not privileged. But privileging includes its negation of the unprivileged element in the pair, a suppressed inclusion that prevents the privilege of the privileged from becoming absolute: *différance*. The differences between the pairs insures that any "last word" is always deferred. It serves as an "ideal, reachable only in principle."[4] Thus, in spite of itself, in demanding ultimate silence (absolute presence), metaphysics demands ultimate loquaciousness. But the "solution" to this metaphysical conundrum is to be found in neither silence nor loquaciousness.

Rather than attempting to re-present one member of a pair by giving it privilege, or privileging the other member by denying what has been previously privileged, Derrida's alternative focuses on the possibility of these binary oppositions (not just the results of them). The point of Derrida's work is to construct a general theory of systems that will take binary opposition seriously without falling prey to the closure generated when one is privileged over the other, as it is in metaphysics (1981b, p. 41).

In taking up a position in which there is no metaphysical closure, no final word, Derrida does not deny truth, meaning, etc.—in metaphysical terms, presence: "in no case is it a question of a *discourse* against truth or against science. (This is impossible and absurd, as is every heated accusation on this subject.) . . . *we must have* [*il faut*] truth" (1981b, p. 58, fn. 32). Like Heidegger, neither does he argue for the subjectivity of understanding and meaning. He says of reading, for example, "Reading is transformational. . . . But this transformation cannot be executed however one wishes. It requires protocols of reading" (1981b, p. 63).[5] Instead of denying truth and meaning, he notes that if there is no transcendent truth to which we can appeal, truth and meaning occur only within systems. Truth and meaning are not the origins of systems and therefore outside system, but they do occur—as parts of systems. Rather than the re-presentation of something atemporal and transcendent, the members of the dyads of philosophy (true/false, being/nothing, space/time) are effects constituted within systems. (However, it is important to note again that presence is not the result of mere subjectivity—cf. Derrida 1981b, p. 29; 1973, pp. 145ff. To believe that presence is the result of subjectivity is to forget that presence and the subject are both "effects" of a system.)

Like Heidegger, Derrida argues that truth is the result of a creative act, a fictive event if we use *fictive* not as a pejorative term, but in line with its etymology (from the Latin *fictio*, "to shape or mold"). To explain something is not merely to lift the veil of ignorance and bring what has always been there into our presence.

To explain is to create, to give birth to the truth as much as it is to reveal it. It is exactly here that Derrida is the most help in thinking about the issues to which Heidegger has directed us. For Derrida discusses and exemplifies to a greater degree than Heidegger what is involved in the fictive event: for Derrida, the possibility of meaning is to be found in the possibility of binary pairs, in the play "within" such pairs. The play of those pairs creates meaning.

For his understanding of creation of presence as value, truth, and meaning, Derrida relies on Friedrich Nietzsche. For Nietzsche and for Heidegger, the alternative to the absolute nothingness that shows itself in the failure of the metaphysical tradition is found in creation, in art if that word is construed in a more Greek than modern sense, as making or producing rather than as the mysterious product of genius.[6] At the end of "Différance," Derrida speaks of the necessity of affirmation: "We must affirm it [what *Being* has heretofore named]—in the sense that Nietzsche brings affirmation into play—with a certain laughter and a certain dance" (1973, pp. 158–59).

But for Derrida, just as for Nietzsche and Heidegger, it is clear that our affirmation is not a matter of caprice or subjectivity, for *affirm* means neither *assent to something a priori* nor *create something ex nihilo*. If one affirms something, one does not theologically create it out of nothing at all (though there is much talk about creativity in the Western intellectual tradition, which takes this point of view). To affirm is a creative act in that it draws attention to what is affirmed, thereby altering its relation to everything else, creating something new in that alteration, and creating something that remains within what was old, illuminating it. For this reason, affirmation is also not merely the repetition of what is already there. Mere repetition is impossible.[7]

Rather than using nineteenth-century natural science as a model for explanation (the usual model for psychology), consider literary criticism and chess mastery. There are no transcendent games of chess apart from and behind the games of chess played by people. The players create chess, including its rules, by playing it, by affirming it, but that affirmation is hardly subjective. Similarly, though certainly not ex nihilo, it makes sense to say that literary critics affirm or create the meaning they show us in the text. The meaning is not there like a metaphysical entity standing behind the text. On the other hand, to the extent that they give us the meaning of the text and not just their own idiosyncratic musings, the meaning is not a subjective creation. (See Hoy 1978 for a cogent discussion of the problem of meaning, especially for a good over-view of the argument against the connection of meaning and authorial intention.)

Given this notion of creation/affirmation and the refusal to postulate a ground for knowledge and explanation, it is clear that no particular approach to knowledge or explanation can claim to be fundamental (though the absence of a fundamental approach does not relegate us to meaninglessness). Traditionally, logic has been the touchstone for language. Such things as rhetoric and grammar have ultimately, therefore, been subservient to logic.[8] Derrida disputes this view.[9] The analogy is fabric: since the text/texture—the object of study, including human behavior—is constituted by all its threads and interstices (and its interstices as much as its threads), no particular thread can be singled out as *the* thread. Since the texture of human existence contains many threads (and the act of picking out any one of them creates, in itself, a new thread), no particular approach can claim to be fundamental. There are, however, threads and interstices, and presumably one could pick at something that turns out to be neither thread nor interstice—lint? Logic is not the touchstone of human understand-ing (as the tradition has insisted), but it is also not to be cast off as so many romantics, dissatisfied with the tradition, have insisted. Logic is a legitimate enterprise. It is one of the threads. It is not in looking to logic that the tradition goes wrong. Neither is some-thing correct to be found in looking away from logic. The meta-physical tradition goes wrong in discovering the fundamental in logic, in privileging logic over the other threads of the fabric. The same argument can be applied to positivist approaches to social science: empirical data and methods are not the end-all and be-all of science, but it does not follow that they are to be ignored.

From Parmenides to G. W. F. Hegel, philosophers have agreed, in one way or another, that "what is real is the rational and what is rational is the real" (Hegel 1970, p. 24). Heidegger tries to offer an alternative to that traditional metaphysics, but according to Der-rida, Heidegger is unsuccessful because he affirms something else as fundamental—namely, temporality.

If Derrida is right, Heidegger is not radical enough. If Derrida is wrong, then he and Heidegger are saying much the same thing.[10] How they are related to each other can be answered only by looking at the basic concept in each, *Ereignis* for Heidegger and *différance* for Derrida, but I argue that Heidegger's thought has an advantage over Derrida's—if they are not saying the same thing.

EREIGNIS AND DIFFÉRANCE

Veronique Foti argues that though there are genuine differences between Heidegger and Derrida, Derrida's critique of Heidegger is inaccurate in that language as *Ereignis* is very much like *différance* (1985). The discussions of both *Ereignis* and *différance* result from a concern with the notion of origin and with a thinking about the possibility of metaphysics. Both can be discussed well in terms of play. Both imply that explanation is a creative rather than a mirroring or discovering act. Neither is an attempt to overthrow metaphysics. Instead, each is an attempt to situate metaphysics, to show the origin of the desire for origins; in other words, each is looking for something static and transcendent in terms of which to make our explanations. But, Foti argues, Derrida's criticism of Heidegger, a criticism that disguises the similarities of their thought, is based on a misunderstanding of the two senses of image in Heidegger and on a too simplistic reading of Heidegger's discussion of presence (*Anwesenheit*).

The complexity of Heidegger's discussion of presence can be seen in a number of places. For example, he explicitly takes up the question of presence as it relates to his work in the essay "Time and Being," saying that how presence is and what its priority means are still unthought (1972c, p. 34). In a related essay he says that presence and absence both depend on something else (the opening—1972a, p. 67), a something that it is difficult to read in terms of simple presence. In addition, for Heidegger, there is something like a direction to the system, what he calls destiny (*Geschick*—1972c, p. 53) and perdurance (*Austrag*—1969, pp. 67–68, 135–36), something not outside the system. (Significantly, *system* is a word never used by Heidegger.) It is this "direction" or "destination" that is the most important difference between Heidegger's and Derrida's thought.

According to Heidegger, as a temporal being, as futural (1976, pp. 327–29; 1975, pp. 374–75), Dasein is *"the original outside-itself"* (1975, p. 377). In other words, because Dasein is essentially temporal, coming from the past and directed toward the future, it is always already beyond the moment. Or, more accurately, the moment itself is transcendental, stretching out beyond the point of the now, both backward and forward. Only in death, when Dasein ceases to be outside-itself (ecstatic) by ceasing to be temporal, can it have reached a point at which it will be finished understanding the world, where there will be nothing left to say, where knowledge will be complete, and where human experience will, therefore, have come to an end. So, *as Dasein*, Dasein is not capable of reaching such a point. Given what it inescapably is, Dasein continues to "say" the world and, in doing so, it is "drawn along" in its temporality—drawn by the very fact of its temporality, by its constant suspension between being born and dying (1976, pp. 372–87), in other words, by the finite possibilities that come to be as Dasein stretches itself out within its "past" and "future." Thus, because it is drawn along by something (which is not some *thing*, some entity) over which it is not master, Dasein has what can loosely be called a fate or destiny (*Geschick*). Or, to avoid the unnecessary fatalistic or mystic overtones that *fate* and *destiny* have, perhaps *destination* is better, though it is a destination that is always deferred, that appears to be always one more stop down the line.

The temporal "movement" of Dasein is not capricious. Capriciousness requires infinity, and Dasein's existence is necessarily finite—that is, bounded. What draws Dasein along is not subjective creation, but neither is it objective reality. It is the movement of possibilities that it both receives and uncovers, which Dasein both creates and receives (1976, p. 384).

An example might help to make the point here. Like a good story or conversation, Dasein is pulled along in a "direction." No one participating in the storytelling or the conversation can tell in advance just where the story and conversation are going, but they are going somewhere or there would be no conversation. The movement of conversation and story is anything but random, even if we cannot give a law for conversation, even if we cannot tell the story's plot until it is over. If conversation's movement were random, it would consist of alternating babbling. Neither is the movement of conversation and story subjective. If it were subjective, we would expect to see the same alternating babbling. Instead, it is a complex interaction of subjects and situations, of possibilities that are both given to and created by those participating.

Gadamer has explicated this movement of Dasein using *effective-historical consciousness* (1972, pp. 266–90). Heidegger speaks of it in terms of the "withdrawal of *Ereignis*," the necessary deferral of pure presence (1972a, pp. 41–42). For our purposes—and keeping the insights of Derrida always in view—Heidegger and Gadamer are saying the same thing: there are limits to the play of temporality (though not static limits), limits that keep the creation of truth from sinking into an abyss of arbitrariness without requiring that we postulate some eternal verity that is transcendent of the world and the ground for truth, but which robs truth of its fictive—created—character. Using the earlier analogy, there are limits to story and conversation, limits that constantly shift but are always—"always already"—there making the story and conversation meaningful. These horizonal limits have their origin in "having-been" and the fact that "having-been" is oriented toward the future. These limits create the so-called fate, the destination, the deferred presence. This limit on play seems essential to the possibility of meaning, but it is something not clearly to be found in Derrida, something that may recommend Heidegger over Derrida.

In the discussion of withdrawal, it becomes apparent that in spite of the similarities of the work of Heidegger and Derrida, they may not be equivalent. In spite of the help Derrida's discussion of play, dyads, and the creation of truth gives us in understanding Heidegger's discussion of being and truth, Heidegger and Derrida may not be saying the same things. Nothing in Derrida's discussion of *différance* seems comparable to Heidegger's discussion of fate or destination in the withdrawal of *Ereignis*. I think this difference between the thought of Heidegger and Derrida is a difference in Heidegger's favor, for it allows the creation of the truth in Heidegger to escape the charge of ultimate arbitrariness, something it is not clear Derrida can escape.

One way to understand the difference between Heidegger and Derrida can be seen in their two views of deconstruction, the name both use to describe their methods (Heidegger 1975, p. 31; Derrida, e.g., 1987, pp. 19–20). Though Heidegger's early notion of deconstruction does seem to be a notion whose function is to lead one to some fundament, some origin of presence (Taminiaux 1986), the later Heidegger continues to think deconstructively (see, e.g., 1954, pp. 249–74, 199–248), but without the search for a fundament.[11] Instead of a fundament, Heidegger's later thinking points to the continual withdrawal of *Ereignis*—the withdrawal (or in Derrida's terms, the deferral) of the eschatological event, of the completion of the story. This, in turn, points to the continuing necessity of activity and the continuing possibility of it, and therefore to the continuing necessity of explanation.

But the continuation of explanation gives Heidegger no advantage over Derrida. Explanation continues for Derrida as well. Heidegger's advantage is that in his work, in addition to necessarily continuing, explanation is drawn along and connected to what came before by what goes before. Not only is there coherence within explanations, there is a kind of coherence between them. This coherence is not the coherence of plot or story-line laid out in advance; it is the coherence of conversation or storytelling when one is in the midst of them.

For Derrida, deconstruction seems to lead to the point where there is no fundament, but neither is there destination. Nothing leads thinking and explanation along. But where there is no destination there is nothing—not nothing in Heidegger's positive sense of "no ultimate thing," but nothing in the sense of nihilism and pure unintelligibility. (For more on Heidegger's sense of nothing, see Heidegger 1972b, esp. p. 104.)

The most common complaint against Derrida is that he elevates arbitrariness to a first principle. I argue that such a complaint is mistaken, at least at the level at which it is made. But though Derrida does not advocate arbitrariness and his thought does not immediately entail it, without something like effective-historical consciousness or the withdrawal of *Ereignis* to give his system at least a quasi notion of direction, I do not think he can escape the criticism of arbitrariness at a higher level. The problem generated by the absence of direction is analogous to, but not the same as, the problem of ideology.

Habermas (1970) criticizes Gadamer and, therefore, Heidegger by arguing that the Gadamerian position makes ideological critique impossible; one must always opt for the status quo if there is nothing but system, if there is no transcendent stance from which one can make a critique. Directed against Heidegger and Gadamer, this criticism is inaccurate. For in the transcendental of withdrawal and fate, Heidegger's early discussion of temporality and the later discussions of *Ereignis* come together to encompass elements that appear to distinguish him from Derrida and make something like ideological critique possible, though not absolute critique of any sort.[12] Without both the movement of deferral *and* the "fate" of temporal possibility, however, something like this criticism does seem to apply to Derrida: if there is nothing but difference and deferral, one's only options are arbitrariness or the status quo.

Though Gadamer's work stems from the early rather than the late Heidegger and may, therefore, be more open to Derrida's criticism, it is this inner-directed movement that Gadamer tries to capture in his discussion of *Bildung* (loosely, *education*), tradition, and the like, in *Truth and Method* (1972)—effective-historical consciousness.[13] Though commonly misunderstood, Gadamer's work supplies a very good explanation of the dynamic aspect of Heidegger's work.[14] Gadamer's talk about play, questioning, authority, and the tradition provide a practical and fairly detailed working out of the implications of Heidegger's early discussion of temporality. On the other hand, the later Heidegger is a continued working out of the same thinking, a continuation that provides a proper antidote to the accusation of conservatism sometimes wrongly leveled against Gadamer. In spite of the change often supposed to be found in Heidegger's work (the turning or reversal—cf. Richardson 1963, pp. 623–28), that which in the early work gives rise to Gadamer's discussion is present too in the late work as destiny, perdurance, and *Ereignis*. This justifies reading the early Heidegger through the later.

If Gadamer's work is not understood as a reading of the early Heidegger, it is not well understood. But it is also true that if Heidegger's early work is not understood in terms of the later continuation of that same thinking, it is not well understood. The early and the late Heidegger illuminate each other. It follows that the best reading of Gadamer is a reading based in the early and the later Heidegger rather than only in the early. As another reading of Heidegger, Derrida's work gives us insight into Heidegger's work, especially the later work (though unlike Gadamer, Derrida does not see himself as working out implications of Heidegger's thought). As such a rereading, Derrida's work can also help provide the antidote to misunderstanding what Heidegger is saying and the lever for understanding Gadamer better.

But perhaps Thomas Sheehan (1985) is right. Perhaps there is no substantial difference between the thought of Heidegger and that of Derrida. After all, in his criticisms Derrida concentrates on only Heidegger's early texts, intentionally ignoring the others. Perhaps what is in order is a kind of ironic reading of Derrida. If so, then the relation I have described between the work of Heidegger and Gadamer is enriched by the addition of Derrida. If, however, there is a difference between Heidegger and Derrida, it amounts to this: there is, for Heidegger, a "standard" or "origin" for truth, something absent in Derrida. But it cannot be overemphasized that this standard is not some *thing*; it is not outside "the system"; it is not immutable or metaphysically transcendent. That is why direction, rather than destination, seems as good a metaphor as any. For

Heidegger, along with openness and play on the one hand and deferral on the other, there is direction, the limits provided in withdrawal.

In conclusion, Heidegger's work offers the ground for a genuine and radical alternative to traditional psychological explanation, an alternative whose nuances are revealed in the encounter with the work of Derrida, but whose work is not surpassed in Derrida's work.

PSYCHOLOGICAL EXPLANATION

In an essay it is difficult to say concretely all that Heidegger, Derrida, and Gadamer mean for psychological explanation, but at least three things can be said. First, psychological explanation must treat both human knowledge and human beings themselves as temporal, where *temporal* means always already ontologically founded in an understanding of being and already engaged concernfully in the world before any reflection or analysis. Theories of human behavior that treat consciousness as reflection do not have to go, but theories that presume with the metaphysical tradition that reflective consciousness is the original or fundamental mode of human being-in-the-world will have to, for reflective consciousness and knowing are fictive—that is, created modes of human being—as is every other mode of human being. Here the Husserlian phenomenologists may have much to teach us about our approaches to psychological study, though the Husserlian terms and methods will have to be rethought in light of Heidegger's attack on essences.

Second, given the impossibility of transcendent critique, existing psychological theories and methods will have to be rethought deconstructively rather than simply destroyed. Charles Scott (1987) and John Caputo (1987) give interesting and interestingly different nonpsychological examples of what such rethinking and deconstruction might involve.

In outline, a deconstructive rethinking involves looking for the seams and cracks in a theory or method to see what is suppressed: if the theory or method emphasizes becoming, the deconstructive reading searches to see the ways in which stasis insinuates itself. On the other hand, if the theory or method emphasizes stasis, a deconstructive reading looks for insinuations of becoming. Exposing these traces of suppressed dyads reopens the theoretical or methodological conversation, allowing it to continue. And it may be that a deconstructive method of therapy is possible or that current effective methods of therapy could be understood as deconstructive, by loosening categories and paying attention to what is suppressed in the "text" of behavior, showing the fissures in the insistence of the patient and the patient's symptoms.

Whatever else it is, however, a hermeneutic-deconstructive approach to either theory or therapy is not a revolutionary approach calling for the overthrow of existing methods and practices. It is more radical than that. Instead of revolution, it calls for a careful and continual rethinking of those theories, methods, and practices, a rethinking done with questioning and deconstruction at its center. It is a kind of radical skepticism that demands not the dissolution of all claims to explanation, but a constant redoing of them. A Heideggerian and Gadamerian hermeneutic approach, with Derrida in mind, would look for ways in which what is privileged in an explanation is also suppressive, and it would look to that suppressed thing to see what could be learned from its suppression.

Thus, rather than throwing out existing methods and practices, we must "loosen them up" so that the problems they address become clear and the problems they overlook can be seen. We need to wear our methods and practices more comfortably, changing or mending as needed, without thinking that the need for such changes and emendations is a sign of defects in our explanations. As the problems psychological explanation addresses and those it systematically ignores become more clear, we may be able to understand our methods and practices better, making us better able to choose among them and to rework what we choose to retain. Gadamer (1975) provides a good model for a hermeneutic approach to scientific psychology.[15]

Such an approach recognizes explanation as a kind of storytelling, the best explanations functioning very much like good dramatic and poetic works. This brings us to the third and, I believe, the most important implication of Heidegger, Gadamer, and Derrida for psychological explanation: understanding psychological explanation as a richly creative, fictive act rather than reportage—or, understanding reportage itself as a richly creative, fictive act rather than the mere reporting back of supposedly objective data (cf. Polkinghorne 1987). The implications of this implication are numerous. If psychological explanation is fictive (but not simply fictional), we must rethink many of our notions—for example, our notions of the function of psychotherapists, and our notions of psychological wellness and illness. To consider descriptions of patients as paranoid or depressed—or even as patients—to be richly creative and useful descriptions rather than quasi-scientific and relatively objective descriptions of an independently existing state of affairs is to consider those descriptions quite differently indeed.

In addition, if we accept the fictive nature of psychological explanation and couple it with Heidegger's possibility that we are self-hidden and self-disclosing as well as world-hiding and world-disclosed, we bring to the fore questions about the relation of mental illness to the de-formations of our society, questions similar to those R. D. Laing, as well as Habermas and other Marxists, have asked us to consider for years. However, in a psychology based on something like Heidegger's work read through the texts of Gadamer and Derrida, there is this difference between what we will come to and what Laing and the Marxists have asked for: we will have a "coherent" view of the world in which to discuss such questions, one that does not replace metaphysics or put a stop to it (because it necessarily incorporates metaphysics), but that understands the place and limitations of metaphysics and, therefore, the place and limitations of its own explanations. We will have a view that continues to speak, incorporating both silence and garrulousness.

Notes

1. These three are not alternates as much as they are successive developments of the same insight and continuations of the same questions. Whatever might differ in these developments, they each very much share in the refusal to appeal to anything transcendent, to anything beyond possible human experience and understanding.

2. It is true that Derrida says we do not get beyond metaphysics—we never escape it—but, as we will see, his approach is to give metaphysics a place and to understand that place, not to get beyond it to something else. The transcendent cannot be overcome by replacement. But if it is not replaced, it remains. The trick is to allow it to remain without allowing it to take over.

3. In spite of the differences between Gadamer and Derrida, differences that normally pit their followers one against the other, Gadamer has a discussion of *play* (1972, pp. 91–127) that I think amenable to Derrida's

use of the word. If the case I make here is correct, that is appropriate, given the indebtedness of both to Heidegger and given the way in which the work of Heidegger and Derrida come together.

4. Thus *deconstruction*, the so-called method of those who follow Derrida, consists of exposing the way a particular explanation already contains the suppressed other of the re-presented.

5. He adds to this: "Why not say it bluntly: I have not yet found any that satisfy me."

6. Ironically, from the point of view of traditional metaphysics, what shows itself in creation is "nihilism," because metaphysics assumes that meaning is found only in the transcendental, which turns out to make meaning impossible. Metaphysics' charge that art is nihilistic is a consequence of art's rejection of the thoroughgoing nihilism of metaphysics.

7. This sense of affirmation and creation seems closely allied to Gadamer's discussion of tradition (1972), a discussion often misunderstood, in spite of Gadamer's cogent arguments to the contrary (cf. 1976), as a kind of reactionary political conservatism transported into human studies. (See Heidegger 1985, p. 138, for an early expostulation of tradition that Gadamer uses as a starting point.)

8. Note, for example, Searle's discussion of fictional language as parasitic (1969, pp. 77–80).

9. Heidegger too reconsiders the status of rhetoric. In *Being and Time*, he says that Aristotle's rhetoric is the first systematic hermeneutic of the everydayness of being-with (1976, p. 138). And Gadamer (1976) is also clearly rethinking rhetoric.

10. This is, for all intents and purposes, the conclusion to which Sheehan comes (1985). As it will become clear, I am very sympathetic with this position, though not fully convinced. On the other hand, Caputo (1985) argues that in seeing with Heidegger that there is no presence to which our thinking can render service with finality and eternal certainty, Derrida goes too far and concludes that there is nothing at all for thinking to serve.

11. And once one has read the later Heidegger, it becomes apparent that even in the early Heidegger there were many indications of what was to come. For example, the discussion of ekstasis in *Basic Problems of Phenomenology* (1975, pp. 377–79) shows clearly the movement toward the later discussion of *Ereignis/Enteignis* ("appropriation/disappropriation") in describing temporality as outside itself and in discussing the movement of that outside itself as an open movement. (See also Scott's analysis of *Being and Time*, 1987.)

12. Note that, a la Kant, the transcendental of *Ereignis* need not be transcendent.

13. Some in the social sciences have found Ricoeur's work more helpful than Gadamer's. (See, for example, O'Grady, Rigby, and Van Den Hengel, 1987). However, it is always unclear whether that is not because Ricoeur retains in some way the notion of the transcendent. Though Ricoeur's work is more accessible to American readers, I think Gadamer's more consistent with what we learn from Heidegger and Derrida.

14. The failure to read Gadamer's work in light of Heidegger's discussion of temporality makes his discussion of historicity and effective-historical

consciousness appear conservative (or even reactionary) and, therefore, necessarily an argument for the status quo. But Gadamer is at pains to make the connection between his discussion of effective-historical consciousness and Heidegger's discussion of temporality (Gadamer 1976; 1972, pp. 240–50). Section 14a of Heidegger's *History of the Concept of Time* also shows this connection clearly (1985, p. 138).

15. Ricoeur (1984, 1985, 1988) may too, but we must be careful that he does not slip metaphysics and the presence of the transcendent back in, as he often seems to do.

References

Caputo, J. (1985). "From the primordiality of absence to the absence of primordiality," *Hermeneutics and deconstruction* (H. Silverman and D. Ihde, eds.). Albany: State University of New York, 191–200.

——— (1987). *Radical hermeneutics*. Bloomington: Indiana University.

Derrida, J. (1973). "Différance," *Speech and phenomena* (D. Allison, trans.). Evanston: Northwestern University, 129–60.

——— (1978). "Edmond Jabes and the question of the book," *Writings and difference* (A. Bass, trans.). Chicago: University of Chicago, 64–78.

——— (1981a). *Dissemination* (B. Johnson, trans.). Chicago: University of Chicago.

——— (1981b). *Positions* (A. Bass, trans.). Chicago: University of Chicago.

——— (1982). "*Ousia* and *gramme*: Note on a note from *Being and time*," *Margins of philosophy* (A. Bass, trans.). Chicago: University of Chicago, 31–67.

——— (1987). *The truth in painting* (G. Bennington and I. McLeod, trans.). Chicago: University of Chicago.

Faulconer, J., and Williams, R. (1985). "Temporality and human action: An alternative to positivism and historicism," *American psychologist*, 40.11 (November), 1179–88.

——— (1987). "More on temporality," *American psychologist*, 42.2 (February), 197–99.

Foti, V. (1985). "Representation and the image: Between Heidegger, Derrida, and Plato," *Man and world*, 18, pp. 65–78.

Gadamer, H.-G. (1967). "Rhetorik, Hermeneutik, und Ideologiekritik— Metakritische Eröterungen zu *Wahrheit und Methode*," *Kleine Schriften*, vol. 1, 2nd ed. Tübingen: Mohr, 113–30.

——— (1972). *Wahrheit und Methode*. Tübingen: Mohr.

Gasché, R. (1985). Public lecture. March 22. Chicago: Loyola University.

Habermas, J. (1970). *Zur Logik der Sozialwissenschaften*. Frankfurt: Suhrkamp.

Hegel, G. W. F. (1970). *Grundlinien der Philosophie des Rechts*. G. W. F. Hegel, Werke in zwanzig Bänden, vol. 7. Frankfurt: Suhrkamp.

Heidegger, M. (1954). *Vorträge und Aufsätze*. Pfüllingen: Neske, 249–74.

——— (1969). *Identity and difference* (J. Stambaugh, trans.). New York:

Harper & Row.
────── (1972a). "The end of philosophy and the task of thinking," *On time and being* (J. Stambaugh, trans.). New York: Harper & Row, 55–73.
────── (1972b). "Die Zeit des Weltbildes," *Holzwege*. Frankfurt: Klostermann, 69–104.
────── (1972c). "Summary of a seminar on the lecture 'Time and being,'" *On time and being* (J. Stambaugh, trans.). New York: Harper & Row, 25–54.
────── (1975). *Die Grundprobleme der Phänomenologie*. Martin Heidegger Gesamtausgabe, Bd. 4 (F.-M. von Herman, ed.). Frankfurt: Klostermann.
────── (1976). *Sein und Zeit*, 4th ed. Tübingen: Neomarius.
────── (1984). *The metaphysical foundations of logic* (M. Heim, trans.). Bloomington: Indiana University.
────── (1985). *History of the concept of time: Prolegomena* (T. Kisiel, trans.). Bloomington: Indiana University.
Hoy, D. (1978). *The critical circle*. Berkeley: University of California.
Kockelmans, J. (1984). *On the truth of being: Reflections on Heidegger's later philosophy*. Bloomington: Indiana University.
O'Grady, P., Rigby, P., and Van Den Hengel, J. (1987). "Hermeneutics and the methods of the social sciences," *American psychologist*, 42.2 (February), 194.
Polkinghorne, D. (1987). *Narrative knowing and the human sciences*. Albany: State University of New York.
Richardson, W. (1963). *From phenomenology to thought*. The Hague: Nijhoff.
Ricoeur, P. (1984, 1985, 1988). *Time and narrative*, vols. 1, 2, and 3. Chicago: University of Chicago.
Sallis, J. (1987). *Deconstruction and philosophy*. Chicago: University of Chicago.
Schrag, C. (1980). *Radical reflection and the origin of the human sciences*. West Lafayette, Ind.: Purdue University.
Scott, C. (1987). *The language of difference*. Atlantic Highlands, N. J.: Humanities Press.
Searle, J. (1969). *Speech acts: An essay in the philosophy of language*. Cambridge: Cambridge University.
Sheehan, T. (1985). "Derrida and Heidegger," *Hermeneutics and deconstruction* (H. Silverman and D. Ihde, eds.). Albany: State University of New York, 201–18.
Taminiaux, J. (1986). Public lectures. *Collegium phaenomenologicum*. Perugia, Italy, July 28–31.

6 • The Metaphysic of Things and Discourse about Them

Richard N. Williams

METAPHYSICS, EPISTEMOLOGY, AND THE ANALYTIC TRADITION

The period of the rise of the analytic tradition in philosophy corresponds roughly with the period of ascendancy of empiricist approaches to psychology. Explicit influences of analytic philosophy on psychology are difficult to trace, partly because of a common disinclination on the part of psychology to consider its own philosophical grounding. There is, however, through the mainstream of the discipline, a spirit in common with this recent philosophical movement. (This spirit is made evident in most histories of psychology; see, for example, the histories of Robinson 1981; Boring 1950.)

I will not attempt to offer an explication of the analytic tradition, for good introductions are available from a number of sources (for example, Stumpf 1977; Weitz 1966). However, I would like to concentrate on certain general themes of the analytic movement, as they are found in common with psychology, which are relevant for the present discussion. Although there is diversity present in this as in all philosophical movements, it nevertheless seems accurate to characterize the analytic tradition, as well as most of twentieth-century philosophy, as a rejection of systematic and speculative metaphysics. (But, as I shall point out later, this is not a rejection of metaphysics per se.)

Earlier philosophy had placed speculation and working out

elaborate systems as the first tasks of philosophy. The early analytic philosophers held, rather, that the establishment of "what is" (the metaphysical question) fell within the domain of science. The task of philosophy was to be clear about the language in which the world was described and in which this science was done. Positivism, including but not exclusively the logical positivism of the Vienna Circle, was a significant part of the analytic movement, although modern analysis has since severed the relationship. Positivism sought to unify all science and thus all investigation, and to tie all knowledge to some type of empirical verification.

Of crucial importance to the task analytic philosophy has set for itself is the careful examination of language. The language of philosophy and science—and by implication, the language of everyday conversations—comes under careful logical and conceptual scrutiny to insure that (1) it is possible within the language to distinguish between true and nonsensical statements, and (2) knowledge is expressed in conceptually clear propositions. This activity of philosophy is, obviously, integrally tied up with the positivist agenda as well. For positivism, language that makes truth claims must ultimately be verifiable by some tie to the empirically demonstrable. This concern for the language of science and its verifiability is a concern for epistemology, and it is this shared concern that has brought positivism and the analytic tradition together. In this sense, then, analytic philosophy has separated the metaphysical task (or question) from the epistemological task (or question) and given preeminence to the latter. We must be clear and confident in regard to our epistemology in order to be so in regard to our metaphysic. This last statement is an important positivist as well as analytic thesis.

Analytic philosophy (considered very broadly) has not, however, given up the metaphysical task altogether. It has merely inveighed against speculative, idealistic metaphysics constructed (chronologically as well as logically) before or with little regard for logico-empirical verification. Because of the emphasis on correspondence in the analytic tradition, some who have worked within the tradition have given the metaphysical task of philosophy entirely over to "cognitive science" (see Dennett 1978; Mischel 1975).

In its rejection of what it takes to be traditional metaphysics and with its concomitant emphasis on truth as correspondence, the analytic tradition has in fact adopted a metaphysic—the "metaphysic of things" (see Faulconer and Williams 1985 for a more complete description of what is captured by this term). This is apparent in the analytic requirement that the operators in logic refer entirely to things, their properties, and the relations among them. Bertrand Russell's "logical atomism," for example, was aimed at expression of truth about "things" as referents. The emphasis in the work of both Russell and G. E. Moore on the separability of the mind and world is in defense of this "metaphysic of things" (see Weitz 1966, pp.1–7). The nature and implications of this metaphysic will be taken up again.

METAPHYSICS, EPISTEMOLOGY, AND THE PSYCHOLOGICAL TRADITION

It is, I believe, unnecessary to do more than state that mainstream American psychology is, or takes itself to be, a positivist, empirical, scientific discipline. Most work on both sides of the issue concerns itself not with whether psychology is a positivist, empirical enterprise, but whether it should be (see, for example, Rychlak 1977; Giorgi 1970; Gergen 1973; Schlenker 1974). Modern psychology, in common with analytic philosophy, has accepted fully the metaphysic of things. In addition, psychology has dedicated itself to a positivistic project of verification through the methods of empirical science. Metaphysics as speculation about a priori, nonverifiable ultimates has no place in the psychological agenda.

While analytic philosophy more or less limited its investigations to the sphere of language, concerning itself with the analysis and clarification of the language of investigation, psychology has retained a desire to do "more." Psychology has set for itself the task of uncovering the ultimate nature and reality of things in the human world. It has been avidly about the business of metaphysics. The methods of positivistic natural science have been adopted as the appropriate methods for the task. Progress in the discipline is equated with the accrual of empirical facts that withstand experimental testing. It is somewhat ironic that, within the discipline of psychology (as well as in most common usage), the word *metaphysical* has come to mean anything that is not empirically verifiable. The rejection of anything "metaphysical" arises from a commitment to a particular metaphysic—the metaphysic of things.

Partly because of its commitment to this metaphysic, psychology, in contrast to analytic philosophy, has been rather unconcerned with questions of language. The emphasis given language by philosophers seems, to psychologists, to be evidence of the lack of substantive problems for the discipline to take up, an activity of unrestrained subjectivity, or, we might suggest, a matter of "mere" (devoid of metaphysical content) epistemology. Psychology has been mostly unconcerned about epistemology because empirical science is taken, de facto, to be the proper and trustworthy method of getting knowledge of the world. The analysis of language is clearly secondary to the gathering of empirical data. It is the domain of the softer disciplines—such as philosophy.

Calls from philosophers to pay more attention to the language in which psychology is being done have largely met with disinterest. Discussions of the language of psychology are "only talk" and do not help us get at the world as it really is. Psychology, on the other hand, wants to get at the real nature of things and thus proceeds with its positivist empirical methods with little regard for questions of language—the language in which work in psychology is done and in which the human world is understood.

One misunderstanding about the perceived advantages of the common metaphysic in which the analytic tradition, positivism, and psychology are grounded needs to be dealt with here. Analytic philosophy rejected so-called speculative metaphysics in favor of a verifiable metaphysic of things. Psychology takes itself not to be doing metaphysics at all, based likewise on a firm grounding in the metaphysic of things and complete faith in empirical verification. It is precisely the possibility of verification among the tenets of both philosophy and psychology that has failed most obviously (see, for example, Lakatos 1970). When verification fails, all physics becomes metaphysics, and all metaphysics becomes, in some sense, "speculative." In psychology this means that rejecting metaphysics is simply accepting a particular metaphysic, the metaphysic of things. The problems inherent in this metaphysic are the topic of the remainder of this essay.

The New Call for the Examination of the Language of Psychology

Recently there has been a new call for psychology to pay careful attention to its language. This call comes most notably from two sources representing two traditions. One is a group of philosophers who might be said to represent the "new" analytic tradition (as seen, for example, in some of the essays in Baynes, Bohman, and McCarthy 1987). This point of view is represented in psychology by the "ethogenic"movement that has emphasized the importance of language, taking its point of departure from the later works of Ludwig Wittgenstein and others in this tradition (see Harré and Secord 1972; Harré 1984). The other major group of scholars calling for psychology to give more consideration to language as a most important human behavior, and to a study of its own language, come from the phenomenological/hermeneutical tradition. There are some important differences between these two groups, but they will not concern us here. What is of more interest is the common point they make concerning language and psychology. I will present a case derived chiefly from the latter position.

The argument for this new call to examine the language of psychology has three major points. First, the importance of language as a human phenomenon has not been fully realized by the discipline. It is argued that all things in the world, including human behavior, exist only in and through language. All that is known, or can be known, is known in discourse about it (see, for example, Gadamer 1982, p. 402; although this point is made throughout his works). The second argument is that the essential feature of human being is that we are born into and live within an ongoing discourse or conversation (see also Harré 1979; Harré, Clarke, and De Carlo 1985). We are what (who) we are only in and through our participation in the discourse. Through our participation, we likewise alter and contribute to the conversation. The third point of the argument follows from the fundamental importance of language and conversation as the grounding of the human world. Metaphysics, in which we concentrate on *what is*, and epistemology, in which we concentrate on what can be *known* and *how* it can be known, become the same enterprise: ontology, in this sense, the examination of the human conversation.

Returning to the current state of psychology, we see that failure to recognize the importance of language in this light has left us without serious grounds for questioning our commitment to the metaphysic of things. Secure in our metaphysical assumption, we pursue knowledge through positivistic, empirical methods, with neither palate nor patience for serious examination of our language—so long as our language does not sound "metaphysical." This has led psychology to adopt and be content with a psychologistic language. The psychologistic language, in turn, prevents the discipline from seeing alternative conceptions. In this sense the problem of psychologism is a fundamental (if not *the* fundamental) problem for psychology.

Psychologism in Psychology

In philosophy, *psychologism* is applied to any theory that tends to give explanatory preeminence to psychological functioning (Bynum, Browne, and Porter 1981). An explanation is psychologistic if it assumes that the only tools for philosophy are introspection and self-observation and that the only way to establish truth is to appeal to subjective constructs. Critics have leveled charges of psychologism at various philosophical points of view for many years.

In psychology, *psychologism* usually describes any theory that implies an inherent process of mentation underlying human behavior and a concomitant metaphysical uniqueness of thinking beings based on such processes. It is usually defended in refutation of rigid environmental determinism such as that espoused in behaviorism (see Block 1981).

I will not attempt to survey all forms of psychologism nor trace the history of the concept. I will, rather, concentrate on psychologism as inherent in modern psychology from the point of view of some within the phenomenological/hermeneutical tradition and on the nature of the problems faced by the discipline as a result. There may be a type of psychologism that does not fall prey to the problems I will outline; however, contemporary psychology does.

From the works of Edmund Husserl, Joseph Kockelmans (1967a and b) has pointed to two major manifestations of psychologism. The first is the "tendency to found the objects of mathematics, logic, epistemology, theory of value, and so on, on subjective psychical experiences" (Kockelmans 1967a, p. 420). This tendency leads psychology to reify and objectify mental or psychological states. Subjective mental states are made the conditions, antecedents, or explanations for human action and experience. Rather than being the direct object of study, psychical experience becomes the basis for explanation of other human activities, which are taken to be the real objects of study. The results of such psychologistic explanation are vagueness and ambiguity because something is used as an explanation that is itself never directly examined. In summary, any theory or system is psychologistic if it assumes that psychological states and experiences enjoy an autonomous existence and that they serve as the foundation of other experiences and human actions.

The second characteristic of psychologism is the adoption of the metaphysics and methods of the natural sciences as appropriate for the study of human beings. Husserl characterized the natural scientific point of view as being a posteriori in the sense that science begins with a theory or point of view and then attempts to put this meaning or interpretation "onto the data." Rather than seeing *what* the data are, natural scientific methods can only ascertain *whether* they are congenial with the way the original presupposition would describe them. We can trace the criticism of this natural scientific approach to explanation in the human world back through Husserl (Kockelmans 1967b; von Wright 1971) to Wilhelm Dilthey and Johann Droysen.

Maurice Merleau-Ponty describes Husserl's philosophical struggle on two fronts (1964, pp. 46–55). First, there was the struggle against psychologism and historicism that would "reduce the life of man to a mere result of external conditions acting on him" (p. 51), which is the accepted mode of explanation from a natural scientific perspective. Secondly, there was the struggle against "logicism." Logicism is attempting "to arrange for us an access to the truth lacking any contact with contingent experience" (p. 51). Ideas (or, in psychology, states of mind) separated from actions and experiences assume an autonomous status and become somehow compelling.

Jean-Paul Sartre (1967) illustrates how psychologism deals with the problem of human emotion, for example. First, psychologism would "isolate the bodily reactions" from the emotional "behavior" and the "psychological state" of emotion. The inner state of emotionality becomes an antecedent condition of which the emotional behavior is a consequent. Psychologism offers a sequential description of behavior with the psychological state generally (but not always) in the earliest position. Sartre explains that psychologism does "not seek the explanation or the laws of emotion in the general and essential structures of human reality, but *in the processes of the emotion itself*" (p. 477, italics in the original). A theory of emotion that isolates the psychological, physical, and behavioral manifestations of the emotion sequentializes the relation between them but does not further understanding in terms other than those inherent within it. Psychologism thus "closes in on itself" (Sartre 1967, p. 477) and does not yield understanding of the essential in human experience. Calvin Schrag discusses this tendency of psychologism to turn in on itself in explanation:

> Psychologism within psychology cannot avoid the application of reductive principles to itself, whereby the conceptualization within

its own discipline becomes simply another expression of psychological intentions, resulting in the displacement of any stable criteria of validation. [1980, p. 1]

Psychologism renames things in terms of its own presupposed theories and constructs. As an explanatory system it is closed; it cannot be validated or applied outside its own constructed world, or in terms other than those it postulates. Of course, no language can ever really "escape itself," but for a language that seeks to be causal and fundamental in the mode of the metaphysic of things, seeking ultimate explanation in a sphere outside itself, this is a fatal, debilitating flaw. This flaw, encumbrance of a psychologistic psychology, precipitates the recurrent crisis in the human sciences that Schrag (1980) describes.

In summary, psychologism entails (1) the reification and objectification of psychological states and experience, endowing such with causal efficacy, and (2) the application of the metaphysical assumptions of the natural sciences and the methods that derive from them to the study of human beings. Space does not permit a detailed consideration of all the theories and approaches in contemporary psychology sufficient to demonstrate that they are psychologisms. However, such an analysis is possible. I will simply assert that mainstream empirical psychology as well as the psychodynamic and common humanistic alternatives are psychologistic, and uncritically so.

We can also summarize the consequences of psychologism for explanations of human behavior offered by psychology. From a psychologistic perspective, psychical experiences (such as emotions) are results either of other psychical states or external conditions. Consequently, all behavior is similarly a result, and human agency is not possible. Further, psychologism leads us to grant that the language of causality is legitimately applied to human action. The causes are either internal states or the external world, operating often without awareness and without agentive participation on the part of "persons."

Psychologism also implies a valid and even necessary separation of the inner experience and the outer experience; the psychological state is separable from the behavior, the inner person (self) from the outer person, and the person from his or her action. Ultimately, as Sartre suggests, the meaning of an act is separated from the act itself (1967, p. 481).

For psychologism, human experience is a sequential process.

Environmental conditions are antecedent to psychological states, and these latter are antecedent to actions. Some mediational processes are necessary also to account for the associations among these components. (See Rychlak 1977 for a critique of mediational psychology.) Psychologism is thus bound to the spatio-temporal. If human experiences are to be understood and explained, they must be separated temporally, because causation (the ultimate explanatory terminus) requires it. (See Faulconer and Williams 1985 for a discussion of the problems associated with such a notion of temporality.)

Psychologism, in its methods, must validate itself. The application of the method of the natural sciences to the study of human psychical experience preempts the discovery of all but psychologistic constructs because this method can only investigate whether a particular postulated reading of an event is consistent with a prediction, not whether the reading is the right one (Kuhn 1970). The essential techniques of this method—operationism, control and prediction, objective observation, etc.—produce psychologistic explanations. (As an illustration of how easily this happens, see Rychlak's 1977 discussion of the S-R bind.) These techniques impose meaning on data in an a posteriori fashion, leading away from direct investigation of human experience and its meaning.

Psychologism and the Metaphysic of Things

The two manifestations of psychologism discussed above arise inevitably from the acceptance of the metaphysic of things in which mainstream psychology is rooted. It is instructive to examine the implications of this metaphysic to see how they lead us into psychologism.

It is fundamental, in the metaphysic of things, that whatever exists, exists as some particular thing. To be at all is to be a thing. This assumption has a long history, dating back at least to Aristotle, through whom it is still influential today (see Faulconer and Williams 1985). Although it is not clear that Aristotle made this mistake, he has been understood in this way. As shown above, this notion of the metaphysical preeminence of things is fundamental even to the modern analytic movement, which has rejected other metaphysical systems. Acceptance of this metaphysic of things is implicit in the emphasis on truth as correspondence and the principle of verification. In relation to language, acceptance of the metaphysic means that the most fundamental part of any language—or part of language—is the referent—that is, the thing to which a word or utterance refers. A referent, if a language expression is to be meaningful, must be a thinglike referent. The thinglikeness justifies talk of truth because it holds out the promise of verifiable correspondences.

Another implication of the metaphysic of things is that things have qualities, properties, or categories attached to them, which, depending on the perspective taken, either determine what the things are, or result from other qualities that are the nature of the things. Explanation of things and their manifestations is legitimately done, therefore, in terms of the properties and qualities of things and their relations. If understanding is possible at all, these properties and their relations must be lawful and consistent. Thinglikeness and this property of lawfulness and consistency make logical analysis possible. For some, the consistency of relations among things is tantamount to logic itself (this is the logicism I referred to earlier). Confidence in the descriptive adequacy of things and categories coupled with the lawful consistency of the relations among categories makes possible (and sensible) the project of traditional analytic philosophy. Such confidence also leads to psychologism.

A third implication of the metaphysic of things follows from the previous one. The study of things seeks to uncover the laws and regularities that operate on or within things because of their properties and their causal and necessary relations with other things. When things come together (actually or conceptually), because of their qualities, they will react in necessary and lawful ways, bringing about events and states. What we must do, then, is uncover the laws and regularities by which these things operate due to their qualities. At the conceptual or philosophical level, this was the original project of the analysts. On the mundane level, this is what the natural sciences, and positivism, have been about all along, and it seems the only legitimate manner of study, even in the human sciences. The acceptance of this view leads psychology into the second manifestation of psychologism discussed above.

To see whether the other manifestation of psychologism also follows, we need to consider how the metaphysic of things deals with a psychological phenomenon like an emotion. If the emotion is to exist, it must exist as a thing. It might be conceived as a biochemical state, or a cognitive/psychological state, but it is a state with thinglike status and specifiable properties. Numerous theories have undertaken to study the qualities or properties of emotions in general or some states of emotion in particular. Prominent among the qualities of emotive states is motivation, or a readiness to respond. Being in a state of anger, for example, is offered as an explanation of other phenomena or behaviors.

In invoking an emotional state as an explanation of behavior we attribute properties to the state sufficient to bring about a behavior. This type of explanation always doubles back on itself because it ends up invoking what it should be explaining. Such explanation gives rise to a scientific-sounding vocabulary that seems to produce knowledge, but does not. For example, a psychological state of "anger" is offered as an explanation of behavior B (this behavior can be, among many other things, a striking out, a physiological change, or a response on a questionnaire). But the only reason for claiming that the psychological state of anger exists at all is that it is a state assumed to have the properties that would produce behavior B, or behaviors very much like B—angry behaviors. It is interesting to note that behaviorists would make an argument like this against a mentalistic psychologism, but they fall back into psychologism just the same because of their devotion to the natural sciences, substituting drive states or stimulus properties for psychological states (see Dennett 1978).

Metaphysical and Practical Discourse

Because of the pervasive psychologism in the discipline, a psychologistic language has grown up for the doing of psychology. This is at the same time (ipso facto) a metaphysical language, appropriate for discourse about things. Psychology exists as a *metaphysical discourse*, a language that has its basis of meaning in the underlying metaphysic of things, and thus has excess metaphysical baggage.

There is an interesting irony pointed out by Amedeo Giorgi (1985, pp. 2–3). We, as psychologists, want to be very careful about our language—the language in which we publish papers and communicate the results of our studies. We have great faith in our ability to adequately and accurately communicate worthwhile data to other psychologists. However, we have no faith in ordinary people's abilities to tell us about human being in their own language. We certainly do not trust their language accounts as data. We have been at the same time concerned and unconcerned about the language of psychology.

The metaphysical language of psychology is such that nearly

every word carries with it a particular theory or metaphysical claim about that to which it refers. The evaluation of such theories or claims of the meaning and nature of psychological phenomena should be the task of psychology. It cannot accomplish its task within a language where the nature of phenomena, their meanings and their metaphysical status, go unchallenged. We *can* evaluate (even, in some cases, empirically) the adequacy of the descriptions of the human world and behavior offered by human beings because we too are human beings rooted in the same world, and scholars of that world and that rootedness. Metaphysical discourse, however, is unassailable. The ultimate evaluation of the metaphysic underlying our language is not possible; the principles of verification and falsification have failed (see, for example, Lakatos 1970). Verification of a metaphysic is certainly not possible by means of a language that instantiates the metaphysic.

To continue to discourse about psychology in metaphysical language cannot produce intelligibility. Metaphysical discourse begs the question of meaning because it has uncritically adopted a particular metaphysic, the metaphysic of things. Questions of the meaning of human actions are deferred and recast as questions regarding the categories and qualities of things. I argue, therefore, that the proper language for psychology is the language within which and through which we live, experience, and what is the same thing, discourse about our meaningful world. I refer to this as *practical discourse* (this of course takes its lead from the attention given by Heidegger to the world of practical involvement, and from what Aristotle spoke of as the practical sciences). It is the meaning of life and world, and the adequacy of expression of any discourse, that form the beginning and sustaining question for psychology; and this question can best be asked and clarified on the level of practical discourse.

The metaphysical discourse that psychology has given us is "relexicalization" (Harré 1984). It requires us to have very uncommon meanings for common words. This discourse substitutes causes for reasons, and entities for activities. This is the essence of psychologism. Thus the vocabulary of psychology is potentially— and to the uncritical, certainly—misleading. The word *motivation*, for example, almost universally denotes a specifiable psychological or physiological state. *Motivated behavior*, then, is the result of an antecedent state, not the action of an agent. Agentive acts cannot find expression in metaphysical discourse. If we are to take agency seriously, we must find it in the actions and descriptions of actions offered by agents, but this is possible only in practical discourse. So we must either "throw out" the word *motivation* or let it be used only on the level of practical discourse.

Similar problems arise with other psychological terms. By *memory*, for example, we can mean (on the level of metaphysical discourse) two kinds of entities: the memory of a particular thing, or a box in which other entities (memories) are found. On the level of practical discourse we see that all talk of memory comes about only because of the concrete act of "remembering." It is the remembering that is fundamental and takes place within practical discourse. On this level, *memory* refers to the act and the meaningful way in which, along with the reasons why, it happens as it does.

Similarly, at the level of practical discourse, anger ceases to be a state or condition for action, but rather a concrete action itself. It is something the person is doing, a being-in-the-world. The meaning of the act is in its contextual expression. We can speak of the emotion of anger, but on the level of practical discourse we are not reducing it to a *thing*, such that its human origins are lost, and its meaning swallowed up in metaphysics.

SUMMARY

The domain of psychology is the domain of practical discourse. The discipline must recognize that people are fundamentally a part of that discourse, from the beginning already underway within it. The world is discourse. It is the task of psychology to evaluate this human discourse and, as a scholarly discipline, to evaluate the adequacy of discourse about the discourse. Taking up this task entails rejecting the metaphysic of things as the obvious and only grounding for "science" along with the epistemology it incites. This move illuminates the pervasion of psychologism throughout the discipline. Having thus cast psychologism as problematic, as a topic for investigation, we have begun to overcome it.

In our evaluation of the world of practical discourse we might profit from empirical study. (Rychlak 1977, for example, has advocated the retention of traditional scientific methods.) When not tied to the metaphysic of things, these methods can yield important information about the experience of the world. Other methods will also be necessary, and such have been developed by a number of scholars, chiefly in the ethogenic and the phenomenological/

hermeneutical traditions (see Aanstoos 1987; de Rivera 1984; Giorgi 1985; Ginsberg 1979; Miles and Huberman 1984; Polkinghorne 1983). What remains is for the discipline as a whole to perceive the problem of psychologism as problematic and its solution as important. The perspective offered by continental philosophy, in its rejection of the metaphysic of things, opens up the grounds for psychology as practical discourse, for a nonpsychologistic human science.

References

Aanstoos, C. M. (1987). "A comparative survey of human science psychologies," *Methods*, 1, pp. 1–36.

Baynes, K., Bohman, J., and McCarthy, T. (eds.). (1987). *After philosophy: End or transformation?* Cambridge, Mass.: MIT.

Block, N. (1981). "Psychologism and behaviorism," *Philosophical review*, 90, pp. 5–43.

Boring, E. G. (1950). *A history of experimental psychology*. Englewood Cliffs, N. J.: Prentice-Hall.

Bynum, W. F., Browne, E. J., and Porter, R. (eds.) (1981). *Dictionary of the history of science*. Princeton: Princeton University.

de Rivera, J. (1984). "Emotional experience and qualitative methodology," *American behavioral scientist*, 27, pp. 677–88.

Dennett, D. C. (1978). *Brainstorms*. Montgomery, Vt.: Bradford Books.

Faulconer, J. E., and Williams, R. N. (1985). "Temporality in human action: An alternative to positivism and historicism," *American psychologist*, 40, pp. 1179–88.

Gadamer, H.-G. (1982). *Truth and method*. New York: Crossroad.

Gergen, K. J. (1973). "Social psychology as history," *Journal of personality and social psychology*, 26, pp. 309–20.

Ginsburg, G. P. (ed.) (1979). *Emerging strategies in social psychological research*. New York: John Wiley.

Giorgi, A. (1970). *Psychology as a human science: A phenomenologically based approach*. New York: Harper & Row.

—— (ed.) (1985). *Phenomenology and psychological research*. Pittsburgh: Duquesne University.

Harré, R. (1979). *Social being*. Totowa, N. J.: Littlefield, Adams.

—— (1984). *Personal being*. Oxford: Blackwell.

——, Clarke, D., and De Carlo, N. (1985). *Motives and mechanisms*. New York: Methuen.

——, and Secord, P. F. (1972). *The explanation of social behavior*. Oxford: Blackwell.

Kockelmans, J. J. (1967a). "Husserl's original view on phenomenological psychology," *Phenomenology: The philosophy of Edmund Husserl and its interpretation*. (J. J. Kockelmans, ed.). Garden City, N. Y.: Doubleday, 418–49.

——— (1967b). *Edmund Husserl's phenomenological psychology: A historico-critical study*. Pittsburgh: Duquesne University.

Kuhn, T. S. (1970). *The structure of scientific revolutions*, 2nd ed. Chicago: University of Chicago.

Lakatos, I. (1970). "Falsification and the methodology of scientific research programmes," *Criticism and the growth of knowledge*. (I. Lakatos and A. Musgrave, eds.). Cambridge: Cambridge University, 91–195.

Merleau-Ponty, M. (1964). *Phenomenology and the sciences of the primacy of perception* (J. Wild, trans.). Chicago: Northwestern University, 43–95.

Miles, M. B., and Huberman, A. M. (1984). *Qualitative data analysis: A sourcebook of new methods*. Beverly Hills: Sage.

Mischel, T. (1975). "Psychological explanations and their vicissitudes." In *Nebraska Symposium on Motivation*, vol. 22, (W. J. Arnold and J. K. Cole, eds.). Lincoln: University of Nebraska, 133–204.

Polkinghorne, D. (1983). *Methodology for the human sciences: Systems of inquiry*. Albany: State University of New York.

Robinson, D. N. (1981). *An intellectual history of psychology*. New York: Macmillan.

Rychlak, J. F. (1977). *The psychology of rigorous humanism*. New York: Wiley.

Sartre, J.-P. (1967). "Psychology, phenomenology and phenomenological psychology," *Phenomenology: The philosophy of Edmund Husserl and its interpretation*. (J. J. Kockelmans, ed.). Garden City, N. Y.: Doubleday, 473–84.

Schlenker, B. (1974). "Social psychology and science," *Journal of personality and social psychology*, 29, pp. 1–15.

Schrag, C. O. (1980). *Radical reflection and the origin of the human sciences*. West Lafayette, Ind.: Purdue University.

Stumpf, S. E. (1977). *Philosophy: History and problems*, 2nd ed. New York: McGraw-Hill.

von Wright, G. H. (1971). *Explanation and understanding*. Ithaca, N. Y.: Cornell University.

Weitz, M. (ed.) (1966). *Twentieth-century philosophy: The analytic tradition*. New York: Free Press.

7 • The Development of Self-Consciousness: Baldwin, Mead, and Vygotsky

Ivana Markova

There is a striking similarity in the work of three social-developmental psychologists whose work has attracted a great deal of attention in recent years: Mark James Baldwin (1861–1934), George Herbert Mead (1863–1931), and Lev Semenovich Vygotsky (1896–1934). They were all interested primarily in the study of the development of the human mind, which they conceived as a process involving mutual interaction between the individual and his or her social environment. Their approach to the study of the mind was holistic rather than atomistic, and dynamic rather than static. They emphasized human agency and action as essential features of the development of self-consciousness.[1]

Baldwin, Mead, and Vygotsky proposed a very broad conception of the development of the human mind, which included ontogenetic, phylogenetic, socio-historical, and cultural development. This broad conception was also reflected in their study of the relationship between the individual and society. The similarity of their interests is apparent in the titles of the books published during their lifetimes, such as Baldwin's *The Individual and Society* (1911), or collections of lectures and articles edited and published after they died, such as Mead's *Mind, Self and Society* (1934), and Vygotsky's *Mind in Society: The Development of Higher Psychological Processes* (1978). In addition, all three were very much interested in wider societal, moral, educational, and political issues. For Baldwin, scientific and moral education based on rationality alone could not secure social progress, and he argued that religion and esthetics were equally important aspects of education (Baldwin 1911, pp. 142–43). Mead's commitment to societal issues was apparent not only in his writing but also through his personal involvement in social issues. For example, he was engaged in the reform of the juvenile penal code and actively participated in a variety of campaigns seeking to achieve justice for minority groups. He was interested in the problems of educational reform leading to integration of general education and vocational training (Joas 1980). Vygotsky, too, was actively involved in educational problems, in his case in the Soviet Union after the October revolution in 1917. The main educational problems at the time were the elimination of illiteracy and the establishment of services for persons with various handicaps, such as mental handicaps and hearing impairment. In spite of his own poor health, Vygotsky devoted much of his energy and ingenuity to these problems (Wertsch 1985).

Baldwin, Mead, and Vygotsky shared a similar fate in the thirties. Although during their lives they occupied prominent positions and exerted considerable influence in psychology, after their deaths they were quickly forgotten and their work lay dormant for several decades. Their recent rediscovery is not fortuitous. After the period of preoccupation with behavioristic, individualistic, and mechanistic approaches to the study of the mind that seemingly provided psychology with scientific respectability, in the last decade or so there has been renewed interest in the study of action, consciousness, the mutual interaction between organism and environment, and ecological principles. This interest goes on alongside similar trends in other sciences such as biology (e.g., Lewontin 1982; Goodwin 1984) and economics (e.g., Boulding 1981). In a similar vein, in literary criticism there is a great deal of interest in socio-cultural development based on the mutuality between the self and others. This interest is reflected, for example, in the attention paid to the Russian semiotician Mikhail Bakhtin (1895–1975) whose work was recently rediscovered and enjoys a resurgence similar to that of Baldwin, Mead, and Vygotsky (Bakhtin 1981, 1984, 1986; see also Clark and Holquist 1985).

The similarity between the work of Mead and Vygotsky has been referred to by Western scholars for some time (Bruner 1962; Luckman 1969; Wertsch 1985), but Baldwin has not been much mentioned in the context of the other two simply because his work is least known (but see Kohlberg 1982).

In terms of their philosophical background, Mead is characteristically associated with pragmatism and with the foundations of symbolic interactionism, Vygotsky is known as a Marxist (Wertsch 1985), and Baldwin as an evolutionary epistemologist (Russell 1978; Broughton and Freeman-Moir 1982). In this essay I shall claim that Baldwin, Mead, and Vygotsky are, primarily and most importantly, Hegelian scholars. I do not mean to say, though, that they manifestly promoted Hegel's philosophy. In fact, for various reasons they were cautious in expressing their allegiance to Hegel, and I shall return to this fact later. However, their approach to the study of the human mind is based on Hegelian epistemology and the logic of their thought is dialectical in nature. Both Baldwin and Mead spent some time in Germany and studied in Leipzig and Berlin. They also read extensively in German and other continental philosophy, and their work shows important signs of that influence. In contrast to Baldwin and Mead, Vygotsky lived all his life in Europe, namely in Russia, which became the Soviet Union in 1917, and continental philosophy permeated his psychological work throughout.

In this essay I shall focus on one aspect of the work of Baldwin, Mead, and Vygotsky only—namely, on their study of self-consciousness. I shall first outline their conception of self-consciousness based on the mutual interaction between the self and others, and I shall point to its close connection with Hegel's theory of the development of mind. I shall then discuss their use of the genetic method with reference to the dyad of inner-outer, as applied to the study of self-consciousness.

BALDWIN, MEAD, VYGOTSKY AND THEIR CONTEMPORARIES

During his relatively short academic career, from 1884 until 1908, James Mark Baldwin was highly productive and undertook the very ambitious task of writing a treatise on the problem of the evolution of the human mind. He was highly critical of individualistic theories of knowledge, according to which persons were assumed to acquire knowledge on the basis of their private sensations and cognitions, and then come to some sort of agreement with others by "matching" their sensations and cognitions with those of the others. Baldwin argued that such theories, which ignore the social origin of knowledge, "have to be laid away in the attic where old intellectual furniture is stored" (1910, p. 78). He was convinced that the mental development of the individual can be understood only in the context of the study of the development of human self- and other-awareness. His book, *Social and Ethical Interpretations in Mental Development* (1897), was intended as a book on social psychology to be used in courses in psychology, ethics, and social science, and was written, he said, because there was no proper understanding of social psychology and no adequate book was available in English at the time. He maintained that social psychology as a discipline did not exist because there was no doctrine of the *socius*—that is, the dialectic relationship between the ego and alter.

During his career Baldwin was perhaps best known for his theory of imitation (discussed later). However, he himself was not happy with this approbation, complaining that his name was too closely associated with that of the French psychologist of imitation, Gabriel Tarde. Thus he said in the preface to the third edition of *Social and Ethical Interpretations in Mental Development*, published in 1902, that in spite of his great interest in the study of imitation he wished to have his work known as the "self" or "self-thought" theory of social organization. Baldwin said his theory of imitation was only a part of his broadly conceived theory of the self. He was convinced that he had succeeded in providing a viable alternative to individualistic theories of the mind and knowledge. To amplify this point, in the fourth edition (published in 1906), he maintained that perhaps the most quoted sentence of his book was "the individual is a social outcome, not a social unit" (1897, p. 96), which means that knowledge is social and under no circumstances should it be considered private property.

This thesis

> should serve to destroy the epistemological atomism and subjectivism of individualistic theories of knowledge, making personal logical thought *an outcome, not an epistemological unit*; very much as the other truth destroys the social atomism of individualistic theories of society and the state (Baldwin 1897, pp. xxi).

Just like Baldwin, George Herbert Mead approached the study of the development of mind from the standpoint of the mutual relationship between the self and the other. He dissociated himself firmly from the Cartesian dualists, who claimed that the spiritual self is a substance different from body. But like most of Hegel's followers, critics and interpreters, he totally misunderstood Hegel, claiming wrongly that Hegel's absolute idealism was hopelessly subjective (Mead 1926; see later). Mead had some sympathy for John Watson's behaviorism, but he rejected it because of its individualism and for reducing consciousness to overt bodily responses and thus denying it altogether.

Just as for Baldwin, for Mead self-consciousness was a result of evolutionary process and was social in nature. In order to clarify the difference between his approach and that of Watsonian behaviorism, he called it "social behaviorism," an unfortunate term that caused Mead to be misunderstood by many. Mead's position with respect to the nature of the human mind and of self-consciousness is most clearly and accurately expressed in his articles published during his life. Since his death, however, six books have been published on the basis of his lectures and unpublished papers (Mead 1932, 1934, 1936, 1938, 1956, 1982), and they differ in the extent to which they accurately reflect Mead's own work. His contribution to the advance of knowledge ranged from general and social psychology to sociology, ethics, philosophy, and the theory of science and of method. Just like Baldwin, at various stages of his life Mead occupied chairs either in philosophy or in psychology.

According to Mead's theory, the human mind develops through communication by means of "a conversation of gestures in a social process or context of experience" (Mead 1934, p. 50). In other words, in order to explain what the mind is and how it functions, one must start from the evolutionarily lower, nonconscious social processes and through them arrive at the evolutionarily higher, conscious ones. Mead argued that Charles Darwin and Wilhelm Wundt each committed a fundamental error in their theories of communication and of interaction of gestures. Darwin did not appreciate that the beginnings of language and communication are to be sought in the interchange of gestures. Wundt, for his part, did not realize that the beginning of a social act can be comprehended without bringing in consciousness or mind. In contrast to Darwin and Wundt, for Mead the starting point for the development of the mind was a nonconscious social act. The conscious mind then emerges as a result of social interaction. Moreover, it is the whole that is prior to the functioning of the individual: "the whole (society) is prior to the part (the individual), not the part to the whole; and the part is explained in terms of the whole, not the whole in terms of the parts" (Mead 1934, p. 7).

Due to his premature death from tuberculosis, Lev Semenovich Vygotsky's academic career was the shortest of the three figures discussed. He was similar to Baldwin and Mead in range and scope of interests, graduating with a degree in law and starting his career as a teacher of literature and psychology. He was very much interested in literature and literary criticism, and in 1925 he presented his dissertation, "The Psychology of Art." The following decade of his life was devoted to the study of the development of the human mind. In the English-speaking world his best known piece of work is the book *Thought and Language* (1962), based on his considerably more extensive *Thinking and Speech* (1934; see also Wertsch 1985). In 1936 a resolution was issued by the Central Committee of the Communist Party proscribing pedology, the Soviet version of educational psychology at the time, and all psychological testing and other evaluative psychological techniques. At the same time *Thinking and Speech* was blacklisted, and Vygotsky was accused of propagating bourgeois and anti-Marxist ideas and of uncritical acceptance of Hegel's idealism (Rahmani 1973). Thus, from 1936 until the late fifties Vygotsky's work was deleted from Soviet psychology and, because of this, he was also unknown to the rest of the world. Only recently has Vygotsky's work been fully appreciated in the Soviet Union, and his previously banned and unpublished work has now appeared in the six volumes of his *Collected Works* (Vygotsky 1982–84).

Vygotsky's work on self-consciousness starts with the claim that the nature of the mind is social and that mental processes can be understood in terms of signs that mediate them. He rejects the Russian form of behaviorism—that is, of Bechterev's and Pavlov's reflexology—as an explanation of self-consciousness. He argues that reflexology obliterates the distinction between animal and human behavior and that by ignoring the problem of consciousness and self-consciousness, psychology deprives itself of the possibility of studying complex issues in human behavior that are, without exception, of social origin. Moreover, by excluding consciousness from the domain of scientific psychology, reflexology gives spiritualistic subjective psychology and dualism the chance of reinstating themselves as the subjects concerned with consciousness and self-consciousness (Vygotsky 1979). Just like Mead, Vygotsky argues that the units of analysis in psychology in general and in the study of self-consciousness in particular must preserve the characteristics of the whole. Just as in Mead's theory of the mind, such a whole is of a social nature, and for Vygotsky, words constitute the basic units preserving the characteristics of the whole. Words express the historical nature of human self-consciousness. Thus Vygotsky concludes *Thinking and Speech*[2] as follows:

> Consciousness is reflected in the word as the sun in a droplet of water. The word is related to consciousness just as a microcosm is related to macrocosm, just as a cell to the organism, and an atom to the universe. The word is a microcosm of consciousness. The meaningful word is a microcosm of human consciousness. [1934, p. 293]

By the time Baldwin, Mead, and Vygotsky started writing about consciousness, self-consciousness, and the human mind, William James (1842–1910) was already the authority on the subject. They all referred to his work with admiration and respect, although neither Baldwin nor Mead accepted James wholesale.

Just like Baldwin, Mead, and Vygotsky, James wished to reject the Cartesian dualism of mind and body. However, in contrast to the other three, his wish remained but a wish. In the preface to his *Principles of Psychology*, in which he expressed his belief that psychology should be a natural science and not metaphysics, he said it was essential to ascertain the empirical correlation between thoughts and feelings on the one hand and definite conditions of the brain on the other (James 1890, I, p. vi).

As Graham Bird (1986, p. 17) maintains, although James wished to reject dualism, he showed that common sense is on its side. However, in James's view the classical dualists did a disservice to the commonsense form of dualism because they became obsessed with the unintelligibilities of traditional epistemology. According to Bird, what James himself attempted was to give a better account of the commonsense distinction between the mental and the physical.

As a radical empiricist James rejected both Kantian transcendental egoism and Hegelian dialectics. He maintained that the only service the transcendental egoists provided for psychology was that they rejected David Hume's bundle of sensations (James 1890, I, pp. 369–70). However, instead of dismantling it, they only tied the bundle together. James was even less kind to Hegelian dialectics, which he compared to a "pantomime-state of mind." Just as in a pantomime all common things can happen in impossible ways, people jumping down each other's throats, old women becoming young men, and everything passing into its opposite, so in Hegelian logic relations must first become impossibilities and contradictions before they are transcended and then identified by miracle (James 1890, I, p. 369).

Bearing in mind that James remained a dualist and that he rejected dialectics, one is faced with the question of the source of Baldwin's, Mead's, and Vygotsky's respect for him. It seems to me that the answer to this question is to be sought in James's conception of "the stream of consciousness." In his work, consciousness was conceived as a process and activity. He strongly denied that consciousness was an entity and insisted, instead, that it was a function of matter. Indeed, he claimed that thoughts are made of "the same stuff as things are" (James 1912, p. 37). James's (1912) article "Does Consciousness Exist?" was applauded by Vygotsky as a partial confirmation of his own ideas. James's claim that the Cartesian and Kantian "I think" should be replaced by "I breathe" also appealed to Vygotsky. Moreover, in the notes to his paper "Consciousness as a Problem in the Psychology of Behavior" (1979), Vygotsky said that he had just learned of the work of behavioral psychologists who, apparently, addressed the problem of consciousness in a similar manner to his own, but could not refer to this work in his essay because it was already in press at the time. These psychologists were John Watson and Karl Lashley, so perhaps it was just as well for Vygotsky that he did not get the chance to acclaim his support for Watson's approach to consciousness.

Mead and Baldwin were more cautious, although they too endorsed James's approach to consciousness as an activity. Mead accepted the notion of the stream of consciousness but adapted it to his own theory. As for Baldwin, the stream of consciousness was left out of his own structural approach to knowledge.

THE CONCEPT OF SELF-CONSCIOUSNESS

Baldwin's conception of the ontogenetic development of self-consciousness is based on the "dialectic of personal growth." By *dialectic of personal growth* Baldwin means a process of mutual interdependence between the self and other selves. As Baldwin puts it, both the self (ego) and the other (alter) are originally crude and unreflective, and largely organic. However, they get "purified and clarified" in the process of mutual interaction: "My sense of myself grows by *imitation* of you, and my sense of yourself grows in terms of my sense of myself" (1897, p. 15; my emphasis). Thus, the individual's awareness of self and other arise together as a give-and-take relationship, and thus they are essentially social.

They manifest themselves by imitation. Imitation is not an automatic repetition of processes but an active responding to the other person, and it has many similarities with Mead's notion of "taking the role of the other person." Through imitation of the other, one comes to know the other's feelings, thoughts, and desires and realizes that the other is a rational, emotional, and volitional being. Baldwin concludes that the ego and the alter are to our thought one and the same thing (1897, p. 18). Consciousness, Baldwin maintains, is the latest and finest adjustment of organisms to their environment (1895, p. 233). The central fact about consciousness, its accommodating element and process, is the focusing of attention. He explains what attention is in the course of his discussion of imitation. Imitation is not just repeating the same process again and again, but every act of attention gives rise to changes on a higher level, resulting in a mental image, memory, an idea.

The growth of ego and alter is based on habit and accommodation. Habit and accommodation are two opposite and complementary tendencies. Habit is the organism's conservative tendency to remain in the state in which it is already. For example, if the organism encounters new phenomena in the environment, it tends to cope with them in terms of the existing structures and processes. Indeed, new phenomena make sense for the organism only to the extent to which the organism can cope with them in terms of its existing structures and processes. For example, an event is perceived as threatening for the organism only to the extent to which it can be anchored to something that already presents a threat for that organism. The other tendency of the organism, quite opposite to habit, is accommodation. Accommodation is the tendency of the organism to cope with new phenomena by performing more complex functions (Baldwin 1895, p. 479). It is the organism's openness to change, trying out new activities, learning, and changing its structure and processes. All the capacities that the organism learns are examples of accommodation. Baldwin points out that accommodation is opposed to habit in two ways. First, accommodation is directed toward the organism's future, or as Baldwin puts it, it has a prospective reference, relying upon past and old movements of the organism (1895, p. 478). Thus accommodation always runs ahead of habit. Secondly, because it involves the selection of new activities, accommodation tends to get into direct conflict with old habitual activities and thus to break habits.

Habit and accommodation are relational phenomena. They are interdependent and their interaction "gives rise to a two-fold factor in every organic activity of whatever kind" (Baldwin, 1895, p. 481). Habit is constantly modified by accommodation, and accommodation is restricted by habit. Baldwin argues that each function of the organism can be understood only in terms of the twofold factor, habit-accommodation, whether it is attention, emotion, or self-consciousness. Thus, just as with other kinds of human social development, the development of self-consciousness involves a conflict, in this case, of self with other selves: "the self meets self, so to speak" (Baldwin 1895, p. 342). In this process, the self of accommodation—that is, the self that learns and changes—collides with the self of habit, of character, and the desire to dominate others. In Baldwin's words, the self of personal agency gets into conflict with the social self. These two components of the self, personal agency and the social self, are thus intrinsically related. As the self develops through imitation, new structures and processes of the social self are incorporated into the older ones of personal agency. In this process accommodation turns into habit, or as Baldwin puts it, "accommodation, by the very reaction which accommodates, hands over its gains immediately to the rule of habit" (1895, p. 480).

Mead expresses his position with respect to the development of self-consciousness in a manner similar to that of Baldwin. According to Mead (1934), one's concept of the self has two components—the self as an agent, the I, and the social self, the Me. They are mutually interdependent and arise together in the process of communication. In this process the acts of each individual concerned serve as stimuli to the other individual, and from the mutual adjustment of both participants to each other one can observe the emergence of the I and the Me, and of self- and other-awareness. It is important that Mead's concepts of the I, the Me, and the Self are different from the concepts with the same names introduced by James (1890). As H. Joas (1980) points out, Mead's social self has a constitutive function in his theory of self-consciousness while for James the social self is just one of many other selves. Mead's I and Me, and Self and Other, have a dialogical, or one could say, dialectical nature, in the sense that they are relational—that is, mutually interdependent—and that the one cannot exist without the other. However, Mead (1909) insists that self-consciousness does not arise through imitation as Baldwin and Josiah Royce claim but that instead social consciousness is a presupposition of imitation. It seems to me, though, that Mead's claimed difference between his notion of communicative adjustment and Baldwin's notion of imitation lies in Mead's misunderstanding of Baldwin's and Royce's use of terms.

While in Baldwin's theory it was attention that represented a barrier to mindless imitation and led to higher levels of self-consciousness, in Mead's (1982, p. 51) conception it was a problem-solving situation that led to an interruption of mindless activities. When a problem appears, and the stream of consciousness is interrupted, one stops and considers available alternatives. This is how reflective thought begins. Mead explains that the method of control over the world is a social technique. A person has an ability to hold in consciousness conflicting stimulations and possibilities of responding to them. It is through self-consciousness that we get hold of our mental material, so as to deal with it through *Vorstellungen*—images or representations.

Vygotsky (1979), too, talked about such *Vorstellungen* in human consciousness, and in this context he referred to Marx's *Capital*. Here Marx discussed the architect's images of his or her product in contrast to the products of a spider or a bee. Both Vygotsky and Marx omitted, however, making reference to Johann Herder's 1771 essay "On the Origin of Language," where the author had given this very same example, talking about the narrowness of the ecological sphere of animals as compared to human reflexive consciousness.

Concerning the nature of self-consciousness as such, here again Vygotsky expressed his views in virtually the same words as Mead and Baldwin: "The mechanism of knowing oneself (self-awareness) and the mechanism for knowing others are one and the same" (Vygotsky 1979, p. 29). He claimed it is wrong to say that we know others because we know ourselves. Rather, we are aware of ourselves only to the extent that we are another for ourselves. There is no difference between the fact that one can repeat one's own word and repeat the word of the other person. Moreover, there are no fundamental distinctions between their mechanisms, because they are both reversible stimuli. Consciousness of speech and of social experience emerge simultaneously and together with one another (Vygotsky 1979, p. 31).

What is fascinating about the similarity of expression of these three social-developmental psychologists is that they either did not know each other's work or if they did they referred to it in such a way that it hardly reflected any recognition of such a similarity. To my knowledge neither Mead nor Baldwin ever referred to Vygotsky. Mead did refer to Baldwin, recognizing the importance of his work, but he was also critical of his concept of imitation and accused Baldwin of dualism. (Just as Mead used the term *social behaviorism*, which was often misinterpreted, so Baldwin used the term *dualism* in his dialectical logic, a usage which was unfortunate.) At least at several places, Vygotsky recognized the importance of Baldwin's work. Yet these occasional references can hardly explain the similarity of Baldwin, Mead, and Vygotsky in expressing their ideas on the nature of self-consciousness. To my mind, the similarity of expression comes from Hegel's writings, although when Baldwin, Mead, and Vygotsky actually refer to Hegel it is at places that do not fully reflect the importance of Hegel's notion of self-consciousness. Moreover, they do it in such a tame manner that one supposes they were worried they might be accused of Hegelianism.

HEGEL'S CONCEPTION OF CONSCIOUSNESS

The idea of mutuality between self and other in the development of self-consciousness—which is the essential presupposition of Baldwin, Mead, and Vygotsky, but not of William James—was expressed by Hegel in his *Phenomenology of Spirit*:

> Self-consciousness exists in and for itself when, and by the fact that, it so exists for another; that is, it exists only by being acknowledged. [1977, p. 118]

Just as Baldwin, Mead, and Vygotsky did later, here Hegel opposed individualistic and dualistic approaches to the study of the mind and human consciousness—namely, rationalism, empiricism, and intuitionism (Harris 1983, p. 47). Hegel acknowledged that Kant had made great progress over his predecessors, such as Descartes, Locke, and Hume, with respect to the understanding of the nature of the human mind, in particular that consciousness synthesizes the individual's experience in the world into a meaningful whole. Moreover, he praised Kant for appreciating that such a synthesis would be impossible if there were no self, a self that for him was a fire consuming "the loose plurality of sense and organizing it into a unity" (Hegel 1873, paragraph 42). However, Hegel pointed out that the Kantian expression "transcendental unity of self-consciousness" and others like it suggest the existence of a monster in the background. What Kant had failed to appreciate, Hegel argued, was that self-consciousness is not simply the activity of a finite self, but that it itself arises in the process of evolution and self-education. It is in this process that Nature eventually becomes aware of itself as an object—that is, becomes reflexively self-aware. Hegel treats this process of the development of self-consciousness in his *Phenomenology of Mind* as a process of transformation of consciousness into its different forms, leading to more adequate forms of knowledge and, finally, to reflexive self-knowledge.

Hegel's critics have often pointed out that he had no conception of any kind of biological evolution and that his forms of evolution are just the evolution of an abstract idea. Of course it is right to say that Hegel's evolution of the mind is not biological evolution. Yet he viewed nature as progressing from its most abstract and undifferentiated forms of knowledge to the most concrete and differentiated ones. Nature starts from simple sentience and sense-certainty and progresses to such forms of consciousness as perception and understanding. In this process consciousness cannot penetrate beyond the appearances of things and so it finally turns its attention upon itself and becomes the object of its study. Consciousness thus becomes self-consciousness. Full self-consciousness expresses itself in practical and theoretical activities, and in morality, law, social order, art, and religion. The highest form of knowledge is philosophy, in which subject and object are united and identified (Harris 1983, p. 21). This final stage of the development of the mind culminates in absolute spirit—that is, thought that thinks reflexively about itself. This thought that thinks reflexively about itself is by no means a hopelessly subjective spirit (as Mead wrongly interpreted it), but the outcome of the mutual interaction between organism and its environment (Harris 1983, p. 209; Markova 1987). Thus phenomenology[3] must be interpreted as a conceptual development in terms of the adequacy of the relationship between the practical and social activity in which people are involved, on the one hand, and their knowledge and self-knowledge that results from that activity, on the other. As E. E. Harris (1983) pointed out, Hegel's view of nature is very modern and it anticipates much of more recent ways of thinking about evolution and development. Hegel develops his ideas in evolutionary terms. Reality for him is a dialectical process of forms, ranging through all levels of natural existence—physical, organic, and psychical—to that point at which spirit (which develops itself through the process) becomes fully conscious of itself.

The *Phenomenology* (1977) was published in 1807 and, as Harris (1983) reminds us, Darwin started his exploratory voyage in the *Beagle* in the year Hegel died. Yet Hegel makes it particularly clear that the development of the mind proceeds by the internalization of natural influences. For Hegel, Harris claims, nature is the external world of reality and the external world is potentially the truth. However, it is not the full truth because the full truth must be cognized, and material nature has not and is not cognition. Nature, though, contains in itself, immanently and potentially, "the seeds of that conscious life which develops out of it" (Harris 1982, p. 129). We must not forget that between Hegel, on the one hand, and Baldwin, Mead, and Vygotsky, on the other, comes Darwin, who enabled the latter three to psychologize and sociologize Hegelian ideas.

THE LOGIC OF INNER-OUTER

One of the most important characteristics of Baldwin's, Mead's, and Vygotsky's work was their use of the genetic or developmental method in the conceptualization of psychological phenomena. As pointed out earlier, all three psychologists had a conception of development that was broad, including not just child development, but also socio-historical and cultural development. Their genetic method was based on Hegel's idea of dialectic logic.

In the history of Western philosophy, traditionally logic has been concerned with identifying the principles of valid inference applicable to all aspects of systematic knowledge. Conceived in this sense, it has been qualified by logicians with such adjectives as *formal, symbolic,* and *mathematical.* Such logic is totally independent of the content of knowledge and of the way knowledge is acquired. Hegel's dialectical logic is different in kind. It is not formal and cannot be formalized. Rather, it is "a concrete theory revealing the ultimate nature of the content of the world" (Harris 1987, p. 154). This logic itself is an outcome of a dialectical development in which less adequate forms of knowledge of the world are transformed into and substituted by more adequate ones. In this process mutual opposites (dyads) such as individual and environment, the self and the other, form and content, whole and part, and inner and outer, interact and mutually determine each other. We have already seen that Baldwin, Mead, and Vygotsky clearly adhered to such a conception of development. For example, Mead pointed out that "the life-process, to be adequately understood, must be considered in terms of their interrelations" (i.e., of organism and environment) (Mead 1934, p. 130). Harris (1983) insists that Hegel's logic must be interpreted with respect to the forms of nature rather than with respect to ideas, and he blames Marx and his followers for the widespread misrepresentation of Hegel. That Harris is right in grounding Hegel's logic in natural (including social) forms of life and not in spiritual entities separate from biological forms of life is clearly documented in the examples Hegel (1812–16, 1830) used to illustrate his claims both in the text and in the notes in his *Logic*.

Let us take, as an example, the mutual opposites of the dyad inner-outer. My reason for choosing this dyad is that it plays an important role in the development of self-consciousness and that it was taken up by Baldwin, Mead, and Vygotsky. In psychology the relationship between inner and outer has often been described as internalization. Children internalize parental influences and culture (Freud 1925–26), and adults internalize attitudes, norms, and beliefs (e.g., Kelman 1958). As already pointed out, the idea of internalization comes from Hegel's *Logic* (1929). Discussing the relation between inner and outer in section 140, he presents the example of the child's socialization. Thus the child appears at first a "mere inward" and the capacity for natural subjectivity is only potential. At the same time this subjectivity takes the form of the "mere outward," which presents itself as parental discipline, teachers' instructions, and the whole gamut of adult authority that environs him:

> The education and instruction of a child aim at making him actually and for himself what he is at present potentially and therefore for others, viz. for his grown-up friends. The reason, which at first exists in the child only as an inner possibility, is actualized through education; and conversely, the child by these means becomes conscious that the goodness, religion, and science which he had at first looked upon as an outward authority, are his own and inward nature. [Hegel 1929, pp. 254–55]

In a similar manner, Hegel discusses examples of adult socialization. In Hegel's conception, punishment of a criminal by an external authority can also be understood in terms of inner-outer. The criminal perceives punishment as an act of external force, but it is through conscience—that is, through the inner force—that the penalty manifests itself. As Harris (1983) points out, this doctrine of society and the state is based on the conception of the mutual relationship between individual and society. The individual is a social product and the aspects of inner and outer, and their relation to each other, express themselves as a mutuality of inner conscience and outer legality. It is because of this mutual relationship between conscience and legality that their effect upon the individual becomes finally the same. As Hegel says, at the end the inner and outer become identical, and their concrete identity expresses itself as actuality.

Genetic logic, on which Baldwin, Mead, and Vygotsky insisted in their work, is based on Hegel's principle that concepts or categories such as "organism," "environment," "subjective," "objective," "part," "whole," "inner," and "outer" are meaningless in isolation—that is, as "either" and "or." Instead, they make sense only in relation to their opposites. In other words, one cannot understand *organism* apart from *environment*, or *subjective* apart from *objective*, or *inner* apart from *outer*.

The dyad inner-outer played an important role in Baldwin's (1906) genetic logic. In this logic, using as he said "a consciously genetic method" (1906, p. ix), in truly Hegelian fashion he proposed a broadly conceived theory of the development of human thought and knowledge from the simplest to the most complex "mode." This genetic development of thought and knowledge, from prelogical into logical and, finally, hyperlogical stages, is based on the growth and transformation of Hegelian dyads of opposites. Baldwin, however, called them "dualisms," which was unfortunate because, as a result, he was misunderstood by many of his contemporaries, including Mead, who accused him of being a dualist. Baldwin's "dualisms" include such dyads of opposites as inner-outer, subject-object, mind-body, and reality-appearance. These dualisms, Baldwin argued, are at first crude and unreflective in the development of thought. Indeed, to interpret Baldwin correctly one should say that these dialectical dyads only appear as dualisms to an untrained—that is, predialectically thinking—mind. They become refined and finally resolved through the development of the mind based on the self-other dialectic. This development includes such forms of experience and education as esthetics and ethics.

The development of thought and knowledge in Baldwin's conception starts, just as in Hegel's *Phenomenology*, from the apprehension of objects through the senses. This mode of thought Baldwin calls prelogical, and it corresponds to the stage that Piaget later called sensorimotor schemas (Lee 1982). To some extent, at each stage of the development of thought the person can control the constructive process through which knowledge is acquired. At the prelogical stage such control is provided by memory. While objects of the senses stubbornly resist the person's control because they exist in the outside world and cannot be got rid of, objects of memory are potentially "liftable" from the context of objects of the senses. Memories are representations of what they represent and can be converted into what they represent. Although children cannot in the first instance control their memories, either by voluntarily testing them or refusing to accept them, children accept the convertible nature of memories. The controllability of memories thus concerns the awareness that something is a memory rather than an object of sense. In other words, the individual becomes aware of a memory as something "inner" and of the object of sense as something "outer," and thus the basis of the dualism "inner-outer" is formed, and so is the basis of the child's awareness of this dualism (Baldwin 1906, p. 68). Thus, the mode of knowledge of the perception of objects and their memory is the very foundation of what, in the process of further development of the mind, transforms into the inner-outer, and the subjective-objective opposites. As Baldwin explains, in the later stage of development, when a person is able to reason and judge whether something is an "inner" image or an "outer" physical object, that person actually exercises control by making decisions as to the course of action. As the child learns to distinguish between memory objects that are convertible into sense objects and "fancy objects" that are not so convertible, awareness of the polarity of inner and outer becomes sharper.

The distinction between the self and the notself, Baldwin maintains, also has a root in inner-outer dualism. The child's awareness that others, too, are selves grows through imitation in play and game:

> The child imitates the act of another, and in so doing what he had only observed, comes to feel how the other feels. He thus learns to distinguish the arena of his direct feeling (the inner) from the larger

range of presentative experience (the outer) from which this feeling was and may still be absent. [Baldwin 1906, p. 87]

Through play and games the child learns to control the inner life and learns that others can do the same. The progression in the distinction of inner-outer resolves itself into the dualism of subjective-objective. In the process of transformation of one kind of dualism into another, the child becomes more and more reflexively self- and other-aware.

Discussing the emergence of self-consciousness, Mead (1982, 1934) puts great emphasis on the progressive development of inner-outer relations. Thus he claims that self-consciousness exists to the extent that individuals are able to respond to their own stimulations in the same way that they respond to those of others. In other words, only when individuals become objects to themselves is reflexive self-consciousness present.

At first, others' speech—that is, the speech of parents, caretakers, and peers—stimulates the child. Other people refer to the child in the third person and so does the child. At this stage, children seemingly stand outside themselves, or as Mead says, the self has not, as yet, been *verinnerlicht*—that is, "spiritualized" (1982, p. 50). The self is an object, but not as yet an object to the child. In other words, it has not become a subjective, an inner, self. At this stage, although children talk to themselves, their thinking and talking appears to them as external. It has not yet been internalized and seems to them, therefore, the same kind of speech as that of other people.

Mead argues that in the process of the development of reflexive self-consciousness the child's vocal gesture plays a crucial role. While originally children are stimulated by the speech of others, gradually they become stimulated by their own speech: "We can hear ourselves talking, and the import of what we say is the same to ourselves that it is to others" (Mead 1934, p. 62). The individual's awareness of self-stimulation is crucial for the development of self-consciousness. Thus the individual's inner consciousness is socially organized because it imports the social organization of the outer world (Mead 1912, p. 406). It thus follows that people are able to introspect and to have an inner conversation with themselves only because they assume a social attitude toward themselves (Mead 1913). Inner conversation is thus nothing but an internalized form of social interaction. As Mead says:

> The internalization in our experience of the external conversations of gestures which we carry on with other individuals in the social process is the essence of thinking. [1934, p. 47]

If persons become stimulated by their own speech, it follows that they are also able to exercise control over and regulate their own responses to that stimulation. Indeed, the difference between the self and others as objects, Mead (1982) argues, lies precisely in one's ability to control one's own stimuli but not those of others. The regulation of one's own stimuli and one's responses to them arises, therefore, from the internalized responses of others. Thus, one's own response to one's conduct becomes a means of social regulation, and consequently there is no sharp distinction between social control and self-control.

Vygotsky's treatment of the dyad inner-outer is very similar to that of Mead. Just like Mead, Vygotsky takes speech to be an essential means of the development of reflexive self-consciousness. It is in the context of his well-known critique of Piaget's concept of egocentrism and of egocentric speech that he developed his own, genuinely social, account of egocentric speech (Vygotsky 1934). Vygotsky (1934, p. 55) summarized Piaget as holding that autism appears to be the original form of thought, with logic appearing relatively late, and with egocentrism the genetic link between them. For Piaget, Vygotsky argued, the roots of the child's egocentrism are to be seen in the child's asocial attitudes and in the specific form of practical activity. For Piaget, practical activity was fundamental for the development of thought. However, Piaget argued that activity was strictly egocentric or egotistic until about the age of seven or eight. According to Piaget, when the child becomes socialized at about this age, egocentric thought does not suddenly disappear but crystalizes itself in the most abstract aspects of purely verbal thought.

Vygotsky rejected the hypothesis that the child is originally an asocial being and that egocentric speech is a manifestation of this fact. Instead, he argued that the primary function of speech, both in children and in adults, is communication and social interaction. Thus child's speech is purely social from the very beginning. Vygotsky (1934, p. 106) pointed out that empirical evidence obtained by K. Buhler (1927) clearly shows that a baby, in the third week of life, responds in a very specific way to the human voice and that a social response to a human voice appears as early as in the second month of the child's life. Recent studies by developmental psychologists have provided even clearer evidence to that effect (cf., e.g., Condon and Sander 1974a and b; Schaffer 1977; Fogel 1977). Moreover, Vygotsky argued that gestures, laughter, babbling, and pointing are important means of social contact from the first months of the child's life. It is wrong to say, as Piaget does, that the child's behavior becomes socialized at any stage, because this presupposes that there is a stage at which the behavior is not social and that it became social in the process of development.

Vygotsky maintained that egocentric speech is very important in the child's development because it signifies a new kind of control: it is a transition from outer to inner control. At about the age of three, when young children start talking to themselves, their speech often represents thinking aloud, and it is the way children exercise control over their own actions. In this way it carries the same function that the speech of other people has for the child. Children then respond to their own speech just as they would respond to that of others. Egocentric speech, Vygotsky argued, is an aspect of the social speech from which it separated itself, and later it transforms itself into inner speech. Egocentric speech is, therefore, a transitional stage from social to inner speech.

To illustrate his claim, Vygotsky gives examples of the function of egocentric speech in his own studies with children. It is often in problem situations, such as when a child drawing a picture does not have a pencil of a particular color or if the tip of a pencil breaks, that children start talking to themselves. Just as Mead claimed that a problem situation leads to reflexive thought, so too did Vygotsky, who referred to Édourd Claparède's view on this question. It is when automatic activity is interrupted that a person becomes reflectively aware of that activity. Egocentric speech is the child's attempt to resolve the situation by means of speech, to plan action that will lead to a satisfactory resolution of the difficulty.

CONCLUSION

In this essay I have tried to show that Baldwin, Mead, and Vygotsky were strongly influenced by the Hegelian way of thinking. One should ask, though, why they themselves did not acknowledge this influence more manifestly. Concerning Vygotsky, Hegel had not been a favorite philosopher in the Soviet Union, for Marx, supposedly, stood him on his head to make him intelligible and applicable to the socialist revolution. Even though Vygotsky was cautious in expressing his support for Hegel's ideas, after his death he was nevertheless accused of uncritical acceptance of Hegelianism. However, no such explanation for the lack of acknowledgment of Hegel's influence is available in the case of Baldwin and Mead.

In developing his genetic logic, Baldwin (1906) made it quite clear that he wished to distinguish it from the metaphysical dialectical logic of Hegel. And on his part, Mead (1926) clearly distanced himself from absolute idealism, which he said had totally failed. Mead saw the reason for this failure in the hopelessly subjectivist perspective that absolute idealism took. Mead argued for the mutuality and objective reality of perspectives between the individual and society, and according to him, Hegel's absolute ego could not fulfill this task.

Baldwin, Mead, and Vygotsky all studied Hegel's work, and it is very likely that they absorbed many of Hegel's ideas without realizing it. It is possible that, having accepted Hegel's conceptual framework, they focused on working out the details of their own conceptions, and on their disagreements rather than their convergences with Hegel. For them, these disagreements may have appeared of much greater importance than their convergences. In a similar way, cognitivism and behaviorism have often been interpreted as alternative conceptions of the study of psychological phenomena, and it has been overlooked that they are essentially the same in nature, both endorsing the conception of the Cartesian dualism of mind and body (Markova 1982). It has been well documented that people take different perspectives of actions when they are actively involved in them than when they are observers (Farr and Anderson 1983), and it is possible that, as creators of their own theories of self-consciousness, Baldwin, Mead, and Vygotsky did not see their similarities with Hegel in the way one can see them as an observer.

Moreover, our own understanding of Baldwin, Mead, and Vygotsky today, just as of Hegel, is itself partially determined by the historical and socio-cultural differences between the times in which they lived and today. Understanding Hegel today is a different matter than what it was in the last century. Understanding Hegel, just like understanding other social and natural phenomena, means understanding ourselves, because it is through us rational human agents that nature recognizes itself and becomes aware of itself.

Notes

1. The concept of self-consciousness in this chapter concerns reflexive self- and other-awareness. Baldwin, Mead, and Vygotsky often used the term *consciousness* when we would use the term *self-consciousness*. In order to follow the usage of the three psychologists, when I use *consciousness* in this essay it is *self-consciousness* that I mean.

2. Page number is given to the Czech edition of Vygotsky's *Thinking and Speech* (1970).

3. *Editors' note*: As Markova uses it in this essay, *phenomenology* refers to Hegel's methods and observations, not to the contemporary philosophical movement of the same name that has its origin in Husserl.

References

Bakhtin, M. M. (1981). *The dialogic imagination* (M. Holquist, ed.; C. Emerson and M. Holquist, trans.). Austin: University of Texas.

—— (1984). *Problems of Dostoevski's poetics* (C. Emerson, ed.). Minneapolis: University of Minnesota.

—— (1986). *Speech genres and other late essays* (C. Emerson and M. Holquist, eds. V. W. McGee, trans.). Austin: University of Texas.

Baldwin, J. M. (1895). *Mental development in the child and the race*. London: Macmillan.

—— (1897). *Social and ethical interpretations in mental development*. London: Macmillan.

—— (1906). *Thought and things*, vol. 2. London: Swan Sonnenschien.

—— (1910). *Darwin and the humanities*. London: Swan Sonnenschien.

—— (1911). *The individual and society*. London: Rebman.

Bird, G. (1986). *William James*. London: Routledge and Kegan Paul.

Boulding, K. E. (1981). *Evolutionary economics*. London: Sage.

Broughton, J. M., and Freeman-Moir, D. J. (eds.) (1982). *The cognitive developmental psychology of James Mark Baldwin*. Norwood: Ablex.

Bruner, J. S. (1962). *Introduction to L. S. Vygotsky: Thought and language*. Cambridge, Mass.: MIT.

Buhler, K. (1927). *Soziologische und psychologische Studien über das erste Lebensjahr*. Jena: K. Fischer.

Clark, K., and M. Holquist (1984). *M. M. Bakhtin: Life and works*. Cambridge, Mass.: Harvard University.

Condon, W. S., and Sander, L. W. (1974a). "Neonate movement is synchronized with adult speech: Interactional participation and language acquisition," *Science*, 183, pp. 99–101.

—— (1974b). "Synchrony demonstrated between movements of the neonate and adult speech," *Child development*, 45, pp. 456–62.

Farr, R. M., and Anderson, T. (1983). "Beyond actor-observer differences in perspective: Extensions and applications," *Attribution theory: Social and functional extensions* (M. Hewstone, ed.). Oxford: Blackwell.

Fogel, A. (1977). "Temporal organization in mother-infant face-to-face interaction," *Studies in mother-infant interaction* (H. R. Schaffer, ed.). London: Academic, 119–51.

Freud, S. (1925–26). *Collected works*, 19, 20. London: Hogarth.

Goodwin, B. C. (1984). "Genetic epistemology and biology," *Evolution and developmental psychology* (G. Butterworth, J. Rutkowska, and M. Scaife, eds.). Brighton: Harvester.

Gruber, H. E. (1974). *Darwin on man: A psychological study of creativity, together with Darwin's early and unpublished notebooks* (P. H. Barrett, transcriber and annot.). London: Wildhood.

Harris, E. E. (1982). "Marxist interpretations of Hegel's *Phenomenology of spirit*," *Method and speculation in Hegel's phenomenology* (M. Westphal, ed.). Sussex: Harvester.

——— (1983). *An interpretation of the logic of Hegel.* New York: University Press of America.

——— (1987). *Formal, transcendental and dialectical thinking.* Albany: State University of New York.

Hegel, G. W. F. (1873). "The encyclopedia of the philosophical sciences, part 1, The science of logic," *The logic of Hegel* (W. Wallace, trans.). London: Oxford University.

——— (1929). *Science of logic* (W. H. Johnston and L. G. Struthers, trans.). Woking: George Allen and Unwin.

——— (1977). *Phenomenology of spirit* (A. V. Miller, trans.). Oxford: Clarendon.

Herder, J. G. (1771). "On the origin of language," *Sämtliche Werke* (B. Suphon, ed.); repr. 1967. Hildesheim: George Olins.

James, W. (1890). *The principles of psychology*, vol. 1. New York: Holt.

——— (1912). "Does 'consciousness' exist?" *Essays in radical empiricism.* London: Longmans, Greens.

Joas, H. (1980). *G. H. Mead.* Frankfurt: Suhrkamp.

Kelman, H. (1958). "Compliance, identification and internationalization: Three processes of attitude change," *Journal of conflict resolution*, 2, pp. 399–432.

Kohlberg, L. (1982). "Moral development," *The cognitive-developmental psychology of James Mark Baldwin* (J. M. Broughton and D. J. Freeman-Moir, eds.). Norwood: Ablex, 277–333.

Lee, B. (1982). "Cognitive development and the self," *The cognitive-developmental psychology of James Mark Baldwin* (J. M. Broughton and D. J. Freeman-Moir, eds.). Norwood: Ablex, 169–210.

Lewontin, R. C. (1982). "Organism and environment," *Learning, development, and culture* (H. C. Plotkin, ed.). New York: Wiley.

Luckman, T. (1969). "Einleitung," *L. S. Wygotski, Denken und sprechen.* Frankfurt: S. Fischer.

Markova, I. (1982). *Paradigms, thought and language.* New York: Wiley.

——— (1987). "On the interaction of opposites in psychological processes," *Journal for the theory of social behaviour*, 17, pp. 279–99.

Mead, G. H. (1909). "Social psychology as counterpart to physiological psychology," *Psychological bulletin*, 6, pp. 401–8.

——— (1912). "The mechanism of social consciousness," *Journal of philosophy, psychology, and scientific methods*, 9, pp. 401–6.

——— (1913). "The social self," *Journal of philosophy, psychology, and scientific methods*, 10, pp. 374–80.

——— (1926). "The objective reality of perspectives," *Proceedings of the sixth international congress of philosophy* (E. S. Brightman, ed.), 75–85.

——— (1932). *The philosophy of the present* (A. E. Murphy, ed.). La Salle: Open Court.

——— (1934). *Mind, self and society*. Chicago: University of Chicago.

——— (1936). *Movements of thought in the nineteenth century*. Chicago: University of Chicago.

——— (1938). *The philosophy of the act*. Chicago: University of Chicago.

——— (1956). *The social psychology of George Herbert Mead*. Chicago: University of Chicago.

——— (1982). "1914 class lectures in social psychology," *The individual and the social self* (D. L. Miller, ed.). Chicago: University of Chicago, 27–105.

Rahmani, L. (1973). *Soviet psychology*. New York: International Universities.

Russell, L. (1978). *The acquisition of knowledge*. New York: St. Martin's.

Schaffer, H. R. (1977). *Mothering*. Cambridge, Mass.: Harvard University.

Vygotsky, L. S. (1934). *Myshlenie i rech': Psikhologicheskie issledovaniva*. Moscow and Leningrad: Gosudarstvennoe Sotsial'no-Ekonomicheskoe Izdatel'stvo.

——— (1964). *Thought and language* (E. Hanfmann and G. Vakar, eds. and trans.). Cambridge, Mass.: MIT.

——— (1978). *Mind in society: The development of higher psychological processes* (M. Cole, ed.). Cambridge, Mass.: Harvard University.

——— (1979). "Consciousness as a problem in the psychology of behavior," *Soviet psychology*, 17, pp. 3–35.

——— (1982–84). *Sobranie sochinenii*, I–VI. Moscow: Izdatal'stvo Pedagogika.

Wertsch, J. V. (1985). *Vygotsky and the social formation of mind*. Cambridge, Mass.: Harvard University.

8 • The Dynamics of Alternative Realities

Simon Glynn

What is reality? More specifically, what is the real world like? The answers to such questions, long of interest to philosophers, are of the greatest significance for psychologists, who, it would seem, would need some fairly clear answers in order to be able to make the judgments that they are called upon to make regarding others' abilities to perceive and conceive the real world. Only if they know what the world is really like, so the commonsense argument goes, can cognitive psychologists judge the subject's ability to perceive it, or can clinical psychologists judge whether a subject is suffering from hallucinations, delusions, or displaying certain symptoms of psychosis or schizophrenia. Strange, then, that while philosophers seem unable to reach any sort of agreement on the nature of the real world, or indeed even on whether such a world exists, psychologists generally express few, if any, reservations concerning their competence to make judgments that presuppose clear answers to such questions.

Of course, it is accepted by almost all who stop to consider the matter that objects in the world look different from different points of view, that my perception of a table may differ from your perception of it by virtue of the fact we are observing it from different visual angles. Further it is accepted that while you and I perceive the table, some other person in another room does not. If, however, that person comes into the room, other things being equal, the person will also see the table. We note also that if you and I change places, our perceptions will be similarly changed. Thus, while our perceptions differ and are constantly changing and interrupted, we do not experience a "boomin', buzzin', confusion." On the contrary, as Husserl has pointed out, we experience something like a "unity of appearances in the phenomenal flux" (1962, p. 59), which is to say we experience the multiplicity of our perceptions as appearances of a finite number of discrete objects. In other words, while undeniably different, interrupted, and changing, our experiences nevertheless display a degree of unity, continuity, and similarity. We resolve this tension between change and stasis by a bifurcation between "appearances," to which we attribute the former properties of our experiences, and "reality," to which we attribute the latter properties. Moreover by drawing a distinction between appearances and reality, common sense is able, within certain limits, to reconcile the admitted differences between our perceptions, which are said to depend upon our points of view, with the claim that we both perceive, or exist within, the same reality.

Nowhere is the mechanism of such bifurcation more visible than where it breaks down, as in the experiment conducted by Ames in which a white ball, in a featureless white room, is kept still but silently and rapidly inflated so that it becomes larger. A subject observing this event reports that the ball is coming nearer. The subject is then informed of what is happening and asked to observe while the process is repeated several times. The subject reports being able to see that the ball is indeed being inflated. Finally the ball, which all the while has been suspended from above on an invisible wire attached to a track out of the field of vision, is not inflated but instead moved smoothly toward the subject, who remains unaware of this movement and still "sees" the ball as being inflated, until it approaches so close that the subject is forced to radically adjust his or her focus.

In the first instance, unfamiliar with natural objects that rapidly change size in the manner of the inflating ball, the subject conceives the real change in size of the ball—due to its inflation—as an apparent change due to its approaching. Informed of the mistake, the subject subsequently reconceives the increase in size of the ball to be a consequence of its inflation, and so misconceives the apparent change in size—due to approaching—as a real change due to inflation. We can see from this how we employ the distinction between appearance and reality in order to reconcile otherwise apparently contradictory experiences, and that our experiences of the "facts" of the "world" depend not only upon our perceptual point of view, but also upon our conceptual perspective.

The significance of our concepts for even our most basic perceptions is further evidenced by the Gestalt Duck/Rabbit and the inverting lenses. The former shows that people with the same retinal impressions can see different things; the latter, the people with different retinal impressions can see the same thing (Kuhn 1970, pp. 126–27), while in similar vein, Arthur Koestler notes:

> If you hold the index finger of the right hand ten inches, and the same finger of the left hand twenty inches, in front of your eyes, you *see* them as being of equal size, although the image on the retina of one is *twice as large* as the other. People moving about in a room do not shrink or grow in size—as they should—because we *know* that their size remains constant. . . . The photographic lens has no such built-in mechanism, it will honestly show the left finger twice as large as the right, and a sunbathing girl's foot stretched out towards the camera as a case of elephantiasis. [1981, p. 78]

If even our most basic perceptions are conceptually mediated in this way, then it goes without saying that more complex cultural phenomena, such as the perceived meaning and significance of a piece of human behavior or of a social event, are certainly no less dependent upon the conceptual framework that we employ to interpret them. As Heidegger confirms, "Whenever something is interpreted as something, the interpretation will be founded essentially upon fore-having, fore-sight, and fore-conception" (1962, p. 191).

We saw how differences in our perceptions could seemingly be reconciled with the belief that we were both experiencing the same reality by regarding such perceptions as appearances whose differences were attributable to differences in our *perceptual* point of view. Similarly we can reconcile the differences in our perceptions of a duck and of a rabbit, of the ball as inflating or approaching, and of the meaning and significance of complex cultural phenomena with the view that we all inhabit the same reality, by attributing such differences to differences in our *conceptual* perspectives. Indeed it has become increasingly commonplace to observe that, while we all inhabit the same reality, we may do so in different ways—that is, from somewhat different perceptual and conceptual perspectives.

Consequently, instead of adopting an "authoritarian" stance, dismissing all worldviews that differ from their own, psychologists and others in the social sciences have increasingly taken a more "liberal" position, suggesting that alternative worldviews be accepted if they demonstrate by their *coherence* with the worldview of the scientist and the society they represent that they too are consistent with, or *correspond* to, reality. However, it is important to note that this liberal position is predicated upon the assumption—which we shall later have reason to question—that the views of psychologists and their society correspond to reality. In other words, while coherence with the norms of society is taken to be a criterion for accepting another's worldview, such coherence does not constitute the ultimate justification for doing so. Rather, because the societal view is assumed to correspond to reality, such coherence is a criterion for acceptance on the grounds that it indicates correspondence to reality. Borrowing and extending an analogy from R. D. Laing, assuming that they are "on course" (i.e., that their views correspond to reality), liberals, unlike authoritarians, do not require absolute conformity. They are prepared to accept the views of all those who are "in formation" (i.e., whose views are coherent with theirs) as similarly on course, rejecting only those who are "out of formation," on the grounds that they are *ipso facto* "off course." However, the formation itself may be off course, in which case, as Laing points out, "the plane that is out of formation may be . . . more or less off course than the formation" (1984, pp. 98–99).

Here, then, Laing is clearly raising a third alternative, the "individualistic" view that those who are out of formation with the society may nevertheless be on course, or in contact with reality, in a way that the society at large is not. Nevertheless, what all these views have in common is that they all *ultimately* seek to justify individuals' perceptions on the basis of their consistency or correspondence to a reality. This reality must therefore clearly be conceived as existing somehow outside or beyond, and thus independently of or transcendentally to, these perceptions.[1]

However, there is another, "anarchist," alternative to all these positions: to deny the possibility of an appeal to any such transcendental perspective or reality, either on the grounds that there is no such perspective or reality, or on the grounds that even if there were, existing as it is supposed to, outside or beyond all actual or possible experience, we could not be aware of it, even in principle. It is just this phenomenological claim that Husserl makes and justifies.

First, suspending judgment upon or bracketing (the phenomenological *epoche*) the hypothesized existence of a quasi-noumenal, transcendental realm of "things-in-themselves,"[2] Husserl turns to describe what remains after the bracketing, in the phenomenologically reduced[3] or quasi-phenomenal realm of our immediate experience. He discovers that we are still able, as before the reduction, to distinguish the experience of the object (appearance) from the object experienced (reality), experiencer from the experienced, subject from object, one object from another, and ideal or so-called mental objects (such as the objects of dreams or fantasies), from each other and from physical objects.

Thus before the reduction it was assumed that such distinctions *must* issue from a separation between experience and a reality existing outside and therefore independently of this experience. However, insofar as it remains possible to distinguish between our experiences of objects, or appearances, and the objects experienced, or "reality," and between ideal and physical objects, etc., solely on the basis of our phenomenologically reduced experiences, then it is obvious that there need be nothing transcendental about reality at all. Clearly then the distinction between appearance and reality is "radically empirical" (Husserl 1965), which is to say intentionally constituted[4] wholly and solely in our phenomenological experiences.

None of this should surprise us unduly. It is, after all, an undeniable truism that we cannot, even in principle, have any direct experience of a realm of reality existing transcendentally to our experience. Consequently, and here we come to the crux of the matter, our experiences cannot in principle provide a *transcendental* basis upon which to arbitrate between them. It follows that the proposals for adjudication between world perceptions made by authoritarians, liberals, and individualists alike, relying as they do on some form of correspondence between our experiences and an independently existing reality, must be abandoned as unempirical in favor of what we have called the anarchist alternative. As W. Werkmeister affirms:

> The correspondence theory . . . breaks down because it demands that I compare something given *in* my experience (the idea) with something which *is and remains outside* that experience (the real thing), and such comparison is impossible. All "comparing" takes place only within first person experience and, as a consequence, only "ideas" [or what we would perhaps better call perceptions or experiences] can be compared with one another. [1968, p. 137]

Nor, as is sometimes claimed, can we adjudicate between competing perceptions of reality by appealing to "sense-data" or its
correlate, sensations. For while from time to time we may seem to
experience simple sensations, such as of pain and pleasure, it is
not in these cases, but in those cases where we experience objects
and events, that we need to be able to appeal to sense data or
sensations as a basis for adjudicating between such experiences.
Yet in precisely such cases, as Husserl tells us:

> . . . one finds anything but color data, tone data, other "sense" data
> or data of feelings. . . . Instead, one finds . . . the *cogito
> intentionality*. . . . "I see a tree which is green; I hear the rustling of its
> leaves, I smell its blossoms," etc.; or, "I remember my school days," "I
> am saddened by the sickness of a friend," etc. [1970b, p. 233]

Again:

> I do not see color sensations, but colored things. I do not hear
> sensations of sound, but the song a woman is singing etc. [cited in
> Lubb 1978, p. 108]

Thus it seems that our experiences of even the most simple and
basic objects and events are always already the product of an
interpretive synthesis of sense data. Consequently, we experience
no unsynthesized or "raw" sensations against which we can judge
interpretive syntheses. This view is apparently supported by
Merleau-Ponty, who tells us that:

> Once perception is understood as interpretation, sensation, which
> has provided a starting point, is finally superseded, for all percep-
> tual consciousness is already beyond it. The sensation is not experi-
> enced, and consciousness is always consciousness of an object. . . .
> Pure sensation . . . is an illusion. . . . [1962, p. 37]

Here we must draw back a little. For if we do not experience
sense data or sensations, but rather objects and events, then we
can have no empirical evidence that our perceptions of objects and
events are the product of the interpretive synthesis of sense data or
sensations. Nor indeed can we even coherently believe that they
could be. For although one may *believe*, albeit necessarily without
direct empirical evidence, that there exists a quasi-noumenal realm
of things-in-themselves, one cannot, even in principle, intelligibly
believe that there exist insensible sense data or sensations. Like
"unperceived perceptions," such a notion is logically contradictory. Sartre points out that, in such cases at least, "sensation is a

pure day dream of the psychologist" (1956, p. 315). As Merleau-Ponty concludes:

> To the world of opinion, perception can appear as an interpretation. For consciousness itself [however], how could it be a process of reasoning since there are no sensations to provide it with premises, or an interpretation, because there is nothing prior to it to *interpret?* [1962, p. 37]

In view of this, while it may initially seem plausible to attribute the differences in our perceptions of the world to differences in points of view or interpretive or conceptual perspectives—that is, to regard these differences as different appearances either of a transcendental reality or of sense data—we now see this cannot be so. If we had access to a reality existing independently of the world given to us in our experience, be it a world of things-in-themselves or a realm of pure sensations, then we could justifiably speak of alternative appearances or interpretations of reality. However, in view of the fact that we have no such access but still have quite *different* experiences from each other, it is unclear in what sense we can claim such experiences to be experiences of the same reality or world. Indeed, under these circumstances it would seem to be more appropriate to speak of alternative constructions of reality, of different "life-worlds" (*Lebenswelt*), or even of alternative realities. As Husserl puts it:

> The contrast between the subjectivity of the life-world and the "objective," the "true" world, lies in the fact that the latter is a theoretical-logical substruction . . . that is in principle not perceivable, in principle not experienceable in its own proper being, whereas the subjective in the life-world, is distinguishable in all respects precisely by its being actually experienceable. [1970b, p. 127]

In other words, caught as we are within the hermeneutic circle, the circuit of our own theoretically or conceptually mediated experiences, we are unable, even in principle, to experience an objective or transcendental reality beyond this circle. The situation is not unlike that of historians, who, in light of the fact that no one can have access to the past except through historical "reconstruction," may come to recognize that what they are doing may more properly be referred to as *constructing* rather than *reconstructing* the past. Similarly, recognizing that we can have no access to reality save through our theoretically and conceptually mediated experiences, we have come to realize that what we are doing may more properly be referred to as constructing reality. As Jürgen Habermas (1978, p. 286) confirms, even "'nature in itself' is a construction." Thus, like historians who seek to justify their "reconstruction" of the past by an appeal to historical "facts" that are no less constructions than the often extensive and complex overarching world-historical views they are invoked to justify, we seek to justify our life-world constructions by appealing to our experiences of more basic "facts" that are, in turn, themselves constructions, albeit at a more fundamental level than the life-world constructions that they are invoked to justify.

Surprisingly enough, nowhere is this more apparent than in the supposedly objective natural sciences. As Heidegger affirms:

> The greatness and superiority of the natural sciences during the sixteenth and seventeenth centuries rests in the fact that all the scientists were philosophers. They understood that there are no mere facts but that a fact is only what it is in the light of a fundamental conception. [1978, pp. 247–48]

Take for example the disagreement in the work of Aristotle and the work of Isaac Newton concerning the motion of an apple. While Newton understood the "fall" of this "massive body" as a manifestation of gravity, Aristotle understood the "striving" of this "earthly body" as a manifestation of its desire to return home; and while both appealed to their perceptions of the "facts" in order to support their theoretical constructions, they did of course see different facts. Whereas Newton "saw" gravity in the very motion of the apple, Aristotle equally "saw" striving in that same motion. Both invoked the facts to support their theories, and both were unaware that they were constructing such facts from within the frameworks of their theories.

In cases where such a Gestalt switch from one construction to another is not so straightforward, the facts may be construed in the light of subsidiary *ad hoc* theories. Imre Lakatos (1970, pp. 100–101) tells the story of a physicist who calculates the path of a newly discovered planet with the aid of laws derived from Newton's theory of gravity, only to find that the planet deviates from the path. The physicist takes this, not as a falsification of Newton's theory, but as proof of another hitherto unknown planet whose mass is responsible for perturbing the orbit of the observed planet. The physicist calculates the mass and position of the unobserved planet and asks an astronomer to look for it. The astronomer's failure to observe such a planet is taken not as a falsification of the theory, but as evidence of the limited power of the astronomer's telescope. A bigger telescope is built, but still the planet cannot be seen. The physicist hypothesizes that this is due to a cloud of cosmic dust that obscures the planet. A satellite is sent up, but no cloud is found. Far from taking this as evident falsification of Newton's theory, and the theory of the perturbing planet, and the theory of the cosmic dust, the physicist suggests that there is a magnetic field interfering with the satellite's instruments, etc., etc.

In other cases, where facts stand in direct contradiction to their theoretical constructions, the scientists may either ignore such facts or simply dismiss them a priori on the grounds that if they conflict with the theoretical worldview they must, *ipso facto*, be illusory. For instance, Galileo proposed that all heavenly bodies moved in circular orbits. Faced with comets, that clearly moved elliptically, he took this not as a refutation of his theory, but as evidence that all comets were illusions, while he dismissed all who claimed otherwise as either incompetent or malevolent. Albert Einstein tells us that, "in reality, it is the theory that decides what we observe" (in Heisenberg 1971, p. 63).

Thus in everyday perception, we hold the theory that physical objects tend to remain the same size or change comparatively slowly. We therefore dismiss the direct evidence of our senses to the contrary. We dismiss as mere appearances our experience of objects getting larger as we approach them and smaller as we move away. So convincing has this construction become to us that most of us would actually claim we directly *saw* objects as maintaining a constant and stable size and shape. Again we dismiss our actual and direct visual perception that oars bend in water as illusory, because it challenges our theory that they remain straight. Those who would claim that our sense of touch gives us independent verification of this fact must explain why they accept that it is the sense of sight, rather than the sense of touch, that is deluded— unless of course they assume that they already know the true shape of the oar in water. And against their attempt to invoke the refraction of light in support of their claim, it may be objected that if one can, like Galileo, dimiss the very evidence of one's own eyes as illusory, it is difficult to see how one could irrefutably establish the refraction of light. After all, proofs of the nature of light, indeed of the very existence of light as we understand it, are inextricably dependent upon that same sense of sight.

From all this it should be clear that theoretical conceptions—

worldviews—do not compete to arrange the same facts, but rather bring with them their own constructions of the facts. Thus Husserl draws our attention to

> the *naivete* of speaking about "objectivity" . . . the *naivete* of the scientist of nature or of the world in general, who is blind to the fact that all the truths we obtain as objective truths and the objective world itself . . . (the everyday world of experience as well as the higher level conceptual world of knowledge) are his own *life-constructs* developed within himself. [1970b, p. 96]

Having established this, let us compare the above account of the activity of science with the activity of the paranoiac. Koestler informs us that

> the most striking feature of the paranoid's delusional system is its inner consistency. . . . Firstly, it claims to represent a truth of universal validity, capable of explaining all phenomena. . . . In the second place, it is a system that cannot be refuted by evidence, because all potentially damaging data are automatically processed and reinterpreted to make them fit the expected pattern. . . . In the third place, it is a system which invalidates criticism by shifting the argument to the subjective motives of the critic. [1981, p. 263]

Like the scientist's view, the paranoiac's view is consistent and claims universal validity. Further, like the scientist, paranoiacs are prepared to construe the facts in the light of the overarching theoretical constructions they hold, and to question the ability, or even the integrity, of those whose views conflict. As even Karl Popper (1959, p. 50) recognizes, "In point of fact no conclusive disproof of a theory can ever be produced," a claim no less true of a psychotic's constructions than of a scientist's. Medard Boss therefore concludes:

> There is no sense in granting one reality priority over another. It would be quite futile for us to maintain that the table before us is more real than your motorcycle spies merely because they eluded my perception and are perceptible only by you. [1963, p. 13]

And those who would object to such a suggestion on the grounds that only the paranoiac has any experience of motorcycle spies would do well to consider the fact that we not only accept the existence of atoms and electrons, of virtual particles, n-dimensional space, antimatter, etc.—despite the fact that no one, not even scientists, have ever claimed to have had *direct* experience of such entities—but we also accept the existence of wavicles, positrons, and so on—despite the fact that, as logically contradictory, no one *could* ever experience them!

All this being so, if as Heidegger (1962, p. 414) confirms "in principle, there are no 'bare facts,'" but only facts as mediated by or interpreted within the frameworks of our theoretical constructs, then quite clearly such facts can provide no conclusive refutation of these theoretical constructions, be they the constructions of the scientist or of the psychotic. Rather, as in the case of historical hermeneutics, *a theoretical construction can be challenged, if at all, only on the basis of an alternative construction*. Therefore, far from being able to dismiss a construction for failing to correspond to the facts, the most one can do is to demonstrate that a construction or worldview is *inconsistent* (cf. Lakatos 1970, pp. 99, 130). Such a demonstration could show that the construction is *intrinsically* inconsistent in and of itself or with the lower-level theoretical conceptions that mediate our basic perceptions of the facts. Or it could show that the construction is *extrinsically* inconsistent with another, higher-level theoretical construction and its accompanying facts.

This raises two related questions. First, what reasons are there, if any, to prefer consistent or coherent as opposed to incoherent constructions? For given that we have no conceptually unmediated experience of a realm of "bare facts," then even if we could show there were such a realm, we should still have no reason to assume it was coherent. Therefore we cannot even justify a preference for coherent constructions or worldviews on the grounds that such coherence is a necessary—though not of course sufficient— condition of their correspondence to reality. Ultimately, is there any reason to prefer intrinsically coherent over intrinsically incoherent constructions? Second, in the event of two constructions being equally intrinsically coherent yet extrinsically incoherent or contradictory, what reason do we have, if any, to prefer one to the other?

In an attempt to answer these questions, let us begin by examining a linguistic analogy. We use the term *red* to designate the color of top traffic lights and Mediterranean sunsets, and the term *green* to designate the color of bottom traffic lights and lush grassy pastures. Insofar as we cannot have each other's private experience, none of us can determine whether the color experiences we have when we look at top traffic lights, Mediterranean sunsets, etc., is the same as the color experience others have when viewing the same things. That is to say, we cannot know if our individual color experiences *correspond*. Indeed it is conceivable that the color experience you have when you look at top traffic lights and Mediterranean sunsets is the same that I have when viewing bottom traffic lights and lush grassy pastures, and vice versa. However, despite the fact that we cannot tell whether your color experiences correspond to mine, this does not mean that there is no reason to prefer any description of my color experiences to any other.

For instance, if I told you who have never visited Britain that British mailboxes are red, you would be able successfully to anticipate what your color experiences of such mailboxes would be (namely, the same as your color experiences when viewing top traffic lights and Mediterranean sunsets). But if I told you they were green, you would incorrectly predict what your color experience would be of such mailboxes (i.e., you would predict that it would be the same as your color experiences of bottom traffic lights and lush pastures).

It is important to recognize that the accuracy of your prediction depends not upon whether my color experience *corresponds* to the color experience you describe by the same term, but upon the consistency or *coherence* of our use of the term. Thus while you could not check whether or not the color experience I describe by the term *red* corresponds to the color experience you describe by the same term, you could nevertheless distinguish coherent color descriptions—color descriptions that enabled you successfully to predict your future color experiences—from incoherent ones; and you would obviously have very good pragmatic reasons to prefer the former over the latter.

In answer to our first question, then, above, it is pragmatism that leads us to prefer coherent constructions of reality over incoherent ones. As Nietzsche confirms:

> Knowledge works as a tool of power. . . . In order for a particular species to maintain itself and increase its power, its conception of reality must comprehend enough of the calculable and constant for it to base a scheme of behavior on it. [1967, section 480]

Further he tells us:

> This *compulsion* to form concepts, genera, forms, ends and laws [or what we would regard as coherent world constructions] . . . should not be understood as though we were capable through them of ascertaining the *true* world, but rather as the compulsion to adapt to ourselves a world in which *our existence* is made possible. Thereby

we create a world that is calculable, simplified, understandable, etc., for us. [cited in Habermas 1978, p. 296]

In answer to the second question, it is clearly for this same purely pragmatic reason that, other things being equal, we should prefer simple and extensive or universally coherent constructions over less simple or less extensive ones. Therefore, being unable to establish even the existence, much less the coherence, of a world beyond experience, we cannot dismiss atypical or less coherent experiences and accounts on the grounds that they are less real or true, in some ultimately transcendental sense, than more typical and coherent experiences. Nevertheless, we can dismiss such relatively incoherent experiences and accounts on the grounds that theoretical constructions that insisted on incorporating them would become increasingly complex and less extensive and would, therefore, be of less utility. Moreover, while in everyday experience, as in science, we are often prepared to dismiss what we *do* experience with our senses as appearances, illusions, or delusions on just these pragmatic grounds, conversely we are prepared on the same grounds to accept the existence not only of entities that we *do not* experience, such as atoms and electrons, virtual particles, antimatter, etc., but also the existence of objects we *cannot* experience, like the quasi-noumenal world of "things-in-themselves" existing outside experience, and even such self-contradictory entities as wavicles and positrons, entities which we are all agreed we *could not* experience. In all these cases, our justification is that such beliefs promote a relatively simpler, more extensive or coherent integration of our experiences than would otherwise be possible. Our justification is pragmatic. Thus it is now clear beyond a doubt, that, as Habermas (1978, p. 137) has put it, it is the ". . . interest in possible technical control which defines the course of objectification of reality," in which case objectivism conceals "the connection of knowledge and interest" (1978, pp. 316–17).

If this is so and our construction of reality is motivated by and justified in terms of its pragmatic utility, then given that things are not useful in the abstract but are only more or less useful in aiding us in reaching particular goals, in relation to particular projects, etc., we might expect that our construction of reality should mirror the practical goals or projects we have chosen, projects that, according to Sartre, define what we are (cf. Sartre 1956, pp. 443, 453, 480, 564). In other words, if "I am nothing save the concrete project" (1956, p. 564), then insofar as my construction of reality is ultimately pragmatic and thus reflects this project, then it should reflect me. Thus as Sartre (1956, p. 200) affirms, "The thing is an instrument or utensil. The original relationship between things . . . is the relation of *instrumentality*," and therefore "it follows that . . . the order of instruments (or things) in the world is the order of my possibilities projected . . . the image of what I am." Further, ". . . the world by means of its very articulation refers to us an exact image of what we are" (1956, p. 463).

Just as my friend's elation and Hannibal's despair at seeing the Alps reflect that my friend is a winter sports enthusiast and consequently has a different project in mind than Hannibal, the fact that the American Indians can not only interpret, but seem even to see signs that others cannot, reflects the fact that they are hunters. Similarly the fact that Eskimo vocabulary has a larger number of different words for what others simply see and call *white* reflects the fact that they perceive differentiations to which others are oblivious; their construction of reality reflects their project of survival within their snow-covered environment, with their level of technology. As Thomas Luckman elaborates:

> World views originate in the shared systems of relevance of historical societies. The systems of relevance are determined by various conditions; the topography of a territory, the ecology of a habitat, dependence on certain plants and animal species, the differentiation of roles in a kinship system, the distribution of power and authority, the level of technology, etc. In combination these factors represent the "factual requirements" of a social structure and form a matrix within which originate shared systems of relevance. The latter in turn influence the social objectification of classification systems. [1970, pp. 88–89]

Moreover, as Husserl insists:

> In our continuously flowing world-perceiving we are not isolated but rather have, within it, contact with other human beings. . . . Thus in general the world exists not only for isolated men but for the community of men; and this is due to the fact that even what is straightforwardly perceptual is communalized. [1970b, p. 163]

Not only, then, is our construction of reality pragmatic, but it is also communalized. Nor should this surprise us, for as we may already be able to see from the above, this communalization is a direct consequence of our pragmatism.

That is to say that insofar as we share common technological means and common projects with others, and insofar as our perceptions/constructions of the world are instrumental or pragmatic, our perceptions/constructions are mediated by these common technologies and goals. It is for this reason that we can expect to share a common world. For example, because they employ a common technology and share common goals in a common habitat, we may expect that traditional American Indians will have an essentially similar world construction, a construction that will differ from that of modern aircraft pilots, for instance (cf. Gurwitsch 1970, p. 50).

Moreover, while the employment of common technologies to achieve common ends in similar environments may not be sufficient to insure a communalized worldview, the overwhelming majority of us depend to a large extent upon the mutual cooperation and effort of others for our very economic survival, and such communicative praxis is greatly facilitated by mutually or extrinsically coherent constructions of reality. This means that we are under the same pragmatic pressure to adopt an extrinsically coherent or communalized worldview as to adopt one that is intrinsically coherent.

In light of this we should not be surprised to learn that broadly similar strategies are employed in both cases. That is to say, just as individuals often devalue, degrade, or even disregard as appearances or illusions those perceptions that threaten the intrinsic coherence and utility of their constructions of reality, so societies and cultures often similarly devalue, degrade, or disregard as bad, mad, or stupid, others whose perceptions threaten the extrinsic coherence or "communalization" (and thus the utility) of their worldview or life-world. As Husserl puts it:

> In this communalization, too, there constantly occurs an alteration of validity through reciprocal correction. In reciprocal understanding, my experiences and experiential acquisitions enter into contact with those of others, similar to the contact between individual series of experiences within my experiential life; and here again, for the most part, intersubjective harmony of validity occurs . . . [establishing what is] "normal" . . . and thus an intersubjective unity also comes about in the multiplicity of validities. . . here again, furthermore, intersubjective discrepancies show themselves often enough; but then . . . a unification is brought about. . . . All this takes place in such a way that in the consciousness of each individual, and in the overarching community consciousness . . . one and the same world achieves and continuously maintains constant validity as the world . . . the world as the universal horizon, common to all men. . . . [1970b, pp. 163–64]

Thus "each individual, as a subject . . . has his experiences, his aspects, . . . and each particular social group has its communal aspects, etc." (Husserl 1970b, p. 164). Consequently we may accept the religious worldview, the scientific worldview, the artistic worldview, etc., etc., as *complementing* our own, and we may even be prepared to regard worlds that are extrinsically incoherent with ours, such as the "world of the Azande" or the "world of antiquity," as *supplementing* our own, at least insofar as they are relatively removed in time or space and thus are not perceived as constituting a direct challenge. Nonetheless we degrade, devalue, or disregard any worldview that cannot be so incorporated by us in any such way. As Laing (1969) has observed, "our perception of reality is the perfectly achieved accomplishment of our civilization."

Ours is a construction of reality that regards *our* world as *the* world, and denigrates alternatives as constructions, even though they may be as intrinsically coherent as ours. The clear implication is that while it is the intersubjective coherence of their experiences which leads others to believe in the independent existence of their worlds, in our case we believe the intersubjective coherence of our experiences is grounded upon the independent existence of the world; that while others believe the world to be such and such because they all experience it to be so, we experience it to be such and such because it is so. In the main, others adopt the same attitude toward us, both sides appealing to precisely that transcendental justification of their experiences that, *qua* transcendental, must *ipso facto* be and remain beyond their grasp.

In this manner, insists Claude Lévi-Strauss (1966, p. 3), "every society . . . tends to overestimate the objective nature of its own thought." However, failing to recognize that ". . . what I live so completely and intensely is a myth [or *construction* as we have called it], which will appear as such to men in a future century, and perhaps to myself a few years hence," (Lévi-Strauss 1966, p. 255) that in Peter Berger and Thomas Luckman's words, "knowledge is socially objectivated *as* knowledge, as a body of generally valid truths about reality," we come mistakenly to regard "any radical deviance from the institutional order . . . as a departure from reality":

> Such deviance may be designated as moral depravity, mental disease, or just plain ignorance. While these fine distinctions will have obvious consequences for the treatment of the deviant, they all

share an inferior cognitive status within the particular social world. In this way the particular social world (or world construction) becomes the world *tout court*. [1967, p. 3]

In order to demonstrate this, let us take as an example the case of a subject who is observed by a psychiatrist apparently "talking to himself." Upon being asked to explain his behavior, the subject reports that he is talking to another person, whom he describes as about five-feet ten-inches tall, thin, and with long brown hair, a person whom he cannot only see and talk to, but also touch, etc., and who, when appropriate in the course of the conversation, will respond by talking back. Asked how often he sees and talks to this person, the subject replies that it is usually at least once a week, and often more. The psychiatrist, unable to see this other interlocutor and therefore perhaps convinced that the subject is suffering from some form of hallucinatory delusion, calls a colleague who confirms the diagnosis as "schizophrenia." Upon further questioning it subsequently becomes clear that such schizophrenic episodes are most frequent on Sundays and happen most often in church, where the supposed schizophrenic, along with a large number of equally "deluded" members of the particular congregation, all make similar, indeed intersubjectively coherent, claims to be literally in the presence of Christ, and thus display themselves as victims of a "mass psychosis."

Most significantly, an analysis that was essentially similar in all relevant respects could be given of the claims of Catholics, for example, who believe in the transubstantiation of the holy eucharist, and consequently take themselves, quite literally, to be drinking the blood and eating the flesh of Christ. However, for significant reasons that will become evident, they are probably less likely to be regarded as mad than the first congregation described. On the other hand, from the viewpoints of both congregations, it is the psychiatrists who, in failing to observe the evident facts of Christ's *literal* presence in church, or of the transubstantiation of the eucharist, may be regarded as deluded, or perhaps even as bad or mad.

Here we can see, clearly displayed, the diacritical relation between our conception of reality and our marginalization of individuals or groups as deviant. Whether we regard the psychiatrists as bad or the congregation as mad is dependent upon our conception of reality. Conversely, what we take to be reality may be made dependent upon whether we regard the psychiatrists as bad or the congregation as mad. The legitimation of a construction of reality and the illegitimation or marginalization of those who challenge it are two aspects of the same process, in which case, madness (at least in the sense of a psychotic "loss of contact with, or failure to grasp 'reality'") is clearly no less a social construction than we have demonstrated reality to be.

As Berger and Luckman confirm:

> Questions of psychological status cannot be decided without recognizing the reality-definitions that are taken for granted in the social situation of the individual . . . psychological status is relative to the social definitions of reality in general and is itself socially defined. [1967, p. 196]

Thus, for example, David Cooper tells us:

> Schizophrenia is a micro-social crisis situation in which the acts and experiences of a certain person are invalidated by others for certain intelligible cultural and micro-cultural reasons, to the point where he is elected and identified as being "mentally ill." [1970, p. 16]

Indeed this is clearly demonstrated by the fact that while there are equally compelling epistemological reasons for the majority of society (who neither literally experience Christ nor literally experience the eucharist as real flesh and blood) to regard those who do as mad, they are nevertheless probably more likely to regard the former as crazy than the latter—though they may well not regard either of the congregations as mad. But this same, let us say Western majority, may well regard as crazy other individuals who "talk to themselves" on the streets, or certain other religious groups, such as Shi'ite fundamentalists whose experience of reality certainly appears no more epistemologically incoherent with the Western majority's experiences than are the Christian groups'. In other words, while those whose conceptions deviate from the socially approved construction of reality may be regarded as crazy, thus evidencing the socio-cultural relativity of such classification, it is clear that they are not necessarily so regarded. Curiously enough, however, far from undermining our general thesis by signifying an asocial, acultural, absolute, or transcendental ground for such judgments, this fact only serves further to illustrate the socio-cultural relativity of such judgments. In order to demonstrate this we have only to ask ourselves what the difference is between those deviants who are "elected and identified as being mentally ill'" and those who are not.

In the first place, unlike the individuals talking to themselves, the particular Christian groups we have mentioned are just that. They are not isolated individuals, but part of a group, an institutionalized group moreover, which finds it much easier to maintain the legitimacy of its reality in the face of opposition than an individual would. But this is not the whole story, for the Shi'ites, who are, after all, members of a substantial, institutionalized group, may well be regarded by many in the West as crazy. In order to understand this difference, let us examine the Christian groups in greater detail.

As well as the fact that they are members of a group, it should be noted that the experiences and behavior of the Christians we have mentioned is highly structured, formalized, and even ritualized. They typically "see" Christ or take communion in the context of a formalized and ritualized service in which only the initiated participate, a service that is, moreover, usually conducted in a privately owned church specially designated for the purpose and which nobody is forced to attend. Let us imagine, however, that instead of confining these experiences and behavior to the church, certain individuals claimed to have the same experiences, and exhibit the same behavior, on the streets, and had open "conversations with Christ" while shopping in the local supermarket. We may imagine that many of the other patrons of the supermarket would feel embarrassed, or even threatened, by such behavior. The manager might be called and a police officer sent for, and even if the individual left the supermarket when asked, he or she would, in all probability, be regarded as mad by many who witnessed these events. Nor would a group of people all exhibiting this same behavior necessarily fare any better in similar circumstances, as is evident from the history of the early church.

As this example may suggest, it would seem that it is the degree of anxiety that an individual or group's construction of reality, as manifested in their behavior or claims, causes in others, which is likely to have a far greater influence on the way they and their construction of reality are regarded than the intrinsic, or even extrinsic, epistemological coherence of their position. For this very reason, the sanity of members of the established Catholic Church is perhaps less likely to be questioned by our society at large than the sanity of members of the other Christian congregation, while neither Christian congregation is so likely to be regarded as mad by Westerners than are the Shi'ites, the more so in view of the fact that, whatever the intrinsic merits of their political claims, the political activities of some Shi'ites are perceived by many Westerners to be disruptive and challenging to the West.

Nor should any of this surprise us, for the point of diagnosing someone as mad, as Cooper tells us, is that "almost every act, statement, and experience of the labelled person (or group) is systematically ruled invalid," along with the reality they posit (1970, p. 10). Only if and to the degree that the individual's or group's construction of reality threatens or causes anxiety in others do these others usually regard it as necessary to attempt to negate the alternative reality and its bearers. As Boss elaborates:

> No psychopathological symptom will ever be fully and adequately understood unless it is conceived of as a disturbance in the texture of social relationships of which a given human existence fundamentally consists . . . all psychiatric diagnoses are basically only sociological statements. . . . [1963, p. 56]

Thomas Szasz agrees: ". . . the laws of psychology cannot be formulated independently of the laws of sociology," he tells us (1974, p. 8).

Denied any natural ground or transcendent perspective from which to arbitrate between conflicting constructions of reality and concomitant conflicting claims regarding the sanity of those who hold them, the social group, the family, the psychologist, or any other called upon to arbitrate does so on the basis of their theoretical preconceptions or prejudices and consequent "perceptions." And while individuals or groups may present their credentials, and even employ arguments in their attempt to be accepted as authoritative arbiters, the decision as to which will be regarded as *an authority* will depend upon the theoretical preconceptions or prejudices, and consequent perceptions, of those who are *in authority*, those who have the power to make such decisions. Therefore, in all societies, it is those who are in authority, who have power, who control the social construction of reality, and concomitantly of sanity and insanity. As Berger and Luckman unequivocally inform us, "He who has the bigger stick has the better chance of imposing his definition of reality" (1967, p. 127)

But this is not to say that the theoretical criteria of coherence and simplicity that we discussed earlier play no part in justifying a particular construction of reality. They may indeed be regarded by the arbitrators as relevant criteria by which to judge the subjects' or groups' worldview and behavior. In the same way, these theoretical criteria may be regarded by those in power as relevant criteria by which to judge arbitrators' reports and recommendations. However, it is to be admitted that an appeal to coherence and simplicity or to the pragmatic utility to which it gives rise will be successful only before those who value such characteristics, a circumstance that may appear to be at odds with the earlier claim that it was just such pragmatic utility that provided the ultimate justification for any particular construction of reality. But while it is true that those in power may temporarily fail to value such pragmatic criteria, they will of course not remain in power for long if they continue to exhibit such failings but will, in time, inevitably be replaced by those who are more pragmatic. For this reason it is indeed pragmatism that provides the criterion by which all epistemological claims will ultimately be judged. For only insofar as it is of great utility, and thus powerful in its own right, or placatory to the powerful—that is, pragmatic in the highest degree—can a worldview or construction of reality and the individuals or groups who adopt it hope to succeed in the evolutionary struggle for survival in the face of challenges from others. It is, therefore, in the dialectical interplay of pragmatism and power that we can now locate the source of our own construction of reality. Thus as even Bacon, that founder of the Enlightenment, recognized, "human knowledge and human power meet in one . . . truth and utility are here the very same thing" (in Roszak 1973, p. 149).

Notes

1. Actually it is not clear that Laing himself, well versed as he is in phenomenology, would subscribe to such an experience transcending reality, in which case his analogy is somewhat misleading.

2. For a detailed exposition of bracketing or the epoche, see Husserl 1970c, sections 30–32; 1962, lectures 2 and 3.

3. For a detailed exposition of the reduction, see, e.g., Husserl 1962, chaps. 5–6; 1970c, lectures 2 and 3.

4. For a full discussion of intentional constitution, see, e.g., Husserl 1962, chap. 4, sections 33–46, chap. 8, section 84; 1970a, esp. pp. 1ff., and lecture 2; 1970a, section 41.

References

Berger P. and Luckman, T. (1967). *The social construction of reality.* Harmondsworth: Penguin.

Boss, M. (1963). *Psychoanalysis and daseinsanalysis* (L. B. Lefebre, trans.). New York: Basic Books.

Cooper, D. (1970). *Psychiatry and anti-psychiatry.* London: Paladin.

Gurwitsch, A. (1970). "Problems of the life world," *Phenomenology and social reality: Essays in memory of Alfred Schutz* (M. Natanson, ed.). The Hague: Nijhoff.

Habermas, J. (1978). *Knowledge and human interests,* 2nd ed., (J. Shapiro, trans.). London: Heinemann.

Heidegger, M. (1962). *Being and time* (J. Macquarrie and E. Robinson, trans.). New York: Harper & Row.

——— (1978). "Modern science, metaphysics and mathematics," *Martin Heidegger: Basic writings* (D. Krell, trans. and eds.). London: Routledge and Kegan Paul, 247–282.

Heisenberg, W. (1971). *Physics and beyond* (A. J. Pomerans and R. N. Anshen, eds.). New York: Harper & Row.

Husserl, E. (1962). *Ideas* (W. R. Boyce-Gibson, trans.). New York: Collier.

——— (1965). "Philosophy as a rigorous science," *Phenomenology and the crisis in philosophy* (Q. Lauer, trans.). New York: Harper & Row, 71–147.

——— (1970a). *Cartesian meditations* (D. Cairnes, trans.). The Hague: Nijhoff.

——— (1970b). *The crisis of European science and transcendental phenomenology* (D. Carr, trans.). Evanston: Northwestern University.

——— (1970c). *The idea of phenomenology* (W. Alston and G. Nakhnikian, trans.). The Hague: Nijhoff.

Koestler, A. (1981). *The ghost in the machine.* London: Pan/Picador.

Kuhn, T. (1970). *The structure of scientific revolutions,* 2nd ed. Chicago: University of Chicago.

Laing, R. D. (1969). *The divided self.* Harmondsworth: Penguin.

——— (1984). *The politics of experience.* London: Pelican.

Lakatos, I. (1970). "The methodology of scientific research programmes," *Criticism and the growth of knowledge* (I. Lakatos and A. Musgrave, eds.). Cambridge: Cambridge University.

Lévi-Strauss, C. (1966). *The savage mind.* London: Widenfield and Nicolson.

Lubb, H. (1978). "Positivism and phenomenology: Mach and Husserl," *Phenomenology and sociology* (T. Luckman, ed.). Harmondsworth: Penguin.

Luckman, T. (1970). "On the boundaries of the social world," *Phenomenology and social reality: Essays in memory of Alfred Schutz* (M. Natanson, ed.). The Hague: Nijhoff, 73–100.

Merleau-Ponty, M. (1962). *The phenomenology of perception* (C. Smith, trans.). London: Routledge and Kegan Paul.

Nietzsche, F. (1967). *The will to power* (W. Kaufmann and R. J. Hollingdale, trans. and ed.). New York: Random House.

Popper, K. (1959). *The logic of scientific discovery.* London: Hutchinson.

Roszak, T. (1973). *Where the wasteland ends.* London: Faber & Faber.

Sartre, J. P. (1956). *Being and nothingness* (H. Barnes, trans.). New York: Philosophical Library.

Szatz, T. (1974). *The myth of mental illness*, rev. ed. New York: Harper & Row.

Werkmeister, W. (1968). *The basis and structure of knowledge*. New York: Greenwood.

9 • Heidegger and the Problem of World[1]

William J. Richardson

Marilyn Monroe died naked and alone under a rumpled bedsheet with the telephone in her hand. Whom had she been talking to, or trying to reach? We do not know. We do know that earlier in the day she had talked with her analyst, Ralph Greenson. We are told that she tried without success to reach Robert Kennedy, her man of the moment, who, father of a family and attorney general of the United States though he was, had promised, she claimed, to marry her and now was apparently trying to put a distance between them. She had talked with some intimate friends and others like Marlon Brando and Peter Lawford and the son of Joe DiMaggio. They noticed the increasing slur in her speech (but it was nothing new for Marilyn)—the autopsy would show blood levels of ten times the normal dose of phenobarbital and twenty times the normal dose of chlorohydrate. Clearly she was groping for whatever support her circle of people and things could give, but they were not enough. They all belonged to the "world" she knew, and it was this that had collapsed. And so, fired from her last film job as unemployable, with her career on the rocks, repudiated apparently by her last lover, Bobby Kennedy, frustrated forever (it seemed) in her desire to become a mother, addicted to alcohol and drugs, this 36-year-old sex symbol, verging on middle age, survivor of thirteen abortions and six previous suicide attempts, looked upon her "world" in shambles and, intentionally or not, died by an overdose of barbiturates—naked and alone.

Why do I write of her? Because she is still very much alive. Gloria Steinem (1986) added one more biography to the forty or so other books that deal with Monroe's life and death. Her image can be found in any poster shop; an exhibition on the history of portraiture in the Sackler Museum at Harvard begins with the earliest recorded death masks of 5,000 years ago but ends with Andy Warhol's tricolor silkscreen of . . . Marilyn Monroe. Thus alive, though dead, she offers us a convenient heuristic opportunity to reflect together for a few moments on what the "world," as we put it, meant to Marilyn Monroe and how it got its meaning, in order to raise the question as to whether another way of experiencing the "world" might have made a difference in the outcome of her life (see Steinem 1986, pp. 132–33).

The nature of the world precisely *as* world took on a new importance for philosophers in the twentieth century largely because of the influence of Martin Heidegger (1889–1976). His thought overflowed into psychiatry through the work of the Swiss psychiatrist and friend of Sigmund Freud, Ludwig Binswanger, who found some of Heidegger's early conceptualizations clinically helpful, and, more recently, through the work of another Swiss psychiatrist, Medard Boss, who elaborated an entire theory of psychotherapy based on Heidegger's terminology. If we are to get some appreciation of how Heidegger, or a Heideggerian, would look upon Marilyn Monroe's experience of the "world," we must begin by asking how the notion of world became problematic for Heidegger in the first place.

He was eighteen years old and at the educational level of a college sophomore (final year at the *Gymnasium* in Constance) when a priest friend gave Heidegger a copy of the doctoral dissertation of Franz Brentano, the well-known nineteenth-century scholastic whose lectures Freud had followed in Vienna. Its title was "The Manifold Sense of 'Being' in Aristotle," where *being* was the Greek *on* (the German *Seiendes*) and meant anything that "is." Now *is* can mean a great many things: if I say that it "is" now ———— P.M. while someone "is" here writing to you with the help of a word processor that "is" in operation while the city of Boston "is" all around him and God "is" (or "is" not) in heaven, *is* means something different each time. Yet there is some kind of common denominator. What is that common thing that supplies every specific being with its *is*? That is Heidegger's question. He calls it the "to be" (*Sein*) of whatever "is" (*Seiendes*)—the Being of beings, or the Is of what-is, as if it imparted to everything that is its power to manifest itself as being what it is.

This is how Heidegger describes, over fifty years later, the experience of reading Brentano's book:

On the title page of his work, Brentano quotes Aristotle's phrase: *to on legetai pollachôs*. I translate: "A being becomes manifest (i.e., with regard to its Being) in many ways." Latent in this phrase is the *question* that determined the way of my thought: what is the pervasive, simple, unified determination of Being that permeates all of its multiple meanings? . . . How can they be brought into comprehensible accord? This accord cannot be grasped without first raising and settling the question: Whence does Being as such (not merely beings as beings) receive its determination? [cited by Richardson 1976, p. x]

Traditional philosophy gave Heidegger no help, but Husserl's newly proposed method of phenomenology, he tells us, suggested a way to proceed. For Husserl, originally a mathematician, had sought to develop a method for philosophy that would be analogous to the rigor espoused by the natural sciences and could guarantee comparable success in the modern world—that is, through a close analysis of the phenomena of consciousness itself. Heidegger adapted the method to his own purposes, taking it to mean essentially "letting be seen/appear" (*legein*) those things "whose nature it is to appear" (*ta phainomena*). But what phenomenon in particular would he examine in this way? Precisely the very being that raises the question, for such a being must have some sense of what *to be* (*Sein*) means if he uses the word *is* all the time. Heidegger calls that being *Dasein* because of its peculiar relationship to being (*Sein*). This is an old German word to which he has given a new meaning that restricts it to designate a human being. He captures the same meaning in the word *existence* that he sometimes writes "ek-sistence" to suggest the notion of the human being as standing (*-sistere*) outside of (*ek-*) itself and toward the to-be/Being of whatever is. Eventually he uses the word *transcendence* to suggest the same thing: the passage beyond beings to Being. Whatever the terminology, this is what he means by the human *self*.

Dasein itself, then, would be the phenomenon that Heidegger must let-be-seen (let-be!) in terms of its awareness of what Being (*Sein*) means. But if we take Dasein as it appears to us in the coming and going of everyday life, the most that can be said about it to start with is Dasein is a being whose nature is "to-be-in-the-world." And so Heidegger begins to work out his approach to the Being-question in his major work, *Being and Time* (1962; first published in 1927), by letting Dasein be seen precisely as "Being-in-the-world," first by analyzing *world*, then the "to-be-in," subsequently the unity of the two in a single experience, and finally the source of this unity that he finds to be in the unity of time itself. And so the great work (*Being and Time*) proceeds.

The nub of Heidegger's analysis of the world that Dasein finds itself "in" lies in a distinction between (1) the network of people and things that surround us and make up the various intertwining segments of our daily lives (professional, personal, social, etc.) and (2) the larger context, the broader horizon of pervasive meaningfulness within which everything that is is encountered and takes its meaning. The former we can refer to as "my" "world" or "your" "world," or as one's "own" "world," or the "ontic" "world" (from Greek *onta* meaning the plurality of what is)—in short, a "world" made up of beings, even if taken in their totality. The latter is for Heidegger *the* world as such. Marilyn Monroe's "own" world on that last desperate day, for example, included the bed, the telephone, the four walls of her messy room, the pills, the swimming pool outside, the people she spoke with (e.g., Greenson) or did not speak with (e.g., Bobby Kennedy), the millions of fans who knew her only on the screen. All these beings had a meaning for her in one way or another, but a larger pattern was always already functioning to make that meaning possible. We become aware of that larger pattern, Heidegger argues, when something goes wrong in our own familiar world of every day. Suppose, for example, you were having a crucial telephone conversation with someone like Marilyn and for whatever crazy reason you were cut off. It would be easy to realize how complex was the skein of people this involved in that moment. Obviously the patient herself with all her tangled relationships would be implicated, but consider the phone itself and all that it involves. First there is the human world that invented it, then produced it. Then there is the physical world out of which it is fashioned, contributing resources that gestated for thousands of years, then the laws of the electromagnetic world reaching out beyond the stars to permit it to function. Yet all these numberless factors do not suffice to make the telephone work, for they presuppose something further— some all-pervasive pattern of meaningfulness that permits them to interrelate in some meaningful way. It is this web of beings plus the matrix that lets them be meaningful that is disclosed in the moment of breakdown. It is the matrix itself that Heidegger understands by *the world*, and since the analysis is made by Dasein and for Dasein, Dasein is its ultimate point of reference.

The tragedy of the Saturday afternoon in August 1962 was that there was no one who could help Marilyn Monroe discern a matrix of meaning beyond the pain of her disappointments, the world as such beyond the sum total of people and things that surrounded her and constituted her own particular "world." In a sense, this was the tragedy of her life. For the crumbling of the "world" about her on the day she took her life seems little more than the final consummation of an experience that took place when she was eight years old. She had already been in several foster homes, for her mother, abandoned by the lover and father of the child the very night that he learned of the pregnancy (Christmas Eve, 1926), had been unable to care for the baby and had paid other families to care for her. By the age of eight she was living with a friend of the mother referred to as "Aunt Grace." But this day Aunt Grace had plans of her own. Marilyn tells the story:

> My mother's best girlfriend at this time, Aunt Grace, was my legal guardian, and I was living in her home. But when she remarried all of a sudden, the house became too small, and someone had to go. . . . One day she packed my clothes and took me with her in her car. We drove and drove without her ever saying a word. When we came to a three-story brick building, she stopped the car and we walked up the stairs to the entrance. I saw this sign, and the emptiness that came over me I'll never forget. The sign read: *Los Angeles Children's Home.* I began to cry. "Please don't make me go inside. I'm not an orphan, my mother's not dead. I'm not an orphan—it's just that she's sick in the hospital and can't take care of me. Please don't make me live in an orphan's home!" I was crying and protesting—I still remember they had to use force to drag me inside that place. I may have been only eight years old, but something like this you never forget. The whole world around me crumbled. [Cited in Steinem, p. 28]

The world that crumbled was the world she was used to—that is, the world of people and things she knew and could presumably count on. The shock of abandonment shattered this world but by that very fact lit up the broader horizon of meaning that made it possible even to say that the ontic world had *lost* its meaning, had "crumbled."

There were other stark moments where her own world might have crumbled: for example, when she was about to be married for the first time she tried to contact her natural father, but when she announced herself as Norma Jeane, Gladys's daughter, he simply hung up on her; she tried a second time as Marilyn Monroe, but this time he directed his wife to give her the name of his lawyer in case she had any complaint. And that was that.

Once Heidegger has discerned the nature of the world to which a human being is exposed, he proceeds to talk about what it means to be "in" such a world. It certainly does not mean to be opposed to the world as a subject is opposed to an object, but rather to be "open" to it, to have access to it in such a way that one passes beyond the people and things that surround us to the world as matrix of meaning by reason of which all these things have relevance. He describes this passage as transcendence and analyzes different components in its movement.

Heidegger speaks first of a component called *understanding* (*Verstehen*), not as an intellectual function but as a power to disclose the world, like a searchlight. He speaks, too, of an ontological disposition (*Befindlichkeit*) as that component by reason of which we are capable of affect. There is, too, a component that makes it possible for us to articulate all this through speech. He calls it *Rede*, sometimes translated *discourse*, though I prefer *logos*. Finally, there is a component in the movement that he calls *fallenness* by reason of which there is a low center of gravity in humans that makes us tend to lose ourselves among the people and things around us and forget the great privilege of being open to Being itself, experienced at this point as the matrix of meaningfulness that is the world.

But Heidegger insists that transcendence thus understood is a very finite thing, permeated by many kinds of negativity. For example, people are not master of their own origin—they discover themselves as already "thrown" into the world. Moreover, particular individuals are not independent of other beings, these people and things that surround each of them. And not only is a person not independent of other beings but is even drawn toward them and tempted to lose oneself in them, like the victim of a cosmic undertow. Again, the person is not capable of experiencing the world in itself but only as not any being within the world, as no-thing (*Nichts*). Finally, the most limiting thing of all is that the person is Being-unto-an-end, and that end is death. He or she is Being-unto-death, not in the sense of being destined one day to die—that is no great news—but in the sense that death, the ultimate ending of every human being, has already placed its mark upon him or her. The moment Dasein begins to be, Dasein also begins to be finite. Dasein is Being-unto-limit, unto-end, unto-death. How is all this experienced in its unity? It is at this point that Heidegger makes his famous analysis of anxiety. For anxiety as he understands it is a foreboding in the presence not of a given thing, like a dentist's drill or an instrument of torture, but precisely of no-thing at all—of what remains when the "world" about us crumbles. It is no-thing and no-where, *das Nichts*.

There are lots of ways to describe the experience of the No-thing. One way is caught by Wallace Stevens in his poem "The Snow Man":

> . . . any misery in the sound of the wind,
> In the sound of a few leaves,
>
> Which is the sound of the land
> Full of the same wind
> That is blowing in the same bare place
>
> For the listener, who listens in the snow
> And, nothing himself, beholds
> Nothing that is not there and the nothing that is.
>
> [1982, pp. 9–10]

But in the presence of the No-thing, what is one to do? For Heidegger, it is the moment of opportunity. For it is then that Dasein hears the voice of a logos that wells up from its depths—this is how he understands conscience—a voice calling itself to become truly itself: transcendence trammeled with finitude. To this finitude Heidegger gives the name "guilt"—surely not moral but rather ontological guilt, the sum total of what Dasein lacks. The call to Dasein is to accept itself as what-it-is-and-is-still-coming-to-be. Heidegger's name for that acceptance is *resolve*. The result is an authoring of oneself both as transcendent and as finite that he calls *authenticity*.

There is one more major step. Heidegger now asks about the source of this experience of Being-in-the-world in this way and sees that it involves a movement in three directions. Dasein comes to itself through its openness to the world/Being—through this openness Being comes to it. This "coming" of Being to Dasein is what is called *future*. But it comes to a Dasein that *already* is—that is, is what it has been up to now—to Dasein as "past." And yet, this "coming" through Dasein as "past" lets the people and things within its "world" become "present" to Dasein and Dasein to them. This "presence" constitutes Dasein's "present." Future, past, and present: these are the dimensions of time. What gives unity to Dasein is the unity of time itself. And for Dasein to be authentic in terms of the temporality that constitutes it, it must say yes to the future as coming through its past, thus rendering possible whatever meaning is to be found in the present. It is at this point only that we can speak of the "truth" and "freedom" of Dasein's "self."

But all this sounds like so much theory. How would it work for a Marilyn Monroe? Between the time when she first felt the crumbling of the world that surrounded her and her last desperate cry against the disintegrating career in 1962, she was clearly dominated by what Heidegger would call (German) *das Man* (the French *on*)—that is, the tyranny of the common mind of what everybody says and does: the "they" of "what *they* are wearing in Paris this year," or "everybody" as in "everybody's doing it," of "people" as in "people will talk."

What "they" dictated to Marilyn Monroe was the primacy of her physical beauty over all else, which, in effect, left her the "prisoner" of her body (Steinem, pp. 137–56). Say if you will, as her biographer does, that she embodied the "big breasted beauty that symbolized women's return to home, hearth, childbearing, and togetherness after World War II. . . . Marilyn was made into a symbol of what a postwar woman should be" (Steinem, p. 95). But there was more to her appeal than a social phenomenon. There was an entire conception of womanhood: "'A woman needs to . . . well *support* a man, emotionally I mean. And a man needs to be strong. This is partly what it means to be masculine or feminine. I think it's terribly important to feel feminine, to act feminine. . . . Men need women to be feminine'" (p. 92).

And femininity for Marilyn Monroe meant becoming an object of physical beauty. "I daydreamed chiefly about beauty," she wrote in her unfinished autobiography. "I dreamed of myself becoming so beautiful that people would turn to look at me as I passed" (p. 138). Her body was her "magic friend," as she described it (p. 141). It may explain her penchant for, and comfort with, nudity. An object, then, for the vision of others. Her craving to be seen even stretched into one of the self-destructive habits that helped sabotage her career: her pathological lateness. "People are waiting for me," she explained. "People are eager to see me. I'm wanted. And I remember the years I was unwanted. All the hundreds of times nobody wanted to see the little servant girl Norma Jeane—not even her mother" (p. 157).

See her, then, in the first blossoming of her career standing in a strapless evening gown and sandals in the freezing cold before thirteen thousand GI's in Korea screaming for her over and over again. "It was the first time," she said later, "that I ever felt I had an effect on people" (p. 64). She was an object for them and an object for herself.

But femininity meant more than physical beauty, it meant sexual compliance as well. Though she entered her first marriage, arranged with a 21-year-old neighbor, innocent and naive, soon afterward she was discovered by a photographer while working in a wartime airplane factory and moved up from model to starlet to star; she learned that sex was the price of success and she paid it willingly. She bragged once that she was never a "kept woman" and refused at least one offer of marriage from a millionaire because she did not love him, but she did feel that sexual satisfaction was the only thing that she had to offer. Eventually she would use it compulsively simply as a way of achieving in however transient a fashion the childlike warmth and intimacy that she had never known. As Steinem summarizes the problem:

> Her sexual value to men was the only value she was sure of. By exciting and arousing, she could turn herself from the invisible, unworthy Norma Jeane into the visible, worthwhile Marilyn. She could have some impact, some power, some proof she was alive. The very compulsion to do that seems to have kept her from accepting her real self enough to find sexual pleasure of her own. Marilyn kept hoping that a relationship with a man would give her the identity she lacked, and that her appearance would give her the man. This impossible search was rewarded and exaggerated by a society that encourages women to get their identity from men—and encourages men to value women for appearance, not mind or heart. [p. 118]

Behind this compulsive need, of course, was that of the neglected child, whose father had rejected her, sight unseen, the very night he heard she was conceived. In any case, the whole masquerade had gone so far that at the end her mannerisms were so extreme that she was almost a female impersonator (p. 119), a parody of herself. As her analyst, Greenson, put it, "The main mechanism she used to bring some feeling of stability and significance to her life was the attractiveness of her body" (p. 154).

Having experienced herself as the female object both in the eyes of others and of herself, her first line of defense was to treat her body as an object and resort to drugs as the preferred instrument with which to deal with it. Some explain her drug dependence as beginning with a resort to drugs to deal with menstrual pain due to what has since been diagnosed as endometriosis. However that may be, in the later years she depended on drugs for everything: to put her to sleep, to wake her up, to stimulate her, to calm her, to relieve her of depression. Add to this her Bloody Marys for breakfast and champagne throughout the day. You can understand, then, how her famous "Happy Birthday" to Jack Kennedy in 1962, Marilyn standing in a transparent dress she had been sewn into, whispering in a doped slowness with long, sexy pauses, that for all its voluptuous seductiveness indicated a mind that seemed to have receded, as Arthur Schlessinger wrote later, "into her own glittering mist" (p. 128).

All of this adds up to the vision of a tortured woman, empty of self-worth, failing in her career, frustrated by her failure to have a child, dependent on drugs and alcohol to relieve her pain: a woman whose own world of people and things had fallen apart.

But in all this "glittering mist" there were signs of transcendence, too. I take this to mean that there was a sense of self that was not exploited by the glamor or the pain of her career as a sex symbol. I find this in that furtive claim on human dignity that could affirm that she was never a "kept" woman, that refused to marry for money when she could not marry for love, that appealed to her last photographer and would-be biographer: "Please don't make me a joke." I find index to this, too, in her well-known aspiration to develop in her a culture that she knew she lacked. She would study Renaissance books on anatomy and hang up studies of Titian and his school in her dressing room. Once an astrologer asked her if she knew that she, as a Gemini, was born under the same sign as Rosalind Russell, Rosemary Clooney, and Judy Garland. Her reply: "I know nothing of these people. I was born under the same sign as Ralph Waldo Emerson, Queen Victoria, and Walt Whitman" (p. 174). Her heroes were Albert Schweitzer, Albert Einstein, and especially Abraham Lincoln (p. 169). On the lot she would carry volumes of Shelley, or Keats, or Thomas Wolfe, or James Joyce, and once between rehearsals for her "dumb blonde" role in *All About Eve* she was found reading Rainer Rilke's *Letters to a Young Poet* (p. 169).

In all this, I take it that there was a yearning for something beyond the "world" of people and things she found about her toward something unknown and undefinable, something to which literary and artistic culture might give her access. Steinem puts it well, I think, when she describes these efforts as using a searchlight to explore the darkened World, the No-thing.

And there was a temporal dimension to this search, perhaps

slightly frenetic, but nonetheless suggesting that time itself was beneficent. In one of her final interviews she interrupted the conversation to say "Let us drink a toast to the future and what it holds in store" (p. 37), and at another moment: "There is a future and I can't wait to get to it." Her wedding picture with Arthur Miller is inscribed on the back "Hope, Hope, Hope" (p. 115).

But the hope she proclaimed and the future she aspired to are not to be found in the ontic world of the everyday. What hope there is in Heideggerian terms is grounded in a future that is still in advent. And the future that is still coming, for which she "waits" or "can't wait," is not just some golden tomorrow that lies over the rainbow "only a day away," but, in Heidegger's terms, the ad-vent of Being and meaning that can come to us only as already what we have been—that is, a future that comes *through* the past.

This means that treatment of Marilyn Monroe in terms of philosophy of "existence" would involve the achieving of authenticity, hence of making her own, of authenticating the past through which the future comes. In her case it would have meant making her own, of "owning," the tendency toward depression that hospitalized both her mother and grandmother before her; of "owning" the abandonment by a mother who could not take care of her, by a father who would not even acknowledge her; of "owning," therefore, the deprivation of the neglected child. This would have meant not only acknowledging the need in her for the parenting she never received and therefore sought in the sexual contacts that never satisfied her, but also the ephemeral transiency of the people and things in which she had placed her trust: her beauty, her youth, her career, her potential motherhood. All these were defined by possibilities that had been exploited and limited by choices that were already foreclosed.

If all had gone well, then, the result would have been the capacity to recognize the sign of death on everything she said or did. This would not have meant the desire to hasten the moment of ontic death, if that is really what happened on August 6, 1962. It would simply have meant that this is the tragic sign of the human condition itself and in her it simply went by her proper name.

Note

1. Presentation prepared for Symposium on Psychiatry and Continental Philosophy at the 140th annual meeting of the American Psychiatric Association, 12 May 1987, Chicago.

References

Boss, M. (1979). *Existential foundations of medicine and psychology* (S. Conway and A. Cleaves, trans.). New York: Jacob Aranson.

Heidegger, M. (1962). *Being and time* (J. Macquarrie and E. Robinson, trans.). New York: Harper and Row.

Richardson, W. J. (1976). *Heidegger through phenomenology to thought*, 3rd ed. Preface by M. Heidegger. The Hague: Nijhoff.

Steinem, G. (1986). *Marilyn*. Text by G. Steinem, photographs by G. Barris. New York: Henry Holt.

Stevens, W. (1982). *Collected Poems*. New York: Vintage (Random House), 9–10.

10 • On Becoming a Subject: Lacan's Rereading of Freud

Debra B. Bergoffen

For Sigmund Freud and Jacques Lacan, to be born a human being is to be given the task of becoming a human subject. Neither analyst considers subjectivity to be a birthright. Both agree that it is an achievement, the outcome of a complex and staged process that requires individuating acts of separation, integration, and self-constitution. They also agree that this achievement is never an accomplished fact. That is, in looking at the process of becoming a human subject, we are not in the presence of a mechanical, linear, developmental process with a clear beginning, middle, and end, but rather, we are confronted with a progressive/regressive movement characterized by breaks, lures, and lurches. Every movement forward requires a letting-go of a given mode of being. A cut must be made. Toward what end? From what motive? Toward a higher, more complex, more complete mode of integration that promises to meet desire's aims more fully. However, if the lure of the bait is falsified in the living of the promise, the dynamics of regression take hold. Lines of nostalgia resurface the breakpoint, and the subject returns to earlier, more secure modes of being. Freud and Lacan agree that the difficulties of this process are reflected in the fragility of the result. The question between them concerns the task at hand.

In what follows I will examine the Freudian and Lacanian accounts of the becoming of the human subject. Beginning with Freud's analyses in *The Three Essays on the Theory of Sexuality* and *The Ego and the Id*, I will describe the ways in which Lacan's appropriation of the Freudian perspective moves the center of attention from sexual identity to language as it questions the ego's claims of occupying the place of the subject.

SEXUALITY: INFANTILE AND OTHERWISE

The scandal of Freud's *Three Essays* was twofold. First, it insisted on the importance of the instincts. The instinct theory and its correlate, the doctrine of the unconscious, challenged all Cartesian notions of subjectivity and all tabula rasa epistemologies. Reason was unseated from its foundational position; the idea that the human being passively absorbs impressions was rejected. Instead of being presented as a thinking subject, the human being was portrayed as an active, desiring being who is neither autonomously rational nor easily assimilated into the social order. The rule of reason and assimilation was replaced with the regime of desire and conflict.

The second scandal of this pioneering work was its refusal of biological determinism. According to the arguments of the *Essays*, biology is not destiny. Though one is born a sexed body, it is not through the physiology of sex, but through the psychology of desire that one becomes a gendered subject. That is, the ways in which one comes to embody or live one's sex, and not the sex itself, effect one's living of desire. Defenders of reason found Freud's instinct theory abhorrent. Advocates of the instincts refused his distinction between sex and gender. To no one's surprise, least of all Freud's, the *Essays* found few early champions.

Though no longer scandalous, the *Essays* remain provocative. A central Freudian text, it introduces us to Freud's theses of sexuality and subjectivity, and schools us in his method of suspicion. As in several of his other works, Freud begins with what everyone takes to be the facts-of-the-matter. He writes:

> Popular opinion has quite definite ideas about the nature and characteristics of this sexual instinct. It is generally understood to be absent in childhood, to set in at the time of puberty in connection with the process of coming to maturity and to be revealed in the manifestations of an irresistible attraction exercised by one sex upon the other; while its aim is presumed to be sexual union, or at all events actions leading in that direction. [1962, p. 1]

And as in many of his other works, Freud immediately begins to subject these so-called facts to psychoanalytic scrutiny.

Introducing the principle of suspicion, Freud devotes the remainder of the first essay to undermining the second and third commonsense truths of sexuality—the idea of the irresistible nature of the heterosexual attraction and the idea that the aim of sexual activity is "union." The challenge to the first of these commonsense truths, that of childhood sexual innocence, will come later. Though it is the falsity of this first idea rather than the falsity of the other two that is critical to his theory of subjectivity, it cannot be immediately or directly attacked; for of all the truths of sexual common sense, this one is held most tenaciously.

The principle of suspicion begins with easier targets. It presents evidence of sexual deviance in such a way as to establish three points: (1) the phenomenon of sexual deviance is too widespread to be dismissed as a mere aberration; (2) what we now condemn as deviant behavior was, in other times and places, accepted as normal and even admirable—for example, homosexuality in ancient Greece; and (3) people whose sexual behavior deviates from the accepted norm cannot be classified as degenerate, their behavior in other areas being quite normal.

The point of Freud's extensive discussion of deviance is not intended to convince us of its normalcy. It is at once more radical and more conservative. Radically, if we read the first essay in light of the second's analysis of polymorphous infantile sexuality, there is no room for the truth of common sense. Conservatively, if we read the first essay in light of the second's reference to perversion and the third's analysis of the Oedipus complex, we find that though Freud refuses to condemn sexual aberrations morally, he nevertheless finds them to be immature expressions of human sexuality and therefore to be less healthy than structurings of desire for heterosexual union. From this perspective, though common sense is clinically mistaken and morally oppressive, it has a point: it is an adequate assessment of psychological maturity and health.

The ambiguities and shifts of the *Essays* reflect the rhythms of the sexual-subjective development they describe. Beginning with comfortable fantasies, we are not allowed to remain with them. The impact of reality forces us to reconsider our position. With each movement away from an illusion, we gather strength for more difficult moves. But there are limits to our ability to confront the truth. When reality becomes too frustrating, too harsh, too difficult to acknowledge, we effect a compromise. As developing subjects we repress the pleasures of infancy so that heterosexual requirements can be met. As a psychoanalyst Freud allows the phenomenon of infantile sexuality to escape repression, provided it allows the standards of heterosexuality to prevail. The aim of the

Essays is to undo the amnesia of repression without threatening the structure of procreative sexuality.

The strategy of the first essay is to justify our suspicion of common sense to the point that we are willing to suspend our belief in the truth of its most powerful assertion: sexuality emerges at puberty. In establishing the distinction between the sexual instinct, its object, and its aim, the first essay undermines the concept of perversion. This undermining carries two important implications: (1) sexuality is not an original gestalt, but a complex integration of distinct elements; and (2) desire is not brought to us from or through the other—it is always already present within us. These implications ground the analyses of the second essay. The doctrine of infantile sexuality develops the meanings of the already-thereness of desire. The doctrines of maturation and development explore the means by which the discrete elements of sexuality evolve into integrated patterns of being.

In affirming infantile sexuality, the second essay transforms human sexuality from a genital activity to a bodily desire. The infant's body is the site of polymorphous sexual pleasure. Instead of simply focusing on the phenomenon of the polymorphous, however, and mapping the multiple sites of infantile desire, Freud refers to infantile sexuality as *polymorphous perverse*. Perverse? After teaching us in the first essay that labeling certain sexual practices *perversions* is a culturally biased rather than an objective judgment, how can Freud introduce the concept *perversion* without being guilty of the same sin he found in common sense? How can he use the term *perverse* and pretend to be offering a scientific-psychoanalytic account of sexuality?

The introduction of the term *perverse* is significant. It marks the ambiguous legacy of Freud's thought. On the one hand, it is a sign of his limitation; for the polymorphous pleasures of the infant can only be called *perverse* from the standpoint of genital sexuality. With the appearance of the term *perverse*, we are warned that however radical Freud's analyses may appear, they are not directed toward dethroning the claims of genital heterosexuality, but rather intended to ground the claims of heterosexual normalcy on psychoanalytic rather than moral principles.

On the other hand, the use of the term *perverse* indexes Freud's theory of sexual identity and development. Recalling that the point of the first essay was not to refute the concept of perversion, but to reject the idea that perversions are unnatural, we find that Freud is making the point that though natural, the perversions are infantile—that is, something to be overcome, left behind.

By linking the infantile polymorphous with the perverse, Freud tells us that the widespread incidence of sexual perversions is not, as moralists would have it, a sign of human depravity, but instead the mark of the powers of memory, nostalgia, repetition, and regression. A comparison may prove helpful here. Mobility, like sexuality, is a developed behavior. Crawling precedes walking. In learning to walk the infant discovers more satisfying, more efficient ways of fulfilling its desire to move about the world. To incorporate walking into its life, however, the infant must give up crawling. This does not happen all at once, but once it happens, it is over. We do not have evidence of cultures that value adult crawling, and we do not discover cases of "closet crawlers."

The situation with sexuality is quite different. Here there is no definitive leaving-behind of the pleasures of infancy. They are either incorporated into accepted adult practices as foreplays or remain pleasures in their own right, perversions. Here, the instinct may find itself in conflict with the requirements of maturation. According to Freud, maturation demands that the polymorphous body orient itself around the genitals. Though adults generally respond to these demands, they never do so completely. Genital sexuality is not analogous to walking. The memories of past pleasures draw us into the dynamics of repetition. Why, how, and when these dynamics threaten particular structures of mature sexuality is a matter of individual psychology. At the theoretical level, Freud's task will be to explain the fragile nature of mature sexuality and, by implication, adult subjectivity.

In exploring the question of infantile sexuality, Freud addresses the questions: Why the centrality of sexuality? Why is sexuality the only instinct intertwined with subjectivity? His answer is brief but powerful: because the sexual instincts are anaclitic. That is, they are neither localized nor specified, but achieve satisfaction by insinuating themselves into other instinctual activities. While hunger instincts can be satisfied by only one bodily organ, the mouth, and one bodily activity, eating, sexual instincts can be satisfied by the entire body (Freud 1962, p. 50, fn. 1) and by a multitude of activities: touching, defecating, sucking, etc. Sexuality pervades our embodied being. As the desire for bodily pleasure, all bodily activities are available to it. It is through the sex instinct that we explore the body and discover its erotic possibilities, and it is through these explorations and discoveries that we articulate our subjectivity. Further, though all instinctive behavior is repetitive, the repetitions of the sex instinct are creative as well as reduplicative.

Freud uses the phenomenon of thumb-sucking to make his points, justifying the identification of thumb-sucking as a sexual activity by appealing to the judgments of others and to the insights of psychoanalytic investigations. Its value as an example lies in its public everydayness. Though people might reject the idea that masturbation is commonplace, they cannot deny the prevalence of thumb-sucking. If thumb-sucking is sexual, then the pervasiveness of infantile sexuality will have to be acknowledged.

Several things are striking about Freud's account of thumb-sucking infantile sexuality (see Freud 1962, pp. 47–48). First, though this sexual pleasure is originally experienced spontaneously and in connection with the satisfaction of a nonsexual need, the first experience generates a new need, the need to repeat, and a new recognition, that the pleasures experienced in taking food were not solely nutritional. In recognizing the distinction between sexual and nutritional pleasures, the infant is led to explore its body for other sources and sites of sexual satisfaction. Further, the bodily exploration has a twofold agenda, pleasure and autonomy. While hunger needs drive the infant toward the other, sexual needs turn the infant toward itself. Hence the plasticity of the sexual instinct provides us with a unique repetition compulsion. While the memory of the original pleasure activates the search for renewed satisfaction, the search is not a simple looking for a lost object. It is, instead, a search for a substitute object. It is a discovery mission. The infant will create its own ways and sites of satisfaction.

There is one more feature of this activity of thumb-sucking that is critical to an understanding of infantile sexuality: though the new form of satisfaction is superior to the old in its availability (the thumb is always ready-at-hand; the breast is not), it remains an inferior source of pleasure (Freud 1962, p. 48). The satisfactions of thumb-sucking cannot compete with the original pleasures of the breast. Freud says that this inferiority will lead the infant from auto-erotic to other-directed modes of sexuality, but he also notes that the power of the memory of the original pleasure draws us backward. The repetition compulsion is not always drawn to serve the developmental dynamics of maturation.

The Ego and the Id will give this power of memory a name, the death instinct, and a crucial psychic function, aggression. A critical feature of psychic life emerges between the analyses of sexuality in the *Essays* and the identification of the death instinct in *The Ego and the Id*—namely, the power of nostalgia. This power may be used to serve or undermine the developmental processes, but however it functions, it is always present. The need to repeat, to return, to refind must be identified as an essential feature of the human subject.

In pursuing the auto-erotic pleasures of desire, the infant's nascent subjectivity is not yet gendered. The purpose of the third of the *Three Essays* is to complete the story of sexual development, to explain how the polymorphous perverse bisexuality of infants and children becomes the differentiated male-female heterosexuality of adults. In this third essay normalcy is equated with mental stability, and the engendering of one's sexuality is identified as the most decisive factor of subjectivity.

Though Freud opened the *Essays* by arguing against the idea that sexuality originates in puberty, he concludes the essays by arguing that sexuality is transformed at puberty. Auto-erotic activities are replaced by other-oriented ones; polymorphous pleasures are moved to specific erotogenic zones; bisexuality is abandoned for heterosexuality. The narcissistic infant becomes a social being. Or put more psychoanalytically, the crises of the Oedipus complex reset the fantasies of the pleasure principle and drive the child to find new ways of re-creating the lost but remembered objects of desire.

As my intention here is to understand Lacan's rereading of Freud, this is not the place to examine the long and difficult history of the Oedipus complex within Freud's thought and within the psychoanalytic movement. What we need to see is how the structures of this complex are said to inform the subject and how they are reread by Lacan. Briefly told, the Oedipal story presumes an analogous sexual development for both sexes. The desiring infant is originally oriented toward itself and its mother. Enclosed in the fantasies of autonomy and omnipotence, it derives satisfaction from its own body and from the idea that it is the sole object of the mother's desire. With this beginning the penis is marked as the critical sexual object. The infant wishes to be the penis desired by the mother. The infant identifies itself with this desire and demands to be recognized as the mother's exclusive object of desire. With the father's entry into the Oedipal scene, the bisexuality of infancy is bifurcated. Sexual distinctions begin to infect desire. Under threat of castration by the father, the boy-child is forced to renounce its mother-directed desire. If it wishes to keep itself as the object of desire of the other (i.e., as the penis), it must find a substitute love object.

The story of the girl-child is more convoluted. Though she too must give up the mother, finding herself already castrated, the father's castration threat cannot be the source of her entry into the social order. His promise can be. He, or rather an uncastrated male like him, can give her the penis she desires. If she transfers her desire from the one who is *like* her (the castrated mother) to one who is like the one *unlike* her (the uncastrated father), she can transcend her castrated condition. A suitable male can give her what she does not have—a baby/penis.

In renouncing the mother as their object of desire, the boy-child and the girl-child accept the incest taboo of the social order, learn the lessons of repression, and incorporate the laws of the community into their psychic structures. There is a double movement here: in giving up the desire for the mother, the child moves out of the family constellation into the social order. The fantasies of auto-erotic narcissism are exchanged for the realities of genital heterosexuality. The child becomes detached from parental authority (Freud 1962, p. 93). With the choice of a proper (i.e., heterosexual) sexual object, the id-ego-superego structures of the subject fall into their appropriate psychic places. We all live happily ever after—at least if all goes well.

But often all does not go well. Infantile sexuality, the core of the human subject, is never obliterated. It may live itself out in sublimations, repressions, or perversions, but live itself out it must. Freud tells us that health resides in the sublimated living of sexuality, but whether this is defined as healthy because it insures an integration of individual, social, and species life, or because it best meets the needs of the human, desiring subject is unclear.

Anticipating *Civilization and Its Discontents*, Freud draws the *Essays* to a close by pointing to the inverse relationship between the free development of sexuality (subjectivity?) and the cultivation of civilization (1962, p. 108). A threat to psychic health, repression is nevertheless key to the psychic development necessary for collective human life. With this ambiguous ending we are left to ponder the place of the subject. Is it to be found in the repressed unconscious, the voice of conscience, or the sublimations of the ego? Is it all of these together? Reason would have us choose all three, but Freud has taught us to be suspicious of reason.

The problem of the subject is taken up again in *The Ego and the Id*. In introducing the concept of the death instinct, and replacing the unconscious, preconscious, conscious description of the psyche with the id, ego, ego-ideal description, Freud pursues his vision of the subject as somehow or sometimes eluding the control of consciousness, as showing itself in consciousness, and as being the point at which our species being, collective being, and individual being intersect. The Oedipal situation and crisis remains central to Freud's analysis. Building on the insights of the *Essays*, he examines the family romance with particular attention to the ego-ideal.

In the *Three Essays* Freud used the universality of infantile sexuality to argue for the universality of the Oedipus complex. In *The Ego and the Id* he uses the universality of the Oedipus complex to argue for the universality of the formation of the ego-ideal (Freud 1960, chapter 3). The complexities of ego-ideal formation illustrate the difficulty of identifying the subject. For while the *Essays* taught us that the subject is bodily, sexual, and gendered, *The Ego and the Id* shows us that living the sexually gendered body is anything but straightforward.

The ego-ideal is the heir of the Oedipus complex: its formation follows the psychic pattern of the ego becoming what it cannot have. Its uniqueness lies in its effect on the ego. For instead of becoming incorporated into the ego, the id initiates a split. Unable to rule as the pleasure principle, the id will rule under the sign of negation. As ego-ideal it will unleash the death instinct against the ego as it allows the libidinal Oedipus desires their due. As representative of the social order, the ego-ideal attacks the ego for its failure to live up to the requirements of morality. Its success in attacking the ego depends on the ego's identifying itself with the laws of conscience. Freud tells us that this identification is motivated by the castration fear, but more than fear is at work here. The law that prohibits the desire is the law of the one (the father) who possesses the desired object (the mother). Submission may be an act of fear. Identification is not. It is a substitution for/delayed satisfaction of the Oedipal wish. The desire to obey the law, as distinct from the fear of violating it, is an identification with the lawgiver, and the lawgiver is the one who has rights to the mother.

The ego-ideal, however, is not just a ruse of the id. It is also a ploy of the ego. For if the ego can represent itself to the id as its lost object, the ego may use its powers of seduction to control the desires of the unconscious. Thus the ego-ideal is also a way for the subject to preserve its primary narcissism. In addition to transforming my desire to destroy the authority who forbids my desire into a desire to be like the one who bars me from my desires, the ego-ideal also allows me to transform myself from an object of hatred to a loved object. The infant's auto-erotic, polymorphous, incestuous expressions of narcissism are called *perverse* and *forbidden*. The loved body cannot be loved in the face of the disapproval of the other. In forming the ego-ideal, I tell myself that I am or can become lovable to myself once more, that I am the one that the other (and I) desire me to be.

Freud calls the ego-ideal the most important development in the life of an individual and the species. We begin to see why. As the heir of the Oedipus complex, the ego-ideal marks the individual's move toward autonomy within the regime of what Lacan will call *the law of the father*. It refigures desire according to the law of repression and becomes the site of the play of the life and death instincts. As the expression of narcissism and the libido, the ego-ideal serves Eros. As the voice of conscience meting out punishment and guilt, the ego-ideal threatens the psyche and serves the instincts of death.

Given the significance of the ego-ideal, we would expect the analysis of its formations and functions to clarify the role of the ego and to show us the place of the subject. It does neither. As attentive readers, we discover that in introducing the splitting of the ego that establishes the ego-ideal, Freud has also created a dichotomy within the ego itself. The ego of the reality principle, the ego as the skin-surface of the id, as that part of the id turned toward the world and as that which mediates between the demands of the instincts and the requirements of survival, has been joined by another ego, the narcissistic ego that seeks to establish itself as the love object of the ego-ideal. This second ego pursues the desires of its narcissistic wish by alienating itself from its immediate libidinal desires. To fulfill its desire to be loved by the ego-ideal, it will become the other desired by the otherness within itself. *The Ego and the Id* seems to take no notice of this bifurcating of the ego. It offers no discussion of the possible relationship between these two strains of the ego and no pronouncement that would allow us to call one but not the other an alienation of the ego.

If we refer to the earlier essay, "On Narcissism," however, we discover that this narcissistic mode of ego-being reflects a primordial structure of the ego. Depending on whether we take *primordial* to mean *infantile* (as in something to be transcended) or *foundational* (as in something that defines), we might privilege or subordinate this narcissistic ego to the ego that mediates desire according to the rules of the reality principle. Our decision would go a long way toward determining whether we see the ego as the site of the subject or its alienation.

In searching for the subject we are confronted with two questions: (1) What is the relationship between the ego and the id, and where in the context of this relationship does the subject lie? And (2) To which depiction of the ego are we referring when we refer to the ego, the ego that pursues the paths of sublimation required by the reality principle, or the ego that submits to the repressions of the ego-ideal?

The quarrel between Lacan and the ego psychologists reflects, in part, the ambiguities of the Freudian text. In situating the subject within the ego rather than the id, ego psychologists identify the ego with the forces of sublimation and the activities of sublimation with the subject. Their claim to be Freud's legitimate heirs is supported by such texts as "psychoanalysis is an instrument to enable the ego to achieve a progressive conquest of the id" (Freud 1960, p. 46) and "analysis does not set out to make pathological reactions impossible, but to give the patient's ego *freedom* to decide one way or the other" (Freud 1960, p. 40, fn. 1).

Lacan rages against this prioritizing of the sublimating ego. He agrees that this "ego represents what may be called reason and common sense" (Freud 1960, p. 15) but reminds us that Freud teaches us to be suspicious of reason and common sense. In refusing to identify the subject with the ego, Lacan is supported by such texts as: "the ego is . . . only a . . . modified part" of the id (Freud 1960, p. 30), and "the ego is that part of the id which has been modified by the direct influence of the external world" (Freud 1960, p. 15), and:

> We shall now look upon an individual as a psychical id, unknown and unconscious, upon whose surface rests the ego, developed from its nucleus. . . . We may add that the ego does not completely envelope the id . . . [and it] is not sharply separated from the id; its lower portion merges into it. [Freud 1960, p. 14]

The ambiguities of the text, however, point to the ambiguity of the issue. They suggest that the subject sometimes seems to be at the site of the ego and sometimes at the site of the id because the demarcation between the ego and the id is elusive. In Freud's words:

> Moreover, one must not take the difference between ego and id in too hard and fast a sense, nor forget that the ego is a specially differentiated part of the id. The experiences of the ego seem at first to be lost for inheritance; but when they have been repeated often enough and with sufficient strength in many individuals in successive generations, they transform themselves, so to say, into experiences of the id, the impressions of which are preserved by heredity. Thus in the id, which is capable of being inherited, are harboured residues of the existences of countless egos; and, when the ego forms its super-ego out of the id, it may perhaps only be reviving shapes of former egos and be bringing them to resurrection. [1960, p. 28]

Perhaps, then, the question needs to be reformulated and refocused. Instead of trying to determine whether to *identify* the subject with either the ego or the id, perhaps we should ask whether and in what sense the ego might be said to *represent* the subject.

SITUATING THE SUBJECT

In his rereading of Freud, Lacan attempts to secure the place of the subject. Beginning with Freud's analyses of (1) embodiment and desire, (2) the Oedipal drama, and (3) the repression/repetition dynamics of the psyche, Lacan attends to the ways in which the question of the other permeates psychic development. For Lacan the alienating power of the other predates the Oedipal crisis and complicates its resolution. While he follows Freud in marking the crucial function of the Oedipal complex, Lacan situates the Oedipal scene within the context of a prior dramatic site, the mirror stage, in which the child sees itself (its signifier) in a mirror and thereby discovers its meaning.[1] The effect of this resiting is to move the center of the drama from sexuality to language and to remove the ambiguities surrounding the question of the ego. For Lacan, the ego is not the subject. As a presence, the ego is a representation of the subject. Insofar as the ego equates itself with the subject and refuses to recognize the spaces that separate the subject from its representations, the ego is an alienating *imago*. In his insistence on the bar that separates the signified (the subject) from its signifiers (its ego manifestations), Lacan presents us with a subject whose presence is best defined as absence (1977, p. 299).

Freud's analyses of infantile sexuality pointed to, but did not focus on, the move from the infant's fragmented experience of its body to its experience of itself as embodied. Though the infant's earliest satisfactions of desire are auto-erotic, according to the *Essays* the narcissism of auto-eroticism emerges only after the infant integrates the discrete sites of its sexual satisfactions into a single body of polymorphous sexual sites. The embodied ego is not a given of infantile sexuality. It is a product of the dynamics of desire.

The discussions of *The Ego and the Id* augment these discoveries of the *Essays* by pointing to the ways in which the embodied ego embodies the egos of others. It will be left to Lacan to resituate the otherness of the ego from its place in the ego ideal and the collective unconscious to a position within the embodied ego. Whereas for Freud the alienation implications of the other begin their play in the Oedipal scene and are played out in the post-Oedipal aggressions of the superego, for Lacan the drama begins much earlier. The impact of the mirror stage is that the dynamics of alienation and otherness are active in the earliest formations of the psyche.

In this sense, the postulate of the mirror stage may be seen as an attempt to answer the question imbedded in Freud's observation that

> it is impossible to suppose a unity comparable to the ego can exist in the individual from the very start; the ego has to develop. . . . There must be something added to auto-eroticism . . . in order that narcissism may come into being. [1959, p. 34]

The imbedded question is, What is added to auto-eroticism that brings narcissism and its ego into being? Lacan answers: the infant's love of its bodily parts becomes a love of its embodiment through the mediation of the mirrored ego *imago*.

This answer does more than fill a gap. It revises Freud's account of the ego on three counts. First, it equates the ego with its narcissistic mode rather than with the perception conscious system (Lacan 1977, p. 6). Second, it describes the ego's narcissism as grounded in a fundamental *méconnaissance* (misrecognition). And third, it collapses the distinction between the ego and the ego-ideal by attributing to the ego the alienations and aggressions of the Freudian ego-ideal. In rejecting Freud's account of the child's entry into the social register, Lacan is not undermining the importance of the Oedipus complex but offering an alternative explanation of its significance. According to Lacan, the Oedipus complex propels the human being into the social order by disrupting the imaginary, not by splitting the ego.

The evidence for the mirror stage is concrete, clear, and concise. The human infant's reaction to encountering an image of itself is profoundly different from the reaction of other animal infants. Whereas other animals soon grow bored with their reflected image, humans react with sustained jubilation. Unlike the chimpanzee that wants to explore the reality of the image, the infant wants to play with it. Unlike the monkey that masters the image and finds it empty, the child is fascinated with the ways in which the image reduplicates its gestures. Though the infant is capable of recognizing itself in its image before the chimpanzee, the infant becomes captivated by its image in ways foreign to the animal.

In recognizing itself in the mirror, the infant mistakes the image for itself, it misrecognizes itself. The clumsy infant identifies itself with an *imago*, setting into play the dynamic whereby the image will determine the infant's identity and future development. In Lacan's words:

> The mirror state is a drama whose internal thrust is precipitated from insufficiency to anticipation and which manufactures for the subject . . . the succession of phantasies that extends from a fragmented body image to a form of its totality . . . and lastly to the assumption of the armour of an alienating identity which will mark with its rigid structure the subject's entire mental development. [1977, p. 4]

The infant's jubilant response to its mirror image is a reflection of its desire to escape its fragmented condition. The image reflects the fulfillment of this desire. Look, it says, you are/can be this self-sufficient, autonomous, integrated unity. If you model yourself on me, you will become the object you desire to be. The vision of the promise is also and at the same time the image of alienation. The process of the ego's domination of the subject begins when the infant/subject submits itself to the specificity of the *imago*. In becoming captivated by its *imago*, the infant/subject rejects both its fragmentation and its fluidity. The infant assumes its image in its fixity and thereby fixes the structure of its development.

In the 1949 version of the mirror stage theory, Lacan accounts for this unique dynamic of recognition/misrecognition/alienation by recalling the premature birth of the human being. Unlike other animals born on time—that is, fully developed at birth—humans are born too early. They enter the world incomplete, uncoordinated, and totally dependent. This human insufficiency establishes a unique relationship between the infant and its image. Whereas the chimp may be said to recognize itself in its image, this cannot be said for the infant. The image of coordinated motor activity, effectively relating to the surrounding environment, is not a reflection of the infant's immediate experience. On the contrary, it is a disconfirmation of the immediacy of experience.

In this early formulation of the mirror stage theory, Lacan isolates ego formation from the dynamics of the social register. The specular I of the mirror stage is distinguished from the social I of paranoic alienation (Lacan 1977, p. 5). After 1953, however, this barrier between desire and the mirror stage is broken. Now the identification of the infant with the image is fueled by the infant's desire to be the desired of the other. According to Lacan's final accounts of the mirror stage, in identifying with its bodily image the infant masks its fragmentation as it identifies itself with a suitable object for the other's desire (Simiu 1988).

In allowing the dynamics of the desire to be the desired of the other to begin their play prior to language, Lacan opens the way to return to Freud's question of the *Narcissism* essay: What is added to auto-eroticism that accounts for the identification by which the narcissistic ego is brought into being? The appropriate response would seem to be, the desire to be the desired of the other. It seems possible, however, to push this dynamic of desire still further. That is, it appears possible to suggest (1) that prior to the desire to be the desired of the other there is the desire to be one's own object of desire, (2) that this desire is born of an experience of lack, and (3) that it is the interplay between this experience of lack and the desire to be one's own desire that brings about the narcissistic identification with the mirror image.

On this possibility the function of the image would be twofold. It would transform the infant's immediate experience of itself as being capable of haphazard activity into a mediated experience of itself as lacking coordination. That is, in referencing itself to the integrated bodily image, the infant would transform its lived experience of being fragmented into an experience of lack. The sight of itself as what it is not would then be seen as a vision that simultaneously images a lack, the cut of desire, and its fulfillment. In identifying with the image, the infant allows desire the power to transform the immediacy of its experience and inform its development. From now on, it will experience itself as/through the image with which it has identified. Thus it is as the disconfirmation of the infant's immediate experience that the mirror can function as the site of the origin of desire.

On this account, in encountering its image in the mirror, the infant encounters the *imago* of its desire. Its experience of lack, however, is a simultaneous experience of the possibility of lack overcome. The image promises the infant that its experience of fragmentation is/will be surpassed as the image lures the infant to structure its desire in the register of the imaginary. Were the mirror's promise grounded in pure recognition, its teleology would simply be a teleology of self-realization. Because the promise is grounded in an identification that is a misrecognition, the teleology of self-realization is also, and at the same time, the bait of alienation.

Lacan's refusal to interpret the infant's jubilation as a sign of self-recognition may be seen as a mark of his break with the traditions of Western philosophy insofar as they are marked by Plato. Further, his refusal to appeal to Freud's allusions to the nirvana phenomenon to explain the mirror stage signals his sensitivity to the dangers of assimilating, instead of disjoining, the Platonic and Freudian discourse of the subject. Had Lacan pursued Freud's allusions to the nirvana principle, he might have surmised that the image of the coordinated body triggers the infant's memories of its prenatal existence, thereby allowing it to recollect its self/itself. On this account, the infant's jubilation might be understood in the following way: the mirror reflection images the infant's fetal experiences of wholeness. It is against these experiences that the infant experiences its lived reality as fragmentation and lack; from these experiences that the desire to transcend the given is born; and for these experiences that the infant recognizes the mirror image as a portrait of its lack overcome. From this Platonic/Freudian perspective, it is only by referring to its prenatal existence that the infant can place the givenness of its haphazard movements under the sign of a lack. From this stance the givenness of the fulfillment of fetal existence renders the facticity of the infant's postfetal existence disjunctive. Within this disjunction, the image of integrated activity reflects the experience of fulfillment and the givenness of random activity registers as an experience of want.

After prenatally experiencing itself as a complete, fulfilled unity, the infant now experiences itself as wanting, fragmented, and uncoordinated. In recalling the infant to its fetal past of fulfilled desire, the image projects the infant toward a future of desire fulfilled. The projection, however, is not straightforward. The present presentation is an image of past and future simultaneously. The image is embraced as a reflection of the present on the basis of a recollected past. The retrospective recognition empowers the image, draws the infant to it, and through it, toward the infant's future.

As an attentive reader of Freud, Lacan cannot have been unaware of these Freudian means of accounting for the infant's fascination with its reflected self. Based on his account of the motivations of the infant's jubilation, we may see this neglect of Freud's suggestive nirvana possibility as a mark of Lacan's understanding of Freud's distinctiveness. For to suggest that the lure of the image is a sign of the power of fetal memories ties the dynamics of the unconscious so closely to the facts of biology and the Platonism of recollection that the meaning of psychoanalysis's break with positivism and philosophy is undone.

Though Lacan's first account of the mirror stage has a biological referent, his final account eschews biology entirely. Further, there remains a crucial difference between Lacan's early biological references and those suggested by the nirvana experience. On the nirvana model, the prenatal infant might be said to experience itself as a subject and might be said to be a subject subjected to amnesia at birth. The implications of this return to the Platonic themes of recollected subjectivity, however, undermine the dynamics of subjectivity proposed by Freud. Sensitive to this danger, Lacan uses biology differently in his original account of the mirror stage. There biology is aligned with the desire to become a subject rather than with the desire to retrieve an already present but forgotten subjectivity. Whether we go by the earlier or later accounts of the mirror stage, and whether we are willing to situate desire prior to the dialectic of self and other, we find that the themes of misrecognition and alienation are crucial. What is unique to Lacan's account of human subjectivity is not simply the claim that it is grounded in desire, but more dramatically the claim that human desire expresses itself in alienated forms and that its alienations are inextricably bound up with the formation of the ego. In comparing the infant with the chimpanzee we find that the human, unlike the animal, is not rooted in the reality principle. The human has no desire to unmask the imagery of its vision.

The story of the mirror stage now reads as follows: in providing the infant with an experience of itself as an integrated whole, the image awakens and structures the infant's desire. In identifying with its *imago* the infant brings otherness into itself; for it is as other that the image elicits the infant's desire, and it is for the other that the infant embraces its image. The identification of the mirror state is not a pure *méconnaissance*, however, for though the infant is not its image, it is as this projected image that it appears in the world among others. Thus the mirror-stage misrecognition is a form of recognition. The figure of myself imaged to me is the figure of myself given to the other. It is as this image that I am the object of the other's desire. Insofar as I recognize the discontinuity between my experienced and imaged selves, I cannot be the desired of the other. The desire of the desire to be the desired of the other asserts itself by repressing the discontinuity. I become the image, an ego, the object of the other's desire.

In addition to delineating the processes of alienation and identification, the mirror stage also helps us understand aggressivity. The mirror stage is one of the points where Lacan joins the problems of aggressivity and narcissism (Lacan 1977, p. 18). According to Lacan, to understand human aggressivity we need to understand

> [the erotic relation] in which the human individual fixes upon himself an image that alleviates him from himself, . . . [in which is found] the passions that he will call the ego is based. [1977, p. 19]

The relationship between this eroticism and aggressivity is explained by John Muller and William Richardson, who write:

> When the unifying image of the ego integrates the original organic disarray the subject experiences . . . a narcissistic passion . . . this energy converts into primitive aggressivity whenever the integration—i.e., the fragile unity of the ego is threatened. . . . The aggressive imago of . . . fragmentation is the inversion of the gestalt of . . . unification. [1982, p. 49]

As the image of the unified body calls forth narcissism and self-identification, the fragility of this subjective identification unleashes aggression. Any threat to its reality must be aggressively negated. In Lacan's words:

> What I have called the mirror stage . . . manifests the affective dynamism by which the subject originally identifies himself with the visual Gestalt of his own body in relation to the still very profound

lack of coordination of his own motility, it represents an ideal unity, a salutary *imago*; it is invested with all the original distress resulting from the child's intra-organic and relational discordance. [1977, pp. 18–19]

From this we are not surprised to learn that

the fragmented body . . . usually manifests itself in dreams when the movement of analysis encounters a certain level of aggressive disintegration in the individual. . . . Correlatively, the formation of the I is symbolized in dreams by a fortress or stadium. [Lacan 1977, pp. 4–5]

The narcissism bound up with the imago-ego is itself bound to the fear and aggression that is unleashed when damage to one's body or regression to the fragmented body is threatened. Aggressive intentions are given magical efficacy by *imagos*, specifically *imagos* of the fragmented body. As these *imagos* are part of the gestalt of aggression, they are also a part of the process of identification.

There is a third piece to this dialectic of the mirror stage, the identification with the other. Because infants first discover themselves in an external image, they confuse themselves with the images of others. We see this misidentification at work in the imitative play of children (eight months) where "the child antici-pates on the mental plane the conquest of the functional unity of his own body, which, at that stage is still incomplete on the plane of voluntary motility" (Lacan 1977, p. 18). Thus the mirror stage comes to an end in paranoiac alienation, in the deflection of the specular I into the social I—that is, in the misidentification of the subject with its own reflection and the misidentification of this reflected image with the image of the other.

From this we learn that the subject becomes an ego by a process of identification mediated by an image and that it is the image of the body that is critical to and central for the process of self-identification. As we first identify with a reflection of our own body, and then with the body of the other, images of otherness imbed themselves in the subject's awareness of itself.

The mirror stage is a paradigm of the dynamics of the imagi-nary. Its analytic importance is linked to the ways in which it articulates the relationship between the imaginary and the struc-tures of the ego, the alienating power of the other, narcissism, and aggressivity. Though a prelinguistic power and pre-Oedipal stage of being, the dynamics of the imaginary are never left behind. As the power of the imaginary is the formative and grounding power of the embodied ego, it is unavoidably entangled with the ego's entry into the field of language and movement through the Oedipal triangle.

The Oedipal situation introduces the child to the power of the symbolic. Without changing the Freudian script, Lacan transforms the meaning of the Oedipus complex. Like Freud, Lacan (1977, p. 311) insists that the dyadic mother-child relationship must become triangulated by the father if the child is to become a human subject. Both Freud and Lacan agree that the desire of the infant for the mother ensnares the child and that the powers of this enchantment-dependent-desire relationship can be broken only by what Lacan calls the *law of the father*. That is, the child must recognize that it is not the object of its mother's desire, that its body ego is not omnipotent, and that there is a law of desire outside itself to which it must submit. In centering their analyses of the psyche on the Oedipus complex, both Freud and Lacan make it clear that subjectivity cannot be equated with autonomy. For both, the human subject lives among others and contains otherness within itself; and for both, it is the otherness of the mother that constitutes a threat to the subject and the otherness of the father that saves the subject from the threat.

To pass through the Oedipus complex is to be transformed. More literal than Lacan, Freud attributes the transformative effect of the Oedipus complex to the collective unconscious and the fear of castration. Less literal than Freud, Lacan attributes the transformative effect of the Oedipus complex to the power of the symbolic. For Freud the fear of castration propels the child into the social order. In giving up its claims to the mother, the child escapes its dependency on her and embarks on the process of individuation. For Lacan the recognition of castration—first of the mother and then of oneself—not the fear of it, marks the significance of the Oedipus complex (Lacan 1977, pp. 282–89). Further, the issue does not concern the penis. It concerns the phallus. Whereas, according to Freud it is the boy-child's desire to keep its penis and the girl-child's penis envy that propel them into the social register, according to Lacan it is the boy- and girl-child's desires to be/have the phallus that place them in the symbolic order. Perhaps to avoid Freud's continued difficulty in deciphering the girl's route through the Oedipus complex, Lacan proposes to "reveal a relation of the subject to the phallus that is established without regard to the anatomical difference of the sexes" (1977, p. 282). Refusing to equate the phallus with a real or imagined organ, Lacan designates the phallus as the signifier of desire and, thereby, of the split within the subject effected by the repression of desire by which we enter the signifying chain of language (1977, p. 288).

By shifting the focus of the Oedipal drama from the penis to the phallus, the castration threat is desexualized. The desiring subject must recognize its finitude. It must restructure its desire to be the desire of the other. As castrated, the subject must recognize that it itself is not the phallus, as it pursues its desire to be recognized as the phallus. Its desire must somehow accept that the real, the promise of fulfilled desire signified by the phallus, is always and necessarily elusive.

In the imaginary play of the mirror stage, the infant identifies itself with the other of the reflected, integrated body. In the symbolic play of the Oedipal situation, the child, in its experience of the cut, comes to recognize the otherness of the other. Because it is not the father, the child cannot have the object of its desire (the mother). Because it is like the father, the child acknowledges the law of the father and uses the metaphoric possibilities of the law, the symbolic, to pursue substitute objects of desire (Lacan 1977, p. 67).

In passing through the Oedipal crisis, the child accepts the order of language and becomes a human subject. In suffering and recognizing its castration, in losing the mother as its object of desire and itself as the object of the mother's desire, the child, motivated by the desire to (re)find the lost object, engages in the metonymic, metaphoric substitutions of the symbolic order.

The pass through the Oedipal to the symbolic is not, however, an exit from the imaginary. Lacan's developmental model, like Freud's, is not linear. The dynamics of regression and repetition prevail. The imaginary is not confined to the prelinguistic; it exists wherever the illusion that the function of the signifier is to reflect the signified prevails (Lacan 1977, p. 150). Formed in the silence of the mirror spectacle, the ego learns to speak. According to Lacan, the voice of the alienating ego is displaced but not silenced by the Oedipal structuring of the subject. More strongly, the ego's speech continues to dominate the subject's discourse of desire. To force the subject to speak, or at least to allow it to be heard, the analyst must refuse to recognize the discourse of the ego (Lacan 1977, p. 130). According to Lacan, the analyst's silence forces the ego to attend to its speech and to recognize that the being it has given itself

> has never been anything more than his construct in the imaginary [and] . . . he rediscovers the fundamental alienation that made him

> construct it *like another* and which has always destined it to be taken
> from him *by another*. [1977, p. 42]

If the ego is the site of the subject's imaginary identifications, where is the site of the subject? Given what we know about the ego-ideal/superego, the only available place would seem to be the unconscious id, the domain of the repressed. But given what we know about the repressed, it hardly seems a likely candidate to be the subject. As the ego is the alienated other of the subject, the unconscious id is the unknown other of the subject. As the desire of the subject that is no longer at its disposal, the unconscious id functions within the subject as the discourse of the other. Its otherness goes beyond its inaccessibility, for when the unconscious reveals itself, it shows itself as the desire of self-recognition, the desire to be recognized by the other as the object it desires (Lacan 1977, pp. 58, 172). Another split, another voice of otherness, another vacant place.

In discovering the elusiveness of the subject, we encounter the domain of the real. As the imaginary is the position of identity and the symbolic is the realm of the cut, the real is the sought for but never found site. As real, the subject is constituted by speech without being what is spoken. It slips behind and underneath the bar of the signifier (Lacan 1977, pp. 160, 163–64). The language of the imaginary, the ego, is particularly unsuited to the task of capturing the subject because in claiming to enclose what cannot be fixed, the ego refuses the movement of language within which the subject shows itself. In Lacan's words:

> For this ego is notable in the first instance for the imaginary inertias
> that it concentrates against the message of the unconsciousness,
> operates solely with a view to covering the displacement constituted
> by the subject. [1977, p. 169]

Lacan's rereading of Freud pursues Freud's insight that psychology not physiology informs the identity of the embodied subject by focusing on the ways in which the subject's identity is a function of the relationship between desire and its representations. In developing the categories of the imaginary and the symbolic, Lacan is developing Freud's analysis of the dual power of language. For according to Freud, though language as the voice of the superego represses my desire and bars me from myself, language as the discourse of free associations, slips of the tongue, errors, and jokes reveals my desire to me.

NOTHING NEW

It is in his tirade against the ego that Lacan has been most frequently accused of veering away from, rather than digging into, his Freudian inheritance. To justify his claim that his attacks on the ego reflect the meaning of Freud's psychoanalytic insights, Lacan cites Freud's statement at the end of the *New Introductory Lectures*, *Wo Es war, soll Ich werden*[2] to insist that Freud identifies the ego as the place of the subject. Reading metaphorically rather than metonymically and noting that Freud does not say *das Es* ("the it/id") or *das Ich* ("the I/ego"), as was his custom when referring to the structures of his topography, Lacan insists Freud is not suggesting that the ego take the place of the id but is attacking the process whereby the ego attempts to dominate the subject. According to Lacan, Freud asks us to consider whether we should allow the ego to enthrone itself as the subject or whether we should insist that the ego recognize the alienations of its fixities and cease its usurpative tactics. Identifying the *Es* as the subject and the *Ich* as the I, Lacan reads *Wo Es war, soll Ich werden* as a statement that recognizes the self's radical excentricity to itself (it is not consciousness—i.e., the ego it believes itself to be) and speaks of our moral duty to pursue the goal of reconciliation. In Lacan's words, "*Wo Es war, soll Ich werden*. I must come to the place where that was" (1977, p. 171).

With this analysis of the text both he and his adversaries claim as their own, Lacan presents his rereading of Freud as having "so little originality even in its verve that there appears in it not a single metaphor that Freud's works do not repeat with the frequency of a *leitmotif* in which the fabric of the work is revealed" (1977, p. 51).

Notes

1. As will be seen, this seeing itself in a mirror need not be taken literally. In the end, the metaphor is the point.
2. One translation is, "Where It (id) was, I (ego) comes to be."

References

Freud, S. (1959). *Collected papers*, vol. 4. (E. Jones, ed.). New York: Basic Books.
—————— (1960). *The ego and the id*. (J. Riviere, trans.). New York: Norton.
—————— (1962). *Three essays on the theory of sexuality*. (J. Strachey, trans.). New York: Basic Books.
Lacan, J. (1977). *Ecrits*. (A. Sheridan, trans.). New York: Norton.
Muller, J. and Richardson, W. (1982). *Lacan and language*. New York: International Universities Press.
Simiu, D. (1988). "A critical look at Lacan's mirror stage theory." Unpublished paper presented at the APA Eastern Division Meetings.

11 • Life-World as Depth of Soul: Phenomenology and Psychoanalysis[1]

Robert Romanyshyn

THE SCIENCE OF PSYCHOLOGY AND THE LIFE OF SOUL

In the seventeenth century, when Galileo conducted his experiments on falling bodies, he wrote to a friend to describe what he had done. In that letter he said, *"I think in my mind* of something moveable that is entirely left to itself"* (in Heidegger 1967, p. 91) and such things fall equally fast. Whether or not Galileo was referring to an actual experiment supposedly performed at Pisa, it is the point of his remark that is decisive. Galileo—and I am using the name to describe a style of vision as much as to refer to a historical person—did not look at what occurred. He thought about it in advance of what occurred. And thinking about things in this way, in advance of their appearance, Galileo, with others, inaugurated a new style of vision. The vision of the living, incarnated eye was replaced by a vision of a thinking mind, while the appearance of things became deceptive. Said in another way, the world as object of mind eclipsed the body as ground of experience.

To be sure, modern science as a style of vision, as an attitude or posture toward the world, was not born with Galileo in one decisive moment. The Copernican earth, which requires the same distrust of embodied experience, precedes the Galileo example, and indeed a persuasive argument can be made to show that modern science begins in the eye of the painter before it is articulated in the mind of the scientist. Brunelleschi's experiments with linear perspective take place in 1425, and in a recent work I have shown how this artistic intention to create the illusion of three-dimensional depth on a two-dimensional plane transforms the canvas into a window on the world, and establishes a new ideal according to which the best way to know the world is to place it as far away as possible (Romanyshyn, 1989b; Levin 1988). Indeed the ideal is to arrange space in such a way that all objects take on an appearance of depth as they converge toward the vanishing point, which in principle lies at an infinite distance from the self behind the window. Within such a space this self is destined to become an observing eye, a spectator, and the world itself a matter of vision, a spectacle. Moreover, the sensing-sensuous body is destined to become useless in a world that has become a matter for the eye alone.

For example, when in 1688 Newton transforms the rainbow into the spectrum, a path is opened toward draining the world's body of its color. Via the *prismatic* eye the world's color, which for the *incarnate* eye is inseparable from the sound, texture, smell, and feel of things, becomes a light matter, a matter of "difform rays some of which are more refrangible than others" (Romanyshyn 1980b, pp. 3–9). In short, when the self becomes a spectator behind a window, the body as carnal knowledge of the world is on the way toward becoming dispensable. At the ideal of infinite distance, at the vanishing point that originally was called the point of flight, the body abandoned translates into a world drained of its color, taste, sound, touch, and smell.

The eye of the painter, Brunelleschi's eye of infinite distance, paves the way for the philosopher's eye, Galileo's eye of mind. This is one outcome. The seeing eye becomes the thinking mind. Another outcome, of course, is that the eye that now surveys the world from afar is destined to become the instruments of technology. The microscope, the telescope, the camera flesh out this new style of vision. They become the body of this new eye, which becomes the world's measure. They incarnate an eye of amplified vision that humanity now needs in order to keep in touch with a receding, vanishing world. At the end of this paper I will return to this theme of technology, but lest these brief remarks on how linear perspective as an artistic invention becomes a cultural convention, a cultural habit of mind, seem too extraordinary, consider these words of the art historian Samuel Edgerton:

Indeed, without linear perspective, would western man have been able to visualize and then construct the complex machinery which has so effectively moved him out of the Newtonian paradigm into the new era of Einsteinian outer space—and outer time? Space capsules built for zero gravity, astronomical equipment for demarcating so-called black holes, atom smashers which prove the existence of anti-matter—these are the end products of the discovered vanishing point. [1976, p. 165]

I begin with this historical example of Galileo and Brunelleschi because it illustrates the first of three themes in this paper. This first theme is that the *science of psychology* is a historical appearance of human psychological life, of humanity's soul if you will, which appearance is inseparable from a new physics of nature (Galileo, Copernicus, Newton et al.) and a new physiology of the body (Vesalius, Harvey et al.). The eye that *"sees"* all objects fall equally fast, like the eye that places the world ideally at an infinite distance the better to know it, is a *style* of vision, a *way of experiencing* the world. It is a worldview that encompasses the manner in which we take up what is real and not real, what is sane and insane, what things are and what the human body is, what space and time are, what matters as fact and what is regarded as fiction, what dreams, images, memories, perceptions are, etc. It is a human psychology that is articulated in this style of vision, an understanding that humanity creates for itself in creating a way of understanding the world.

René Descartes makes it very clear that this view of the world, a style of vision that establishes a physics of nature and a physiology of body, *is* a view of ourselves, a psychology. He writes in *The Dioptrics* that we will be more certain of the life of vision if we study the eye of a newly dead person.[2] A vision of seeing is already sketched here in terms of the anatomical eye, a vision that imagines the seeing eye to be like a camera. The irony, however, in this piece of cultural-psychological history is that when in two hundred years we flesh out this image with the actual invention, the relation between the seeing eye and the camera is reversed. Instead of celebrating the imaginative power of the living eye to envision its vision as a camera, the science of psychology reduces that power by explaining the vision of the seeing eye in terms of the camera. Or said another way, what begins as a metaphorical vision of the seeing eye ends as the literal conditions that explain it.

The second theme of this paper is that phenomenology and psychoanalysis are each in their own respective way responses to this historical appearance of human psychological life as the science of psychology. Insofar as psychology's claim to be a science has meant that soul has been dichotomized between body and mind, phenomenology and psychoanalysis share a critical rejection of this dichotomy. In the next two sections of this paper this critical rejection is discussed in terms of three prejudices that characterize the science of psychology: the objective world, the ego, and the empirical fact as the datum of psychology.

The paper's third theme is that a convergence of phenomenology and psychoanalysis leads toward a phenomenological depth-psychology that acknowledges that a style of vision, a psychology, is fleshed out in the way in which an age paints its paintings and builds its buildings, creates its laws and practices its sciences, manages its money and worships the gods, etc. Soul incarnates itself as world, and the final section of the paper specifically explores this theme in terms of how the technological world embodies the soul of the science of psychology. Indeed, I want to propose in that final section that the world, including the technological world as the incarnation of the soul of science, is a *symptomatic* embodiment of human psychological life. The world is not only the flesh of soul, it is also the *suffering* flesh of soul. In short, the conclusion I wish to draw in this paper is that via phenomenology and psychoanalysis the science of psychology, recovered as a cultural-historical appearance of psychological life, opens a path toward a phenomenological depth-psychology that treats the cultural-historical world, the lived world, as a symptom of soul and offers a therapeutics of culture and history (cf. Romanyshyn 1984).

PHENOMENOLOGY AND THE SCIENCE OF PSYCHOLOGY: THE PREJUDICE OF THE OBJECTIVE WORLD AND THE LANDSCAPING OF EXPERIENCE

In the world of everyday life, the world as it is experienced immediately by the living body, the body of flesh and blood, the sensing-sensuous body whose perceptions of the world are also always involvements within the world, heavier objects fall faster than lighter ones. This world lies near at hand. Indeed more than near at hand, this world *surrounds* us, envelops us. We are always in the midst of this world, engaged with things and with others, solicited by their presence, seduced as flesh by the flesh of the world.

Phenomenology is the science of this world, the *logos* of its paths and spaces, its volumes and its depths, its rhythms and its textures, and in this respect phenomenology is the *reversal* of the world of science, that world where all objects do fall equally fast, or where seeing is a matter of what meets the eyeball, the eyeball of anatomy, the anatomical eye of the corpse. Reversal, however, is not quite accurate.[3] *Return* perhaps is a better description. Phenomenology returns humanity to the world from that distance, infinite in the ideal, from which we practice a scientific vision.

The Copernican earth is an apt symbol of this distant vision. It is a fitting image of the world that we create for ourselves within that distance, a world that as a creation of mind no one can inhabit, an earth upon which no one can dwell, an earth finally that we are not able to embody. The difference between the world of this Copernican earth and the real world of everyday life is nicely summarized in these lines of Martin Heidegger:

> Let us think of the sun. Every day it rises and sets for us. Only a very few astronomers, physicists, philosophers—and even they only on the basis of a specialized approach which may be more or less widespread—experience this state of affairs otherwise, namely as a motion of the earth around the sun. But the appearance in which sun and earth stand, e.g. the early morning landscape, the sea in the evening, the night, is an appearing. This appearance is not nothing. Nor is it untrue. Nor is it a mere appearance of conditions in nature which are *really* otherwise. This appearance is historical and it is *history*, discovered and grounded in *poetry* and *myth* and thus an essential area of our world.
>
> Only the tired latecomers with their supercilious wit imagine that they can dispose of the historical power of appearance by declaring it to be "subjective," hence very dubious. [1959, p. 105; italics added]

Phenomenology appreciates this difference. Indeed it grounds itself upon it; and as a method of return, phenomenology practices a fidelity to appearances, to those paths and spaces, volumes and depths, rhythms and textures that constitute the world as it is bodily lived. One might suggest, then, that phenomenology as a return from distance to proximity is a science of remembering, a praxis of recovering out of forgetfulness the world as it is experienced. And in this respect one might add that phenomenology is a psychoanalysis of the bodily experienced world. Phenomenology does for this world what psychoanalysis does for the person: it remembers what is otherwise forgotten.

Phenomenology calls the bodily experienced world the *Lebens-*

welt (the lived world) and thereby distinguishes it from the world realized in distance, the objective world.[4] This objective world (the world of the Copernican earth, for example) is for us an object of vision realized in distance. It is a world upon which we operate and into which we have insight. It is also by definition a world from which we are apart.

Returning us from distance, phenomenology suspends the claims of the world as an object, this world that confronts us and that we assault with a frontal ontology that transforms the world into an object for our use (see Levin 1985). Phenomenology suspends the claims of this world to be the condition or cause of our experiences, and in doing so it makes possible a remembrance of the world as the setting within which our experiences occur. In short, phenomenology brackets the prejudice of the objective world and inquires into the world as the setting where experience takes place (see Romanyshyn 1980a, pp. 153–78).

For descriptive purposes and with acknowledged indebtedness to many other phenomenologists, I call this work of bracketing and remembering the moment of landscaping experience. It is the moment in which phenomenology is supreme, the moment in which the world as the *where* of experience is remembered and described. Whether it be a description and protocol analysis of anxiety, depression, anger, perception, remembering, imagining, hoping, dreaming, attention, etc., phenomenology recovers the structures of these experiences as they are lived as worlds.[5]

We can, I believe, better appreciate the strength of phenomenology, and we can better understand the meaning of world as the *where* of experience, if we suggest that the life-world as landscape of experience is like the stage setting of a drama.[6] Like a stage, the life-world is a place where experience takes place and action occurs. Indeed, it is a place inseparable from that experience and action. The spaces and times of the life-world, like that of the stage, are structured in relation to the experiences and actions that happen there. More specifically, the things that make up our space, like the things of the stage world, are "props" that mirror or reflect the experience and the action that occur there. The volumes and densities, the paths and byways, the colors, textures, tones, and luminosities of the world when one is depressed are no less a stage setting that reflect one's experience than is the lone tree that dots the center stage and forms the landscape of Estragon's and Vladimir's homelessness as they wait for Godot. And just as we cannot imagine a drama apart from a stage or a setting, just as every drama needs a stage, even if it "only" converts an ordinary street into a setting for an impromptu performance, I am suggesting that human experience as it is lived is enacted within a world that is a stage.[7]

The suggestions that all the world is a stage and that our lives are enacted performances are not new. Role theorists have been telling us that for many years. Nevertheless, the suggestions matter because they turn phenomenology toward two questions: *Who* inhabits the landscape? And *what* story is enacted there? If the life-world as landscape of experience is a stage setting, then the questions of the characters who enact a drama within that setting and the story enacted there arise as specific issues. Unfolding the *where* of experience, phenomenology is led to the themes of the *who* and the *what* of experience. The prejudice of the objective world that phenomenology overcomes moves it toward a confrontation with the prejudices of the ego and the empirical fact as the datum of psychology. And here phenomenology converges toward psychoanalysis.

PSYCHOANALYSIS AND THE SCIENCE OF PSYCHOLOGY: THE PREJUDICES OF THE EGO AND THE FACT, AND THE FIGURING AND STORYING OF EXPERIENCE

Perhaps the primary lesson of psychoanalysis is that it has taught us to regard home as a stage where human life is dramatically enacted. Said in another way, Freudian psychoanalysis has taught us to regard the spaces of the home, its rooms, like the bedroom and the bathroom, as settings for the enactment of stories between characters *disguised* as husband and wife, as parent and child. We recognize each other in these ways, as husband and wife, as parent and child, and yet within the setting of the home, the center of one's life-world, we encounter tyrannical fathers and seductive mothers, oedipal children and multiple parents, remembering here that Oedipus had four. We recognize an appearance *and* we encounter a depth. Maurice Merleau-Ponty has made this same point the other way around. He writes that "we struggle with dream figures and our blows fall on living faces" (cited in Wilshire 1982, p. 218).

Psychoanalysis has sensitized us to our own multiplicity. It has cautioned us never to assume the who or the what of experience. It has taught us to suspend the claim of the ego to be the locus of action and to suspend the claim of the past to be an empirical history. As a science of remembering, it brackets the prejudice of the ego as the agent of psychological life, and the prejudice of fact (especially the past as merely causal fact) as the datum of psychological life. In doing so it recovers the multiple figurations of psychological life (for example, id, ego, superego, eros, and thanatos); it also recovers the historical past as an imaginal story that one creates or makes in re-membering it as much as it is a story already made, waiting to be discovered (see Romanyshyn 1987, pp. 297–305).

For descriptive purposes, and to complement phenomenology's moment of landscaping experience, I would call these psychoanalytic contributions the moments of figuring and storying experience. A quick and ready illustration of these two moments is offered by the experience of regarding oneself in a mirror (see Romanyshyn 1982).

A phenomenology of the mirror experience indicates that the image is a depth we see with our living eyes, a depth as far on that side of the mirror as we are on this side of it. Moreover, that depth is a deepening of experience that refigures the person as a character in a tale: we never encounter merely a duplicate of ourselves in the mirror reflection. On the contrary, through the image we recognize and encounter ourselves as *familiar-stranger*. In addition, the phenomenology of the mirror experience indicates that we live through this encounter with the imaged depths unknowingly, forgetfully, much as we live forgetfully through the world as landscape of experience. In this respect, psychoanalysis, like phenomenology, is called to be a discipline of remembering. We need add here only that the mirrors through which we live the imaged depths are not merely or primarily actual ones. Rather, these mirrors are the things of the world and the presence of others that give me back to myself in deepened and refigured fashion.

However much we recognize the mirror experience as a moment of refiguration, a question persists about the relation between the person on this side of the mirror and the figure encountered in the depths on the other side of the mirror. Considering this question will help to clarify the sense of experience as a figured and storied reality.

The psychological relation between person and figure is, perhaps, best understood by analogy with the dramatic relation between the actor and the character he or she portrays. On the one hand, this analogy tells us that a psychological figure of experience can no more exist apart from the person than a dramatic character can apart from an actor to enact him or her. To be sure, dramatic characters do exist on paper, but they are more akin to dream figures before one awakens and carries them into the world. They await, as do our dream figures, a *muscular incarnation*, and they depend, as do our dream figures, on the person to provide it. We might say, therefore, that between person and figure there is a relation of *identity*, and saying so we could add with respect to theater that it is this relation of *identity* that makes the dramatic performance believable. Insofar as the actor as person *is* the character, theater as a piece of make-believe is believable.

On the other hand, this identity must give way to a *difference* lest one transform fiction into history. In the theater one sees, for example, Hamlet-as-performed-by-Burton.[8] One does not see only Prince Hamlet. One sees the prince enacted, and insofar as the actor as person *is not* the character, the believable remains a piece of make-believe. In analogous fashion, the relation of person and figure is also a relation of *difference*.

The analogy indicates, therefore, that in the psychological figuration of experience one is faced with the paradox that one *is* and *is not* who one is. The *familiar*-stranger whom I recognize and encounter through the mirror *is* me, and I dwell there comfortably in his appearance and gestures as much as he dwells in mine. But I also sense, sometimes vaguely and sometimes with a sense of foreboding, that the familiar-*stranger* is *not* me, for surely I do not carry such a passive, expressionless face, or surely I do not wear such a menacing frown. Moreover, the same paradox of being and not being who I am haunts my relations with others. The look that darts across your face when I "sincerely" tell you that I love you reflects back to me an uneasiness whose depths I fear to know. Between I who speak and I who fear, there exists, however vaguely, this relation of identity and difference. That look, hardly noticed if at all, brings into question *who* is speaking.

The analogy, person is to figure as actor is to the character portrayed, also clarifies the meaning of experience as storied. It indicates that the storying of experience is precisely the apprehension of it as neither a fact nor a fiction. Elsewhere (Romanyshyn 1981, pp. 3–19) I have shown how this domain between fact and fiction characterizes psychological life as a metaphorical reality, and here, for the sake of brevity, I wish only to demonstrate this point by way of an example.

Consider how the staged drama already locates us within that space of the metaphorical between fact and fiction. There before me on the stage is Willie Loman, the protagonist in Arthur Miller's *Death of a Salesman*. It is this figure whom I see, and through him, like a mirror, something of myself. He moves me, and my emotional, embodied response betrays an involvement between me and the character who appears. There is no mere fiction here in the sense of something unreal, which does not matter, or which is, after all, only a matter of mind. And yet it is Willie Loman as enacted by Dustin Hoffman, and this too is what I see, what I experience. It is a kind of double vision I have, and it is this double vision, this way of experiencing the character Loman *through* the actor Hoffman, that keeps me from mistaking the fictional drama for a factual event. There before me on the stage I am invited to witness the unfolding of a tale that takes place in a domain between the fictional and the factual, the mental and the empirical, the ideal and the real.

In like manner the story revealed through the mirror figure also inhabits a domain between the material fact and the immaterial fiction. The mirror image, which sketches out the story's theme, is there before me and I see it. And yet it is not empirically there. I look in the mirror and through it I may see a pathetic figure, and while my awareness of the figure might reside in a mood of sadness, I do not move, literally, to embrace it, because, like Narcissus's reflection, one *knows* it will disappear. That figure haunts me on this side of the mirror, and the mood it reflects attests to its reality as more than a piece of unreal fiction. It matters in the conduct of my living, and yet my behavior in relation to it attests equally that it is not a matter of fact.

Psychoanalysis attunes us to this dramatic landscape where human experience matters insofar as it is a believable story. Indeed the storying of experience to which psychoanalysis introduces us indicates that human life as we live it in the world with others— that is, before we philosophize about it and before we reduce it to the level of our explanations, whatever they may be—is less a matter of what we know and more a matter of what we believe and can believe. The *what* of experience is as much, and perhaps even more, a matter of the faith of the human heart than it is the knowledge of the human mind. Even our perceptions bear witness to this dimension of belief. An age perceives what it is able to perceive and the shifts in perception between one age and another, the shifts that, for example, allow one age to see the presence of the gods in the world and another to be blind to them, are not reducible merely to matters of fact, to the question of empirical evidence. More than a thousand years before Copernicus, Aristarchus of Samos knew that the earth moved round the sun. But there was no world to sustain a belief in that perception. There was no world where such an experience was believable.

Closer to home we know that the experience of remembering the past is inextricably bound to what we can and what we need to believe of it. Indeed psychoanalysis is born in this recognition. The stories of seduction were not empirically true, yet the genius of this vision was to understand that they were not for that reason false. We *remember* the past precisely because we *re-member* it. We *preserve* what was precisely because we *transform* it. We *discover* the past precisely because we *create* it. And this work of re-membering, of transforming, of creating is a matter of what is believable and as such bearable. Truth, understood psychologically, is a matter of what one can believe.

The storying of experience suggests that human life is a work of making, a *poesis* in the root sense of this term (see Romanyshyn 1987). This work of storying indicates that in living in the life-world we are engaged in a poetic history, in a making of what is already made, whether that be the givenness of the present or the past, or the givenness of the other, the world, and one's own body.

In a sense we have come nearly full circle insofar as the storying of experience has led us toward the recognition that human experience is a given to be made. The gestures that define me to others are, it is true, given to me by others, especially significant archaic others, and yet they are not me until they are made between me and others in the world we share. And while it is true that psychoanalysis understands this world in a dramatic way—for example, things as symbols of libidinal attachments—it is phenomenology that opens up the world as the stage or setting of human life. Psychoanalysis, therefore, is led back toward phenomenology because phenomenology has taught us so well that, in human psychological terms, the world itself is not a fixed matter. It has taught us so well to appreciate the world as the landscapes of our experiences.

I do not mean to suggest at this point any easy or comfortable rapprochement between phenomenology and psychoanalysis. If I have emphasized a convergence, it is not at the expense of forgetting their differences. One such difference is the notion of the symptom. Both the multiple figurations and the storylike character of human experience announce themselves in psychoanalysis through the symptom. The convergence, then, sparks a creative tension, because it suggests that the landscapes of the life-world, within which stories are enacted, are symptoms of soul. It suggests that the world as it is lived, the life-world, the cultural worlds in which humanity houses itself, are to be regarded as symptoms.[9] In the final part of the paper I wish to explore this suggestion briefly.

PHENOMENOLOGICAL DEPTH-PSYCHOLOGY: A THERAPEUTICS OF CULTURE

I have attempted to indicate how phenomenology and psycho-analysis open the world as a landscape where the figures of soul enact their stories. My intention, however, has been more than theoretical, because I believe that such a psychology in its praxis and research can and must address the critical questions of our time. For me the question of technology and soul has been para-mount, specifically the expressions of technology in the world events of space flight and nuclear weapons. *What psychological story or stories is the human soul enacting within these technological land-scapes?*

To illustrate the path of such a psychology, I want to focus the question of technology and soul by considering the fundamental equation that lies at the foundation of our technological thinking: $E=mc^2$. This equation, which defines for us the physical relation between energy and matter, is a psychological story (see Romany-shyn, 1989b). What is that story and who is speaking it? Besides being a mathematical formula, the equation is also a symbol of our age, a condensed myth. Moreover, it is also a symptom. By symptom, however, I do not mean something negative. I do not mean disease. On the contrary, recalling our psychoanalytic per-spective, I want to emphasize that the symptom is a call to re-member what is otherwise forgotten, that the symptom is an invitation to give the forgotten its place. Thus, a symptom may very well be a *dis-ease* (an uneasiness), but as such it is an uneasi-ness that arises out of neglect. To say, then, that $E=mc^2$ is a symptom is to invite us to attend to the world within which this psychological story of the equivalence of energy and matter is enacted. In doing so I am proposing that a phenomenological depth-psychology performs a therapeutic work upon culture, be-cause it uncovers the story of who we are when we landscape the world in such a way that matter becomes a matter of energy.

The equation $E=mc^2$ establishes, at least indirectly through the notion of mass, an equivalence between matter and energy (see Capra 1975). Indeed it proposes a convertibility such that matter matters as energy. "Matter is energized," we might say, and in this respect the equation suggests that a story of *dematerialization* is being told. Two questions, however, arise. First, in what sense is this dematerialization intended? Second, how is it achieved psychologically?

Initially consider the second question. The relation of equivalence between matter and energy is an equivalence that characterizes the physical processes that occur in the sun. In this respect $E=mc^2$ is a vision of matter and energy that is, as Hannah Arendt says, *astrophysical* rather than *terrestrial* (1958). The vision, therefore, belongs to one who is a cosmic, universe-al figure. It belongs to one who is an alien with respect to the earth. Surely the perception of matter as a little sun, as a fiery ball of cosmic energy, is an alien vision for us who inhabit the material earth. The equivalence, then, between matter and energy presumes a distant vision. It presumes that we who take up that vision have become psychologically strangers to the earth.

The reply to the second question, to how this equivalence is established, already suggests a reply to the first question regarding the meaning of dematerialization that this equivalence implies. The alien perspective that defines this vision belongs to us, and if it is we ourselves who have become estranged from the earth, then this estrangement betrays a motive. Have we become estranged from the materiality of earth because of our ambivalence toward matter? Does the estranged vision betray a wish to escape the earth, a desire to depart?

A symptom is ambiguous, and thus we can never be certain of our replies or our questions. Nevertheless, just as the individual symptom is always embedded within a wider context, there are several themes that surround and support these questions. With respect to the issue of ambivalence for matter, it is significant to note that an emotional ambivalence with regard to the material body appears at roughly the same time that this apparent ambivalence with regard to the material earth appears. Interestingly, Einstein's papers on relativity, which establish this equation, appear in the same year, 1905, as Freud's *Three Essays on a Theory of Sexuality*. If the former as a theme of dematerialization suggests an ambivalence on the part of soul with regard to matter, the latter uncovers a motive for this ambivalence: the material body is repressed (forgotten) because it is erotically alive. Thus we ask of the symptom $E=mc^2$, "Does the repression of the erotic body find its counterpart in the physicist's equation that describes (landscapes) a world where the energizing of matter is a libidinal dream from which we must escape?" Do we become alien with respect to a material earth that now has become threateningly energized in much the same fashion that the hysteric became alienated from the erotic body? After several centuries of "Newton's sleep," a phrase of the visionary poet William Blake to describe a deadened nature, are we faced with an awakening eros both on the level of body and earth? Is the physicist's equation, like the hysteric's symptom, a sign of a neurosis, a sign of what has been forgotten? Is $E=mc^2$ a symptom of a planetary neurosis?

Material nature reawakening with energy, with the energy of desire! In the late nineteenth and early twentieth centuries, it is the poet and the painter in addition to the physicist and the psychoanalyst who bear witness to this erotic explosion. One need only recall here the French Symbolist poets—Baudelaire, Rimbaud, Mallarmé—to realize that their experiments with language, often erotic and highly charged, were efforts to reconnect things, and to connect with things. And the painters, like Cézanne or the early Mondrian, with his experiments with color, were rediscovering the vital interconnection among things.[10] Mondrian's "Woods Near Oele," for example, displays a landscape that moves with an eroticism characteristic of the sensuous body and illustrative of a feminine presence. In the eyes of the painter, surely, the material earth has come alive, erotically and in a feminine fashion. Is the physicist's equation, then, an acknowledgment of a reawakening of *Mother* earth, and is it the body of Mother earth, like the feminine body of the hysteric, that we seek to escape?

Dreams of escape fueled by awakened desire make one possible story of soul lived out within that technological landscape where matter is energized. But this energizing of matter, its revitalization, is the wish *and* the dread of soul. The wish and the dread are contained in the same equation, like the symptom itself contains both the desire and its prohibition. Contemporary physics, in which this energizing of matter plays such a key role, forces upon us the most radical recognition of nature's vitality. Insofar as it informs us that particles are connections and not entities connected, might we suggest that particles do not desire each other but are in essence desire, that the particle itself is libidinal desire?

In this respect might not the story of soul embedded in physics be awakening us to the discovery of the libido at the heart of matter, to the discovery that at its root matter is erotic?

This same physics, however, also provides us with that cosmic, alien, estranged perspective apart from the awakened earth, and in doing so it expresses the dread of soul in the face of that awakened desire. And within this context of dread, on this side of the ambivalence, the energizing of matter is not a revitalization but a final dematerialization, the dematerialization that we imagine today as a nuclear cloud, a dematerialization that is a final escape from the earth. The mushroom cloud, which is more than a fact in the empirical world, *which is a landscape of soul*, is the vaporization of the material world, an energizing of matter, which is, one might say, a gnostic inspiriting of it. Will the soul's response to the awakened eroticism of matter end in its denial, in the spiritualization of desire? Will the light of nuclear annihilation be the energy released in matter, a light to cleanse the earth, the soul, of desire?[11]

A phenomenological depth-psychology, which I have only very briefly illustrated, asks such questions, because in asking them it seeks to uncover the landscapes within which world events unfold *as* stories enacted by soul. In closing I would like to say that such a psychology indebted to phenomenology and to psychoanalysis, especially as both of these perspectives are replies to the tradition of scientific psychology, places the psychologist as a servant of soul in the service of the world. It does so because it begins and ends with the world. And it begins and ends there because it acknowledges that in designing the world, we design ourselves.

Notes

1. An earlier version of this paper was delivered as an invited address at the annual meeting of the Human Science Research Conference, West Georgia College, Carrollton, 1984.

The term *soul* is quite foreign to contemporary psychology, which understands itself as a science of behavior or mind. I use it here, however, to indicate that the kind of psychology toward which phenomenology and psychoanalysis converge is a science neither of behavior nor mind. And I use it here in the sense of psychological life as a metaphorical reality, as the domain of experience that is between matter and mind, fact and fiction, thing and thought, the objective and the subjective. For a fuller treatment of the metaphorical character of psychological life, see

Romanyshyn 1982. The metaphorical character of psychological life is developed there within the context of the mirror reflection, further indicating that soul is a matter of image that deepens the given by transforming the empirical as story and refiguring the person as a character in a tale. I should also mention that I am indebted to the work of James Hillman on this issue of soul. See, for example, *Re-Visioning Psychology* (New York: Harper & Row, 1975). It was in part from reading his work that I discovered the convergence of phenomenology and depth-psychology. The phenomenological critique of the history of the science of psychology that I gave in the book *Psychological Life*, a critique much indebted to the metabletic work of van den Berg, converges toward the theme of soul, which Hillman develops out of the Jungian context and the mytho-poetic tradition of our Western heritage.

2. For a more detailed treatment of this issue, see Romanyshyn 1982. In addition to developing the metaphorical character of psychological life, this work shows how the science of psychology is a cultural-historical appearance of psychological life or soul. Again I acknowledge my indebtedness to van den Berg's work in metabletics. For an illustrative overview of van den Berg's work, see the festschrift edited by Kruger 1984. For a very fine introduction to van den Berg's metabletic psychology, see van den Berg 1961, 1974.

3. If not quite accurate, it is nevertheless suggestive. Considered as a reversal the relation of phenomenology to science can be described by an analogy to Greek drama. Phenomenology, then, would be the epistrophe of the strophe, that moment when the chorus turns and begins a reverse movement. That moment occurs when the flaws of the hero are being revealed, when insight is about to dawn. Is the appearance of phenomenology, then, a moment of insight in the cultural drama of modern science?

4. For a discussion of the notion of the *Lebenswelt* in relation to the rise of modern science, see Husserl 1970.

5. See, for example, the four volumes in *Duquesne Studies in Phenomenological Psychology* (1971, 1975, 1980, 1984).

6. Wilshire 1982 cautions us about the limits of the metaphor, life is theater. He is right in his warnings. Nevertheless, his work misses the full psychological significance of the metaphor. We are saying that the life-world is theaterlike. Wilshire cautions that the carryover of theater to the world of life results in a breakdown of the metaphor. And here the caution bears psychological fruit. The life-world is theaterlike as a moment of breakdown, that is symptomatically, or stated the other way around, the psychological symptom is the enactment of a dramatic reality. It is the carry-over of a dramatic figure and story into daily life where the result is breakdown. One need only recall here what Freud has taught us about the *home*. It is the stage of dramatic performances where daily life is figured and storied symptomatically.

7. To envision the world in this fashion, as the stage upon which experience takes place, is to understand that experience is visible through and as a world, that the world and the things of the world mirror or reflect the landscapes of psychological life. For a discussion of the notion of the visibility of experience, see Romanyshyn 1989a.

8. Much of my discussion here is indebted to Wilshire 1982.

9. When psychology attends to the life-world as a cultural therapeutics, when it attends to the shadows and symptoms of culture, it
performs the work of deconstruction. In this respect a phenomenological
depth-psychology of the cultural-historical world is to be found in the
work of Foucault 1967.

10. In the last chapter of my recent book (1989b), there is a lengthy
discussion of how impressionism acknowledges the awakened erotic
character of the world.

11. It is perhaps unfair to allude with only an adjective to the gnostic
vision of modern science and technology. It is, however, an important
point. For a fuller treatment of this connection, see Voegelin 1968. For a
detailed presentation of gnosticism itself, see Jonas 1958 and Pagels 1981.

References

Arendt, H. (1958). *The human condition*. Chicago: University of Chicago.
Capra, F. (1975). *The tao of physics*. New York: Bantam.
Edgerton, S. Y., Jr. (1976). *The renaissance re-discovery of linear perspective*.
New York: Harper & Row.
Foucault, M. (1967). *Madness and civilization*. New York: New American
Library.
Heidegger, M. (1959). *An introduction to metaphysics* (Ralph Manheim,
trans.). New Haven: Yale University.
——— (1967). *What is a thing?* (W. B. Barton, Jr., and V. Deutsch, trans.).
Chicago: Regnery.
Husserl, E. (1970). *The crisis of European sciences and transcendental phenomen-
ology* (D. Carr, trans.). Evanston: Northwestern University.
Jonas, H. (1958). *The gnostic religion*. Boston: Beacon.
Kruger, D., ed. *The changing reality of modern man: Essays in honor of J. H. van
den Berg*. Cape Town: Juta.
Levin, D. (1985). *The body's recollection of being*. London: Routledge and
Kegan Paul.
——— (1988). *The opening of vision*. London: Routledge and Kegan Paul.
Pagels, E. (1981). *The gnostic gospels*. New York: Vintage Books.
Romanyshyn, R. (1980a). "Experience takes place," *Dimensions of thought:
Current explorations in time, space and knowledge*, vol. 2 (R. H. Moon and
S. Randall, eds.). Berkeley: Dharma Publishers.
——— (1980b). "Looking at the light: Reflections of the mutable body,"
Dragonflies: Studies in imaginal psychology, 2.1 (Winter), 3–7.
——— (1981). "Science and reality: Metaphors of experience and experi-
ence as metaphorical," *The metaphors of consciousness* (R. Valle and
R. von Eckartsberg, eds.). New York: Plenum.
——— (1982). *Psychological life: From science to metaphor*. Austin: University
of Texas.
——— (1984). "The despotic eye," *The changing reality of modern man*
(D. Kruger, ed.). Cape Town: Juta.

—— (1987). "Mirror as metaphor of psychological life," *Self and identity: Psychosocial perspectives* (K. Yardley and T. Honess, eds.). New York: Wiley and Sons.

—— (1989a). *Technology as symptom and dream*. London: Routledge and Kegan Paul.

—— (1989b). "Psychology and the attitude of science," *Existential-phenomenological perspectives in psychology* (R. Valle and S. Halling, eds.). New York: Plenum.

van den Berg, J. H. (1961). *The changing nature of man*. New York: Norton.

—— (1974). *Divided existence and complex society*. Pittsburgh: Duquesne.

Voegelin, E. (1968). *Science, politics and gnosticism*. Chicago: Regnery.

Wilshire, B. (1982). *Role playing and identity*. Bloomington: Indiana University.

Index

About the Authors

DEBRA B. BERGOFFEN is professor of philosophy and chair of the General Education Task Force at George Mason University. Dr. Bergoffen received her Ph.D. in philosophy from Georgetown University in 1974. Her publications include: "Posthumous Popularity: Reading, Privileging, Politicizing Nietzsche," in *Soundings* (1990) and "On the Advantage and Disadvantage of Nietzsche for Women," in *The Question of the Other* (SUNY Press, 1989).

JAMES E. FAULCONER is associate professor of philosophy at Brigham Young University. Dr. Faulconer is the coauthor of "More on Temporality in Human Action," in *The American Psychologist* (February 1987) and "Temporality in Human Action: An Alternative to Positivism and Historicism," in *The American Psychologist* (November 1985). Dr. Faulconer received his Ph.D. in philosophy from the Pennsylvania State University in 1977.

SIMON GLYNN is assistant professor of philosophy at Florida Atlantic University. He received his Ph.D. from the University of Manchester. Dr. Glynn has been a contributing editor to *Sartre: An Investigation of Some Major Themes* (Gower, 1987) and *European Philosophy and the Human Social Sciences* (Gower, 1986). He is also the author of *The Logic of Intuition and Creativity* (The Open University, 1984).

JOSEPH J. KOCKELMANS is professor of philosophy at The Pennsylvania State University. He received his Ph.D. in philosophy from the Angelico, Rome, and completed postdoctoral studies at the Husserl Archives in Leuven, Belgium. His publications include *Heidegger's "Being and Time"* (1989), *Heidegger on Art and Art Works* (1985), *On the Truth of Being* (1984), *The World in Science and Philosophy* (1969) and *Husserl's Phenomenological Psychology* (1968).

IVANA MARKOVA is head of the Psychology Department at the University of Stirling, Scotland. She received her Ph.D. in philosophy in 1962 and in psychology in 1964 at Charles University,

261

Prague. She is the author of *Human Awareness* (1987) and *Paradigms, Thought and Language* (1982). She is also the editor of *The Social Context of Language* (1978).

DONALD POLKINGHORNE is professor of counseling at the California State University, Fullerton. He previously served as president of the Saybrook Institute from 1976–1987. Dr. Polkinghorne received his Ph.D. in psychology from the Union Graduate School. He is the author of *Methodology for the Human Sciences* and *Narrative Knowing and the Human Sciences*, and he is a licensed psychologist in California.

WILLIAM J. RICHARDSON is professor of philosophy at Boston College and a practicing psychoanalyst. Dr. Richardson received his Ph.D. from the Higher Institute of Philosophy, University of Louvain, Belgium, in 1960. He is the author of *The Purloined Poe: Lacan, Derrida and Psychoanalytic Reading* (1988), *Heidegger: Through Phenomenology to Thought* (3rd ed., 1976), and coauthor of *Lacan and Language: Reader's Guide to the "Ecrits"* (1983).

ROBERT ROMANYSHYN is professor of psychology at the University of Dallas and a visiting lecturer in arts and humanities at the University of Texas, as well as a practicing clinical psychologist. Dr. Romanyshyn received his Ph.D. in psychology from Duquesne University. He is the author of *Technology as Symptom and Dream* (Routledge Chapman & Hall, 1989) and *Psychological Life: From Science to Metaphor* (University of Texas Press, 1982).

CALVIN O. SCHRAG is the George Ade Distinguished Professor of Philosophy at Purdue University. Dr. Schrag, who received his Ph.D. from Harvard University in 1957, was the recipient of a Guggenehiem Fellowship in 1965–66. His publications include *Communicative Praxis and the Space of Subjectivity* (Indiana University Press, 1986), *Radical Reflection and the Origin of the Human Sciences* (Purdue University Press, 1980) and *Experience and Being* (Northwestern University Press, 1969).

RICHARD N. WILLIAMS is associate professor of psychology at Brigham Young University. He received his Ph.D. in personality and social psychology from Purdue University in 1981. Dr. Williams is the coauthor of "More Temporality in Human Action," in *The American Psychologist* (February 1987) and "Temporality in Human Action: An Alternative to Positivism and Historicism," in *The American Psychologist* (November 1985).